Violet to Vita

Violet to Vita

The Letters of Violet Trefusis
to
Vita Sackville-West,
1910–21

With an Introduction by Mitchell A. Leaska

EDITED BY
MITCHELL A. LEASKA
and
JOHN PHILLIPS

VIKING

VIKING
Published by the Penguin Group
Viking Penguin, a division of Penguin Books USA Inc.,
375 Hudson Street, New York, New York 10014, U.S.A.
Penguin Books Ltd, 27 Wrights Lane, London W8 5TZ, England
Penguin Books Australia Ltd, Ringwood, Victoria, Australia
Penguin Books Canada Ltd, 2801 John Street,
Markham, Ontario, Canada L3R 1B4
Penguin Books (N.Z.) Ltd, 182–190 Wairau Road,
Auckland 10, New Zealand

Penguin Books Ltd, Registered Offices:
Harmondsworth, Middlesex, England

First American Edition
Published in 1990 by Viking Penguin,
a division of Penguin Books USA Inc.

10 9 8 7 6 5 4 3 2 1

LIBRARY OF CONGRESS CATALOGING IN PUBLICATION DATA
Trefusis, Violet Keppel, 1894–1972.
    Violet to Vita: the letters of Violet Trefusis to Vita Sackville-
West, 1910–21/edited by Mitchell A. Leaska and John Phillips;
with an introduction by Mitchell A. Leaska.
    p.   cm.
ISBN 0–670–83542–0
    1. Trefusis, Violet Keppel, 1894–1972—Correspondence.
2. Sackville-West, V. (Victoria), 1892–1962—Correspondence
3. Novelists, English—20th century—Correspondence.   I. Leaska,
Mitchell Alexander.   II. Phillips, John (John Nova)   III. Title.
PR6039.R39Z493   1990
823'.912—dc20   90–50062
[B]

Printed in the United States of America

Contents

Illustrations

Preface

This volume contains virtually all of the surviving letters of Violet Trefusis to Vita Sackville-West, written from 1910 to 1921, now preserved in the Beinecke Rare Book and Manuscript Library at Yale University. Altogether they consist of some 1,600 holograph sheets, a few written in ink, most of them in pencil, and all in varying degrees of legibility.

Determining their exact position in the sequence of events presented enough of a problem to require a little explanation here. One does not have to read very far into the letters to sense their characteristic haste and urgency. Violet typically scrawled her messages across the page, ignoring the date, the place of origin and often a beginning and ending; when she had something to say, she said it 'on the spot', as it were, without premeditation or concern for context. We have thus had to rely on the postmark on the envelope – where this has fortunately survived – in order to establish a precise chronology. In the absence of these postal markers, the dates, inserted within square brackets, have been conjectured from internal evidence. In some cases the month and the year could be determined but, in rarer instances, only the year. With regard to the location of origin: when Violet was not writing on printed stationery, she usually did not trouble to provide such information, so that often we had to deduce her whereabouts from clues contained in the letters themselves – sometimes successfully, sometimes not.

Several other matters also deserve brief mention. On a number of occasions, Violet haphazardly stuffed into one envelope long rambling letters of seven or eight sheets – all of them un-numbered, and with no indication of paragraph divisions. The page numbers we were able to establish from the sequential content of the letter but the paragraph breaks remained a matter of (careful) guesswork. Then came those troublesome letters strewn with sentences that begin in English, curl into French, then twist into Italian, momentarily lapse into gypsy, return to English and finally end in a string of question and exclamation marks. And next to these, fortunately rare, linguistic marvels came the desperate, the frantic, the imploring letters (of which there are many) where all conventional punctuation was abandoned to the service of dashes, ellipsis points and other frenzied configurational oddities. Just how we were to proceed with such a hodgepodge of languages and lead marks to make the letter accessible to the reader posed a serious problem. Our solution was to preserve as much of it as possible without sacrificing Violet's tone and meaning, for difficult as such matters were to deal with editorially, it is precisely from these scriptured jumbles that the letters derive their characteristic vibrancy and colour.

Further, if we were to capture the uniqueness of these letters and remain faithful to their intent, it became clear in the early months of our work that certain editorial policies had to be established. Among them was our decision to translate in footnotes, no matter how common the phrase or expression, all the foreign languages that appear in the text of the letters – including whatever gypsy we were able to decipher. We agreed too that when dashes came in such abundance as seriously to impair the meaning or give rise to unnecessary ambiguity, they would be replaced by more conventional marks of punctuation. The few ampersands scattered throughout the text were also expanded to 'and'.

The matter of ellipsis points, however, was the most troublesome to settle. Violet was one of those rare individuals whose speaking voice is preserved in her letters. More than that, she repeated herself almost as much in writing as speakers ordinarily repeat themselves in the rush of spontaneous speech. To permit such redundancy to remain in the text would, we assumed, have an adverse effect on the reader; and so it was necessary to delete much of the repetition and to insert ellipsis points to indicate those deletions. It soon became apparent, however, that Violet's own very liberal use of ellipses, in addition to ours, would have made of the printed page an eyesore of dots. We agreed, therefore, to omit *some* of our ellipses – but only when we were certain that the authenticity of the letter's content was in no way being compromised, or its tone falsified or impaired.

In all other matters of punctuation and spelling, we have remained staunchly faithful to the original text. Violet, in her younger and calmer letters, showed herself dutiful to the traditions of epistolary form, and would remain so in her later years. She was also, on the whole, fastidious in her spelling. Occasionally of course an inadvertency crops up, but nowhere have we inserted a [sic], even to placate the most ardent purists among us. We wanted least of all to introduce into this volume that note of pedantry which such editorial intrusions invariably carry with them.

Regarding the amount and kind of annotation, we agreed to provide notes only when we were sure they would deepen the ongoing narrative or clarify allusions which might otherwise have remained obscure. And to assure the readers' sense of continuity, brief connecting narratives have been inserted at regular intervals to fill in the time gaps as well as to provide a context for the principal characters playing a significant part in the unfolding drama. Such at least was our intention. We hope we have, in some measure, succeeded.

Several published books were helpful to us in the editing of these letters. The first and most important – in fact, the companion to this volume – is, of course, Nigel Nicolson's *Portrait of a Marriage* (1973). The rest, in alphabetical order, are Victoria Glendinning's *Vita: The Life of V. Sackville-West* (1983), Philippe Jullian and John Phillips' *Violet Trefusis: A Biography* (1976, 1984), James Lees-Milne's *Harold Nicolson: A Biography, Volume I, 1886–1929* (1981), Henrietta Sharpe's *A Solitary Woman: A Life of Violet Trefusis* (1981) and *The Last Edwardians* (Boston Atheneum, 1985). We offer our thanks to these authors as well as to Jack A. Siggins and Marjorie G. Wynne of the Beinecke Rare Book and Manuscript Library, Yale University, to William Cagle of the Lilly Library, Indiana University, where the Nicolsons' correspondence and Vita's and Lady Sackville's diaries are housed, to Count Jacques R. de Wurstemberger, whose aid in deciphering Violet's writing and translating from French and German was invaluable, to Helen McCutcheon Nelson, to Alejandro Gaytan de Ayala for his assistance with Spanish translations and notes, and to Cécile Wajsbrot, Violet's first French biographer. Nigel Nicolson granted us permission to quote from Vita and Harold Nicolson's letters and diaries as well as from Vita's 'confession', for which we are indeed grateful. We want also to acknowledge our debt to Dr Elmer E. Baker Jr of New York University for generously supporting Professor M. A. Leaska's application for a sabbatical leave of absence during which to complete his work on this volume. Under Ann Wilson's watchful eye the letters gained immeasurably in editorial consistency. Our final thanks go to Elsbeth Lindner, our editor at Methuen London, who marshalled the work of this volume through publication with ease and efficiency and provided us with much sound advice along the way.

M. A. L. and J. P.
New York and Vevey
February 1989

Introduction by Mitchell A. Leaska

'One of the truly fascinating – and civilized – books of this year, and the years to come,' wrote Leon Edel, Henry James's celebrated biographer, when *Portrait of a Marriage* was published in 1973. 'Vita Sackville-West's journal of her Sapphic and transvestite passion will live in erotic history as a supreme document ... of the spiritual as well as physical conflicts of androgyny.'

In his preface to the book, Nigel Nicolson, Vita's son and executor, tells of the locked Gladstone bag he found in the tower of Sissinghurst Castle in 1962, just after Vita's death. 'The bag contained something – a tiara in its case, for all I knew – and, having no key, I cut away the leather from around its lock to open it. Inside there was a large notebook in a flexible cover, page after page filled with her neat pencilled script. I carried it to her writing-table and began to read. The first pages were abortive drafts of a couple of short stories. The sixth page was headed "July 23rd 1920", followed by a narrative in the first person that continued for eighty more. I read it through to the end without stirring from her table. It was an autobiography written when she was aged twenty-eight, a confession, an attempt to purge her mind and heart of a love that had possessed her, a love for another woman, Violet Trefusis.'[1]

As long as Vita's husband, Harold Nicolson, and Violet Trefusis were alive, there could be no question of publishing so extraordinary a confession, but with Harold's death in 1968 and Violet's in 1972, this 'supreme document of erotic history' was made public. The *Portrait* remains to this day a remarkable tale of passion and pain.

As it happened, Violet's husband, Denys Trefusis, burned all of Vita's letters to Violet when their marriage had reached its most destructive pitch and, with Vita's side of the correspondence obliterated, only the confession itself was left to illuminate her part in

[1] *Portrait of a Marriage* (1973), p. vii.

the affair, making it in essence Vita's story. But Violet has been dead now for eighteen years and the letters published here, most of them for the first time, document her side of this ill-starred passion. That is the sole justification for this volume.

The emotional bond that was to attach Violet to Vita for life began when they were both still children, and dominating that childhood stood two formidable women: their mothers – Alice Keppel and Victoria Sackville-West – both of them adored and idolized by their daughters. The beautiful and spirited Alice Frederica, younger daughter of Admiral Sir William Edmonstone, descended from a long line of Scottish baronets, married in 1891 the handsome George Keppel, third son of the 7th Earl of Albemarle. In 1894, their first child, Violet, was born. Four years later, Alice Keppel, aged twenty-nine, succeeded both Lily Langtry and Daisy Brooke (the Countess of Warwick) in the glittering firmament of the Prince of Wales, who was then fifty-seven and soon to become King Edward VII, the 'Uncle of Europe'.

The Prince was invited to dine with the Keppels at 30 Portman Square on 27 February 1898 and, as Sir Philip Magnus phrased it, 'an understanding, which arose almost overnight, was unclouded until the end of King Edward's reign'.[1] She was perhaps 'the most perfect mistress in the history of royal fidelity'.[2] Until the King's death in 1910, Alice Keppel remained 'La Favorita', as she was dubbed by the Austrian ambassador, Count Albert Mensdorff. And just as Edward VII ruled over England, so Alice Keppel ruled over him. Wherever he was, not far away one was sure to find 'Dear Mrs George', as Edward called her.

All Europe knew of the relationship and accepted it with equanimity. Even George Keppel did not resist his sovereign's choice of mistress. Only 'three bastions of morality' closed their doors to her: the Duke of Norfolk at Arundel, the Duke of Portland at Welbeck and Lord Salisbury at Hatfield.[3] Otherwise she was welcomed everywhere and treated with deference. In France she was received in a way that Madame Pompadour or du Barry might have been in their own day. At Biarritz, where she accompanied the King each year at Easter, Alice Keppel was as much the Queen of England as Alexandra herself.

---

[1] Philip Magnus, *King Edward VII* (1967), p. 353.   [2] Giles St Aubyn, *Edward VII: Prince and King* (1979), p. 378.   [3] Loc. cit.

With Queen Victoria's death on 22 January 1901, the Prince of Wales acceded to the throne and if Mrs Keppel was to move now in a style appropriate to the King, she would need a great deal more money than her husband was in a position to provide. In order to fill the family coffers, then, the Honourable George Keppel was obliged to accept a job offered him by Sir Thomas Lipton (King Edward's millionaire yachting friend) in his Buyers' Association. (Sir Thomas would again come to the Keppel family's assistance in 1910 when they stayed at his tea plantations in Ceylon.) Alice Keppel was an ambitious, determined and powerful woman, however, and if she had all the tact her position demanded, she had also that fine sense of discretion that made her acceptable even to Alexandra.

When the King lay dying at Buckingham Palace, the Queen, in a gesture commensurate to her station, sent for Mrs Keppel so that she might bid her lover a last farewell. Immediately after his death, Lord Hardinge of Penshurst, Permanent Head of the Foreign Office and Viceroy of India, wrote in his personal file the following memorandum:

> I take this opportunity to allude to a delicate matter upon which I am in a position to speak with authority. Everybody knew of the friendship that existed between King Edward and Mrs George Keppel, which was intelligible in view of the lady's good looks, vivacity and cleverness. I used to see a great deal of Mrs Keppel at that time, and I was aware that she had knowledge of what was going on in the political world.
>
> I would like here to pay a tribute to her wonderful discretion, and to the excellent influence which she always exercised upon the King. She never utilized her knowledge to her advantage, or to that of her friends; and I never heard her repeat an unkind word of anybody. There were one or two occasions when the King was in disagreement with the Foreign Office, and I was able, through her, to advise the King with a view to the policy of the Government being accepted. She was very loyal to the King, and patriotic at the same time.
>
> It would have been difficult to find any other lady who would have filled the part of friend to King Edward with the same loyalty and discretion.[1]

[1] Magnus, pp. 323–4.

'In Alice Keppel,' wrote one biographer, 'the King had found not only a woman who, in the evening of his life, would excite him physically as well as relaxing him mentally (a rare combination in itself). On top of that he had found ... a mistress who could cherish him as fondly as a wife. No man, not even a monarch, could ask for more.'[1] And at the time of his death, Mrs Keppel, with the help of Sir Ernest Cassel, the King's financial advisor, had amassed a fortune, and through Cassel the King had made, in addition, a generous financial provision to ensure that the woman he loved 'should lack for nothing'.[2]

Throughout her twelve years as Edward's mistress, whatever her moral deficiencies, Mrs Keppel never lacked discretion: she kept no diaries, saved no letters, put nothing in writing that might one day incriminate her. Looking back today, after more than three quarters of a century, we find a considerable archive of Alice Keppel the public figure, but almost nothing about the private woman – the wife, the mother. To one social contemporary, Consuelo Vanderbilt Balsam, Duchess of Marlborough, 'Alice Keppel was handsome and of a genial and easy approach; nevertheless she knew how to choose her friends with shrewd appraisal. Even her enemies, and they were few, she treated kindly which, considering the influence she wielded with the Prince, indicated a generous nature. She invariably knew the choicest scandal, the price of stocks, the latest political move.'[3] Dame Rebecca West, meeting her in the 1920s, saw her as 'a theatre sister in a well run hospital, quite determined that all had to be for the good of the patient'.[4]

Violet, Alice Keppel's favoured daughter and 'the pride of her parents', wrote many years later in an unpublished memoir that as a child 'she saw Mamma in a blaze of glory, resplendent in a perpetual tiara'. Sonia, Violet's junior by six years, who suffered from 'nervous asthma', remembered in her autobiography *Edwardian Daughter* that 'throughout her life, Mamma was irresistibly attractive to bank managers'[5] and recalled two small incidents that cast Alice Keppel in a rather different light. After a childhood accident in which Sonia had somehow managed to break her collar-bone, 'Mamma took me to a doctor and, because he was rough setting it, she boxed his ears'.[6] The other incident took place in Holland. Sonia

---

[1] Gordon Brook-Shepherd, *Uncle of Europe: The Social and Diplomatic Life of Edward VII* (1976), p. 144.   [2] Gordon Brook-Shepherd, p. 359n.   [3] *The Glitter and the Gold* (1952), pp. 152–3.   [4] *1900*, 1982, p. 151.   [5] Sonia Keppel, *Edwardian Daughter* (1958), p. 28.   [6] Ibid., p. 11.

had written some wildly romantic stories that she treasured. But they were evidently too romantic for Mrs Keppel, who found them lying on a table, read them quickly and promptly threw them into the fire. 'Dumbly, I looked at Mamma. ... Did she not realize all the toil and trouble that had gone to the compilation of these brimming gifts? ... And Mamma, reducing my masterpieces to ashes.'[1] Alice Keppel was clearly a woman who knew her mind and let you know soon enough, often in the most beguiling way, that you too had better know *her* mind.

In *The Edwardians*, Vita Sackville-West described Mrs Keppel (in the character of Romola Cheyne) as 'a woman who erred and aspired with a certain magnificence. She brought to everything the quality of the superlative. When she was worldly, it was on a grand scale. When she was mercenary, she challenged the richest fortunes. When she loved, it was in the highest quarters. When she admitted ambition, it was for the highest power. When she suffered, it would be on the plane of tragedy. Romola Cheyne, for all her hardness and materialism, was no mean soul.'[2]

But whatever Alice Keppel was in reality, to her elder daughter Violet she represented that high romance where materialism has no weight and morality no measure. When Mrs Keppel discovered that Violet behaved contrary to her wishes, she did what it was in her nature and temperament to do: she withdrew her love – and all that went with it. That withdrawal represented the most extreme form of punishment a mother can inflict upon a child, and many of the letters published here for the first time give a picture of the woman that no biographer has yet discovered: a woman who could be as tyrannical as she was charming and as merciless as she was gracious.

Violet's close friend in her later years, John Phillips, recalls that 'often Violet spoke to me, always in superlatives, about her mother, whom she never for a moment descended from the pedestal. One characteristic of her conversations with me was that she would say certain things with such extreme emphasis that instinctively I felt that the exact opposite must be true, that a sort of defence mechanism in her was reacting.'

Violet Keppel was born in Wilton Crescent, London on 6 June 1894 and would not have a sibling to rival her until her sister Sonia arrived on the scene in 1900, when Violet was six. Very little

---

[1] Ibid., p. 97. [2] *The Edwardians* (1930), p. 183.

survives, if indeed anything ever existed, to document her opening years. One gets the impression from the early letters, however, that she was a highly emotional child, extremely sensitive to criticism, and as vulnerable in childhood as she was voluble, vivacious and vocal in adulthood.

Her mother was unquestionably the dominant force in her childhood and spoiled her greatly not so much from an excess of love as from the excess of 'things' that she showered upon the child to defray the deficit of her own exclusive preoccupations. Violet, whose sister was too much younger to be a companion in these early years, found herself alone in the vast world of childhood, and made that place inhabitable by living increasingly in an imaginary world of her own making.

Alice Keppel's 'preoccupation' was of course the Prince of Wales, who entered Violet's life in 1898 when she was four and under whose shadow she lived until his death in 1910. Jean Cocteau was to say in later years that as a child, Violet 'rolled her hoop with a sceptre'. Certainly Edward – 'Kingy' to the Keppel sisters – was very fond of this restless and precocious child, and his influence on *mon petit*, as he called her, was considerable, especially during the annual three weeks' holiday at Biarritz where he was installed in the Hôtel du Palais, with Alice and her daughters staying in the adjacent Villa Eugénia. Growing up in the company of England's monarch, in a world of confusing morals, inevitably had its effect upon so impressionable a little girl, and the fairytale quality of life added to the fantasy world Violet had already begun to construct for herself. Small wonder that in later years she sought spaciousness, needed ever new excitements, grew quickly bored, lived with only the slightest grasp of reality. Small wonder too that, immersed in an atmosphere of hushed conspiracy and high proprietorial claims, Violet should learn in childhood to 'read' people's faces, voices and gestures, to emulate her betters and imitate her elders, to believe in her own opinions and powers of divination, to float vaguely in a frothy world of make-believe where truth and falsehood merged and mingled, and above all to feel that no matter what she had, it was never enough. And these lessons were to prove extremely harmful to herself and to others in the years ahead. For King Edward and her mother were in a sense her primary models of a man and a woman in love, and the glamour of their illicit romance was siphoned into the emptiness of her childhood years and somehow combined with her own craving for affection to produce the most unrealistic notion of what love and happiness must be. Violet saw her mother looking after a kingdom, amusing a pleasure-seeking king, warding off royal boredom. These became collectively her earliest conception of love.

Fortified with this specious conception, Violet met Vita Sackville-West in childhood and attached herself in a way that would one day bring England's pillars of morality crashing down upon both their heads. But if Alice Keppel, the model, had succeeded in her own dangerous enterprise of the heart, then why indeed should her daughter not succeed as well? This, or something very close to it, must have been the underlying governing logic upon which Violet proceeded in her adolescent years to seduce and eventually to lure Vita away from the security of her home and family. The one major obstacle, however, was Vita's mother.

Victoria Sackville-West was born in Paris in 1862, the second child of Pepita, the internationally famous Spanish dancer, christened Josepha Duran. Although Pepita was legally married to her former dancing teacher, Juan Antonio de Oliva, her two sons and three daughters were the children of the unmarried English diplomat, Lionel Sackville-West, whose mistress she had been for ten years at the time of Victoria's birth. On Pepita's death in 1871, Victoria, then aged nine, was sent with both her sisters to a convent in Paris, where she remained until she was eighteen. In 1880 Lionel removed his illegitimate family – all five of them – to England, but the stop was brief. Appointed British Minister to Washington in 1882, Lionel Sackville-West proceeded to America with Victoria. Here, as a hostess in Washington society, she overwhelmed the Americans with her remarkable beauty and seductive charm, and seems to have bewitched the eligible male population, for in later years she claimed to have received marriage proposals from twenty-five of the numerous diplomatic suitors who swarmed around her during the six-year residence.

In 1888, the family returned to England where Victoria's uncle Mortimer, the 1st Lord Sackville, died, making her father the 2nd Lord Sackville and inheritor of Knole, the great 365-room ancestral house, originally granted to Thomas Sackville by Queen Elizabeth in 1566. At Knole, Victoria met her first cousin, also named Lionel Sackville-West, five years her junior, who 'never took his eyes off me during dinner'[1] and succumbed almost at once to her perfectly

---

[1] Susan Mary Alsop, *Lady Sackville: A Biography* (1978), p. 87.

orchestrated repertoire of titillations. He was a shy, modest young man who seemed no obvious match for Victoria's strong personality, but he offered one certain great attraction: he stood to inherit Knole and the title at his uncle's death, and that was evidently reason enough for Victoria to keep his heart firmly within her grasp. Eighteen months after her return from Washington – on 17 June 1890 – the enchanting and increasingly extravagant Victoria married her gentle cousin Lionel in the chapel at Knole. In the private diary she kept for most of her life, Victoria recorded meticulously during her first months of marriage 'where, when, how and how often'.[1] She was as highly sexed as her shy young husband, and as her daughter would one day be.

On 9 March 1892, Victoria and Lionel's first and only child, Vita, was born. The responsibility of parenthood and the fading of early marital bliss, however, affected Victoria adversely and with time transformed her from the ravishing belle of Washington in earlier days to a rapacious, egotistical and destructive woman. Her beauty vied with her ruthlessness, and her extravagance only partially concealed a gnawing self-doubt. Her love for Vita was erratic and smothering, and throughout her stormy childhood, Vita tried to understand this capricious mother who pampered her at dawn and brutalized her at dusk, who proclaimed the little girl beautiful one minute and condemned her as ugly the next. All through her adult life Vita lived in the shade of this imperious and power-hungry woman who simultaneously wounded and fascinated her. No matter how much abuse and pain her mother inflicted, however, Vita, humiliated and impotent as she might be, never faltered in her adoration. 'I would have murdered anyone that breathed a word against her,' she wrote in later life. 'I would have suffered any injustice at her hands.'[2]

Before and even during her marriage, Victoria Sackville-West had attracted countless suitors and continued, after her separation from Lionel in 1919, to attract many more – Sir John Murray Scott, Pierpont Morgan, Sir Edwin Lutyens, William Waldorf Astor – men of great influence and wealth. As she grew up, Vita must have seen that powerful men were part of her mother's turf and reasoned that if she was to remain in her favour, she had better stay clear of competition with her. But for whatever reason, in accommodating herself to the whims of an overwhelming parent, Vita seems to

[1] Victoria Glendinning, *Vita: The Life of V. Sackville-West* (1983), p. 5.
[2] V. Sackville-West, *Pepita* (1938), p. 252.

have suppressed the feminine side of her nature and nurtured the masculine part in the form of male pursuits, reckless games and boyish mannerisms. What better way was there of avoiding confrontation with her mother in the contest for male favour than becoming, in fantasy, a male herself? Had Vita in fact been born the only son rather than the only daughter of Lord Sackville, she would have inherited a historic title, a considerable fortune *and* Knole. It is not hard to see, in these terms alone, why she grew up wanting so badly to be a male – to be 'crested' rather than 'cloven'.

It was from a childhood of loneliness and confusion that Vita emerged, full of damaging contradictions. She was now reticent, now aggressive; expansive and courageous in public, withdrawn and timid in private. She wanted love and friendship, but equally she needed solitude. The outward show of bravado was countered by a haunting sense of inadequacy. Such were the contraries and inconsistencies that tangled and strained her emotional and moral fibre.

Thus dominated by a tyrannical and erratic mother, Vita soon learned that if she was to find anything resembling coherence, she would have to create it herself, and this she did through writing. In childhood and adolescence, she sat endlessly spinning out romances and tragedies, all of them chilling tales of unearthly valour, foresaken love and copious bloodshed, with herself always cast in the role of unvanquishable hero. Writing was a solitary occupation and the writer was an unsociable child. It was a retreat into a past that protected her from the violence and disorder of the present.

Vita had behind her the romance of Knole, just as Violet would have behind her the enchanted Duntreath Castle in Stirlingshire. Thus wrapped in the gauzy veils of history, the girls, when they finally met, would both be brimming with the magical spells of their ancestors and the alluring opacities of antiquity.

It was at Miss Wolff's private school in South Audley Street, London, that the sultry and passionate Violet first laid eyes on the reticent, close-fisted Vita – an awkward, tight-lipped girl of twelve, all 'knobs and knuckles'.[1] They came face to face for the first time at a tea-party. Violet would later write:

> There I met a girl older than myself, but, apparently, every bit as unsociable. She was tall for her age, gawky,

---

[1] Violet Trefusis, *Don't Look Round* (1952), p. 70.

9

most unsuitably dressed in what appeared to be her mother's old clothes. I do not remember who made the first step. Anyhow, much to my family's gratification I asked if I might have her to tea. She came. We were both consummate snobs, and talked, chiefly, as far as I can remember, about our ancestors. I essayed a few superior allusions to Paris. She was not impressed; her tastes seemed to lie in another direction. She digressed on her magnificent home in the country, her dogs, her rabbits.

I thought her nice, but rather childish (I was ten). We separated, however, with mutual esteem. The repressions of my short life immediately found an outlet in a voluminous correspondence. I bombarded the poor girl with letters which became more exacting as hers tended to become more and more of the 'yesterday-my-pet-rabbit-had-six-babies' type. Clearly no letter writer. Our meetings, however, atoned for this epistolary pusillanimity. . . . Our friendship progressed all that winter. I was invited to stay at Knole.[1]

Here is Vita's account of that meeting:

I was twelve, she was two years younger, but in every instinct she might have been six years my senior. It seems to me so significant that I should remember with such distinctness my first sight of her; we met at a tea-party by the bedside of a mutual friend with a broken leg, and she made to me some little remark about flowers in the room. I wasn't listening; and so didn't answer. This piqued her – she was already spoilt. She got her mother to ask mine to send me to tea. I went. We sat in a darkened room, and talked – about our ancestors, of all strange topics – and in the hall as I left she kissed me. I made up a little song that evening, 'I've got a friend,' I remember so well. I sang it in my bath.[2]

Such was the beginning of a friendship in 1904 that would fourteen years later explode into a historic love affair. From the start, the twelve-year-old Vita dimly sensed that she could 'possess' the ten-year-old Violet, but *that* was a secret she confided to no one.

[1] Ibid., pp. 41–2.   [2] Nigel Nicolson, *Portrait of a Marriage* (1973), pp. 21–2.

In subsequent visits to the Keppels' house in Portman Square, Vita found the atmosphere bristling with excitement: King Edward, 'Kingy', might be upstairs regally closeted with 'Dear Mrs George' – the charming mistress whom Victoria Sackville-West had in earlier years quietly discouraged from visiting Knole. On those days when the King was there, signalled by the small one-horse brougham waiting outside, the butler would sweep Vita into some dark hall-corner with 'One minute, miss, a gentleman is coming downstairs'.[1]

The friendship held a greater excitement, however. In the stumblings of adolescence, Vita had discovered someone who found the past as romantic as she did and who loved with the same passion Rostand's *Cyrano de Bergerac*, which they both knew by heart. And though she was not the sophisticated epistolary mistress Violet deemed herself to be, Vita did write – far too much for her mother's taste. The time she spent alone with her manuscript notebooks was almost obsessional, but Vita saw herself as 'horribly unattractive – rough, and secret'[2] and was determined to be clever if she could not be popular.

In May 1908, Violet accompanied Vita and Rosamund Grosvenor, and their respective governesses, to Pisa, Milan and Florence. Rosamund was madly in love with Vita and murderously jealous, but it was here in Italy that Violet first declared her love and, by way of confirmation, gave Vita the fifteenth-century Doge's lava ring she had coaxed out of Sir Joseph Duveen, an art dealer, when she was six. A great many tears were shed when Vita left Florence.

When Victoria's father, the 2nd Lord Sackville, died in 1908, it was assumed that, because he had no legitimate male heir, Knole and the title would go to his nephew Lionel, Vita's father. Victoria's brother Henry, however, no longer satisfied with earlier monetary settlements, now claimed his 'rights' as the legitimate heir by contending, first, that old Lionel Sackville-West had in fact secretly married Pepita and second, that she had never been legally married to her former dancing teacher. Victoria and young Lionel set out to prove her brother wrong on both counts. Many months were spent in searching French and Spanish record offices in addition to the many thousands of pounds spent in legal fees.

The succession case opened at last, on 15 February 1910, and Henry lost. The affair was a sensation and added more fuel to the

<hr />

[1] Glendinning, p. 23.   [2] Ibid., p. 26.

romantically overcharged Sackville family. Cameras clicked end-lessly and newspapers kept up daily accounts of the courtroom scene. At its conclusion, Victoria (now Lady) Sackville scored an enormous victory. The years of worry were finally over and Vita and her parents returned to Knole triumphant.

Later that year, on 29 June, Vita met Harold Nicolson for the first time and found him captivating. Four days later he was invited to Knole, where he returned several times during that summer. Rosamund Grosvenor twitched with jealousy.

Vita's 'coming out' the previous year had been subdued by the succession case, but it was King Edward's death on 6 May 1910 that suppressed most social activity during this period of national mourning. Alice Keppel, England's 'unofficial widow', was flattened with grief: 'How people can do anything I do not know, for life with all its joys has come to a full stop, at least for me ...'[1] she wrote to Lady Knollys, wife of the King's Private Secretary. In her practical wisdom she decided to leave England for an extended period and thus avoid the 'embarrassments of curiosity and com-passion and the depressing realization of all the changes at Court and in society'[2] that would come about during King George V's sovereignty. And so one morning, quite out of the blue, Mrs Keppel announced some 'good news' to Violet and Sonia: 'I am taking you to Ceylon for the winter. In my opinion no young lady's education is complete without a smattering of Tamil.'[3]

Accordingly, the dwelling in Portman Square was exchanged for a new house at 16 Grosvenor Street, 'one of the most remarkable houses in London',[4] and some time in late November 1910 the Keppel family sailed for the East. King Edward's friend Sir Thomas Lipton, who had earlier helped George Keppel during a period of financial strain, once again rose to the occasion and lent the Keppels his house at Dambatenne, in the midst of his vast tea plantations. 'Monkeys gambolled on a small precarious lawn,' Violet recalled in later years. 'Parrots streaked from tree to tree, tiny humming-birds skimmed huge greedy-looking flowers; I shared a room with a tame snake [used to catch rats] and a wild governess.'[5]

Before sailing, Violet bid Vita farewell and, as they drove round and round Hyde Park, kissed her – a gesture Vita found 'extremely

---

[1] Brook-Shepherd, p. 359.   [2] John Phillips in *The Last Edwardians* (1985), p. 24.
[3] Trefusis, p. 56.   [4] Osbert Sitwell, *Great Morning* (1947), p. 239.
[5] Trefusis, p. 58.

disturbing'.[1] Violet, then aged sixteen, had done her best to lure Vita into coming to Ceylon but Lady Sackville, fearing that a lingering summer flu might turn into pneumonia, took her daughter to the Château Malet, in the sunny warmth of Monte Carlo, where they stayed until April of the following year. Harold was invited to stay with them.

From Ceylon, Violet wrote on 4 December: 'Do try not to get married before I return.' 'After all, I'm only a girl,' she continued on the 14th. 'I ought to have foreseen that perhaps at your age [Vita was then eighteen] a masculine liaison would come about. I would be wise to accept this. ... For a long time I've asked nothing of you, so grant me this.'

After three months George and Alice Keppel went on to China. Violet saw Vita briefly in San Remo and gave her some rubies she had brought back from Ceylon. Then, accompanied by Hélène Claissac ('Moiselle' often shortened to 'Mell'), the Keppel sisters went to Munich, where they studied German for over a year. From here Violet wrote solemnly: 'Oh Vita, I get so sad when I think how like we are to two gamblers, both greedy to win, neither of whom will risk throwing a card unless the other throws his at the same time! You won't tell me you love me, because you fear (wrongly, most of the time) that I will not make the same declaration to you at the same moment!' This was Violet, aged seventeen.

During that summer of 1911, however, Vita 'was very much in love'[2] with Rosamund Grosvenor. It was a purely physical attraction, even though the friendship remained technically chaste. In fact, Rosamund 'always bored me as a companion ... she was quite stupid,'[3] Vita would later write in her autobiography.

Harold returned from his post at the Embassy in Madrid and spent the Christmas holidays at Knole. Vita found him as vivacious as ever, and certainly very handsome and clever. She liked him 'better than anyone, as a companion and playfellow',[4] and, despite some scepticism, hoped that he would propose to her before going away in the New Year to Constantinople. Lady Sackville, fond of Harold as she was, had many reservations. His post in the Foreign Office as third secretary brought him an annual salary of only £250, even if he was destined to emulate the career of his father, Sir Arthur Nicolson (later Lord Carnock), in 1912 a distinguished diplomat

---

[1] Nicolson, p. 28.   [2] Ibid., p. 30.   [3] Loc. cit.   [4] Loc. cit.

and Permanent Under-Secretary of State for Foreign Affairs. Surely Vita could do better than that? There was no dearth of admirers. Earlier in Italy Vita had won the heart of Orazio Pucci. Then Lord Lascelles, heir to the Earl of Harewood, had fallen in love with her, and later the Marquess of Granby, heir to the Dukedom of Rutland. And then there were Patrick Shaw-Stewart, Edward Horner and Ivan Hay.

On 17 January 1912, however – a day before the Hatfield House ball when Harold did in fact propose to Vita – Sir John Murray Scott ('Seery') died, leaving Lady Sackville as his principal beneficiary, and at the centre of another court case. According to the terms of his will, she would inherit £150,000 in cash, in addition to all the French furniture in Seery's Rue Lafitte apartment (which she later sold *en bloc* to a Paris dealer for £270,000). The Scott family contested the will and brought a suit against Lady Sackville that opened in June of the following year and lasted two weeks. Victoria Sackville-West, very much in the spirit of her days as the 'Belle of Washington', emerged once again triumphant. She had made a fool of the opposing counsel, confided tearfully in her audience, charmed the judge, seduced the jury, and was soon in possession of a Rolls Royce costing £1,450. 'Mother has been buying chefs, and gardeners, and people, it is such fun,' wrote Vita to Harold in Turkey. 'Yes, she is a splendid person, and I told her you had said so. She is more wonderful every day.'[1] Just as Violet was to worship her mother unconditionally throughout her life, so too would Vita, neither of them conscious of the wide chasm that separates adoration from love.

George and Alice Keppel returned to England in 1912, installed in their fine new house at 16 Grosvenor Street, where Alice resumed her place as one of London's leading hostesses. 'Mrs Keppel possessed an instinct for splendour,' Sir Osbert Sitwell would later write, 'and not only were the rooms beautiful, with their grey walls, red lacquer cabinets, English eighteenth-century portraits of people in red coats, huge porcelain pagodas, and thick, magnificent carpets, but the hostess conducted the running of the house as a work of art in itself.

'I liked greatly listening to her talking,' he continues. 'If it were possible to lure her away from the bridge table, she would remove from her mouth for a moment the cigarette which she would be

[1] Glendinning, p. 45.

smoking with an air of determination, through a long holder, and turn upon the person to whom she was speaking her large, humorous, kindly, peculiarly discerning eyes. ... Her talk had about it a boldness, an absence of all pettiness, that helped to make her a memorable figure in the fashionable world.'[1]

Violet Keppel, now almost eighteen, returned from Germany in April 1912 for her 'coming out' ball in Grosvenor Street. It was a grand affair with a vast tent spanning the garden and Casano's band playing in the background as dinner was served at little tables to countless guests. The young débutante acted the 'cynical, critical, the blasée woman of the world' who had spent 'several years' in Munich studying art.

Shortly after the coming out, Mrs Keppel informed her daughter that they were spending the weekend at Knole. 'Now, though I had not seen Vita for two years, we had kept up a desultory, somewhat misleading, correspondence. ... I had sent her a snapshot of myself as a fully matured German, complete with plaits and silver watch sporran. That had silenced her – at any rate, for a time.' Violet expected to find Vita still 'perpendicular and gauche'. No one had told her that Vita, at twenty, had turned into a beautiful woman: 'The knobs and knuckles had disappeared. She was tall and graceful. The profound, hereditary Sackville eyes were as pools from which the morning mist had lifted. A peach might have envied her complexion. Round her revolved several enamoured young men, one of whom [Ivan Hay] had presented her with a bear, inevitably christened Ivan. Bears had taken the place of rabbits.'[2]

Anxious for Vita's approval after their long separation, Violet approached her with: '*Tu me trouves jolie?*' '*Tu as beaucoup de chic,*' replied Vita, very much on guard. And Violet, wanting desperately to make an impression – good or bad – proceeded to flirt outrageously with a young man. But even then Vita only responded with 'amused condescension'.[3] Certain now that Violet was in her thrall, Vita slipped the very probable noose and fled to Florence in the late spring, again with Rosamund, for whom she still felt a passion that made her head swim.[4]

Harold returned on leave from Constantinople in August and spent two months at Knole. Lady Sackville insisted that their engagement be kept secret and their behaviour beyond reproach.

[1] Sitwell, pp. 239–40.   [2] Trefusis, p. 70.   [3] Ibid., pp. 70–1.
[4] Nicolson, p. 53.

Rosamund was beside herself, but still the young women set off once again for Italy in October. Harold, on his way to Constantinople, accompanied them as far as Bologna.

Despite the candour Vita affected with Harold, she withheld the truth of her feelings for Rosamund, just as he withheld from her his homosexual infatuation with Pierre de Lacretelle, an employee of the Ottoman Bank in Constantinople. From Italy, she wrote of Rosamund's subservience: 'It is a pity and rather tiresome. But doesn't everyone want *one* subservient person in their life? I've got mine in her. Who is yours? Certainly not me!'[1] Thus the stage was set for a 'complex marital relationship with Harold'. She did not, during this Italian autumn of 1912, writes Victoria Glendinning, Vita's biographer, 'conceal from him how happy she was – "it is hot, and the *grilli* sing, and I love the Rubens lady [Rosamund], and somewhere in the world there is you" – and asserted her right to her private friendships: "Don't let's hate each other's friends, and anyhow we can give and take about it can't we?..."'

'This is not so worldly-wise as it sounds,' Glendinning goes on. 'Her instincts were sophisticated, but her knowledge was limited. She knew that there were "effeminate" men (and Harold was not effeminate) but she did not know the physical realities of male homosexuality. Neither did she know that there was a name for the love she and Rosamund felt for one another.'[2] 'You should have warned me,'[3] Vita would write to Harold a half-century later.

On Christmas Day 1912, Harold, nervous about Vita's increasing indecisiveness, wrote to her, stating firmly that he wanted to announce the engagement in April, with the marriage ceremony to take place in September. Vita consented 'almost gratefully, as if that was what she had been waiting for'.[4]

But the New Year brought new complications. Relations between Vita's parents were becoming progressively strained. Rosamund's possessiveness was getting out of hand, and Vita once more began to vacillate over the engagement. To add to the confusion, Violet, who was now seeing Vita more often than ever before, again declared her love. In April, Vita escaped to Spain with Mrs Charles Hunter, sister of the composer Ethyl Smyth. There she feasted on memories of her exotic grandmother, Pepita, and indulged in an orgy of gypsy dancing and snapping castanets. Spain was a place of

---

[1] Glendinning, p. 47.   [2] Loc. cit.   [3] Loc. cit.   [4] Ibid., p. 52.

high romance for her, and there she felt happy and free and Bohemian. It was her 'own country', she wrote to Harold, where her poor, proud relations lived, all of them descended from Lucrezia Borgia – 'Spain and Italy rolled into one'.[1]

In May, Vita returned to England by way of Italy and stopped in Ravello to visit the Keppels, who were staying at the villa of Ernest William Beckett, 2nd Baron Grimthorpe (reputed to be Violet's natural father). A few weeks later Violet came to stay at Knole again, made her way to Vita's bedroom again and once again declared her love. Vita said nothing to Violet of her engagement to Harold.

During the summer months, relations between Vita's parents grew worse as Lord Sackville sought consolation at the bosom of the singer Olive Rubens, who was spending more time at Knole than propriety allowed or Lady Sackville could tolerate. And Violet, after a brief flirtation with Lord Gerald Wellesley – a colleague of Harold's posted in Constantinople – became engaged to him, also briefly. 'My reputation as a flirt,' Violet wrote later, 'was finally established.'[2]

Harold returned to England on 3 July and on 5 August the engagement was formally announced in the newspapers. Rosamund was inarticulate with grief, but Vita was suddenly 'as cold as ice'.[3] She loved Harold as never before. 'Now there's no doubt,' she wrote in her diary. 'At first, I loved him one day and not the next; but now I think of nothing but him.'[4]

At the end of August the happy couple, accompanied by B. M. (Bonne Maman, Harold's name for his future mother-in-law), travelled to Switzerland, where Lady Sackville was joined by the elderly millionaire, William Waldorf Astor, whom she now had in tow, leaving the newly betrothed unchaperoned. But Vita had no doubts about Harold's intentions: 'Some men are born to be lovers, others to be husbands.'[5] Harold clearly belonged to the latter category; for him her feeling was 'unalterable, perennial, and *best*',[6] by which she meant that her love for him was pure.

The nuptials were performed in the chapel at Knole on 1 October. Vita's former suitors sent lavish presents. Lady Sackville declared herself too unwell to attend the ceremony and remained in bed for

[1] Ibid., p. 55.   [2] Trefusis, p. 71.   [3] Nicolson, p. 37.
[4] Glendinning, p. 59.   [5] Nicolson, p. 33.   [6] Ibid., p. 34.

the day. Violet Keppel was absent too. All the jurymen from the Scott case crowded together at the reception: they were all there, of course, at Bonne Maman's invitation.

The newlyweds, after three days at Dorothy Heneage's Coker Court, set off for Florence and stayed in the same cottage that Vita had shared eighteen months earlier with Rosamund. The gesture was, as the new bride herself said, a 'dreadful *manque de délicatesse*'.[1] In November, they went to Constantinople to live in a marital contentment that was to remain 'intact', according to Vita's calculation, 'for about four and a half years'.[2]

In June 1914, they returned to England, where their first son, Benedict, was born on 6 August (two days after the declaration of war with Germany). 'At her own sarcastic request',[3] Violet Keppel was made one of Ben's three godmothers, Olive Rubens and Rosamund Grosvenor being the other two. The two women saw little of each other during the winter months. Pregnant again by December, Vita had become too domesticated for Violet, who was no doubt disturbed by Harold's presence being so unalterably in view; his work at the Foreign Office had given him complete exemption from military service. Nor did she see much of Vita in 1915, when the Nicolsons bought Long Barn, a Tudor cottage in Kent, two miles from Knole. The place was 'too self-consciously picturesque for my taste', said Violet. Life in the Tudor cottage was 'like living *under* the furniture instead of above it'.[4]

When war had broken out, the Keppels were in Holland at Clingendaal, the eighteenth-century house situated near The Hague belonging to Baroness Daisy de Brienen. Violet was there, surrounded by her usual flock of admirers – 'all the brilliant, doomed young men the war was to annihilate',[5] among them Patrick Shaw-Stewart and Julian Grenfell.

Vita's second child, due in September 1915, was not delivered until 3 November. It was a nine-pound boy, born dead. By late April, however, Vita was pregnant again.

At Knole, where she and Harold spent the Christmas of 1916, the atmosphere was close to flash point. Lord Sackville had converted the laundry into an apartment for his mistress *and* her husband. Lady Sackville, about to explode with fury, made everyone

[1] Ibid., p. 38.   [2] Ibid., p. 39.   [3] Loc. cit.   [4] Trefusis, p. 71.   [5] Ibid., p. 72.

miserable, but Harold comforted Vita as much as he could. Early in the morning on 19 January 1917, the new baby, Nigel, was born at Ebury Street, the house in Pimlico that the Nicolsons had bought a year earlier. In late April, they moved back to Long Barn for the spring and summer, and Violet, who had been seeing a lot of Vita in London while carrying on a flirtation with Osbert Sitwell, now swooped down on her for occasional weekends, distasteful as she found her hostess's blissful domesticity.

Some time in 1917, Margaret (Pat) Dansey briefly entered the story. She was the niece of Lord Fitzhardinge of Berkeley Castle in Gloucester, a place that was to become very special to Violet. Pat seems to have become rather quickly a close friend of Violet at about this time, and was forced, it appears from the few scraps of evidence that survive, to listen to endless stories about the extraordinary Vita Sackville-West, who had by now become the subject closest to Violet's heart. From Dorothy Heneage's Coker Court, Violet wrote on 29 October that Vita would become 'smug to an intolerable degree if the vagabond – what Dorothy calls "rackety" element – as supplied to me, is indefinitely withheld from you. We mustn't let that happen. We are absolutely essential to one another, at least in *my* eyes!'

At precisely this time, however, a shadow was cast over the Nicolsons' private life which would have far-reaching consequences. Harold suspected he had contracted a venereal infection in late October. His suspicions were confirmed by laboratory tests, and his physician insisted that Vita be told of this and, worst of all, that she too, for her own protection, submit to the tests.

The situation was humiliating. In revealing to Vita his condition, Harold would have to confess many other things about himself – his male infatuations, his sexual excursions and numerous other small privacies that he had up to this time only lightly touched upon. The obligatory 'talk' took place on 6 November and on the following day Vita went to Oxford to absorb the shock alone and in her own way. 'I fear it will make you loathe me,' Harold wrote to her from London. But he was wrong. 'Vita's response to Harold in this embarrassment, and subsequent explanations and revelations, go a very long way to explain his almost superhuman tolerance of her behaviour to him in the following three years.'[1]

---

[1] Glendinning, p. 90.

Harold was subsequently pronounced to have been clear of infection since January 1918, but was advised to refrain from physical intimacy until 20 April. Engaged in important diplomatic work at the Foreign Office and living in London most of the week, he passed this news on in a letter to Vita at Long Barn, hoping that she would not 'turn from me in abhorrence'.[1] Two days before that crucial date, however, his wife would be a different woman and their domestic bliss at an end.

On 13 April, Violet invited herself to Long Barn for two weeks, going to London during the day and returning in the evening: the air-raids frightened her. 'She had been here I think about a week,' wrote Vita in her autobiography, 'when everything changed suddenly ... changed my life. It was the 18th of April.' From ten o'clock that evening until two in the morning, Vita talked in a way she had never done before. Violet had ferreted out the secret of her dual nature and Vita no longer tried to conceal it from Violet or from herself. 'I talked out the whole of myself with absolute sincerity and pain, and Violet only listened.' There was no interruption, no movement. Violet had waited a long time for this moment. Now it had finally come. 'I might have been a boy of eighteen, and she a woman of thirty-five. She was infinitely clever – she didn't rush me, she didn't allow me to see where I was going.' Violet lay back on the sofa, watching Vita's every move. With her red velvet dress, her pale skin and thick tawny hair, she was very seductive. 'She pulled me down until I kissed her. ... Then she was wise enough to get up and go to bed; but I kissed her again in the dark. ... She let herself go entirely limp and passive in my arms.'[2] This moment was the turning point.

Violet was clever, indeed, for she knew that her most powerful weapon was her passivity. Only this show of submission would seduce Vita completely. For the next five days, 'I made her follow me on wild courses all over the country,' Vita continues, 'and, because she knew she had me only lightly hooked, she obeyed'.[3] The grand passion that in three years' time would end in heartbreak and bitterness had at last begun.

They went off on 28 April to Polperro in Cornwall, where Hugh Walpole had lent them his fisherman's cottage, and did not return

[1] Nicolson, pp. 103–5.   [2] Ibid., p. 107.   [3] Loc. cit.

until 10 May. It was the first time Vita had ever been away from Harold, but his letters, three and four a day, did nothing to bring her back to the now-dubious family hearth. Domestic bliss gave way to romantic bliss. Four days after their return, on 14 May, Vita began writing *Challenge*, a novel about themselves – two young lovers: the erotic Julian (Vita) and the erratic Eve (Violet). Soon the mercury of their passion would soar.

By June, Violet, now calling herself Lushka, was writing letters to Vita (sometimes Julian, sometimes Mitya) that plumbed the heart of Vita's fantasies of masculine power, letters that deliberately accentuated Violet's passivity and helplessness. Vita had bent Violet to her will, shattered her poise – 'away from you I am nothing but a useless puppet! an empty husk'. This emotional realignment for Vita was apocalyptic. 'It was like beginning one's life again in a different capacity.'[1]

To Cornwall they fled again in early July, this time too for a fortnight. Their involvement was deepening, becoming more serious than Vita had anticipated. They began using secret expressions adapted from Spanish Romany, a gypsy dialect probably picked up from George Borrow, and wrote to one another in words no one else could decipher. The web of emotion was growing tighter, more exclusive. Throughout the summer they were together constantly. Violet was either at Long Barn, with Vita increasingly in the masculine garb of breeches and gaiters, or Vita was at Grosvenor Street, where at some point she met Violet's confidante Pat Dansey.

Vita loved her new freedom and tried to explain it to Harold as something good: 'I feel that Violet and people like that save me from a sort of intellectual stagnation, a bovine complacency.'[2] And with Harold in London much of the time, Violet was free to glut her lover with all the illusory ideals she could think of. 'The only two things that matter,' Violet scrawled across the page, 'are love and beauty. . . . Heaven preserve us from all sleek and dowdy virtues. . . . What great man was ever constant? What great queen was ever faithful?' She went further. She wanted to instil in Vita a mixture of guilt and shame for her own 'dowdy virtues' as a wife. They must free themselves, thumb their noses at traditional wisdom, cast off the restraints of custom and respectability. 'What sort of life can we lead now? Yours, an infamous and degrading lie to the world,

[1] Glendinning, p. 92.   [2] Nicolson, pp. 108–9.

officially bound to someone you don't care for. ... I, not caring a damn for anyone but you.'

During the summer months of 1918, Denys Trefusis, to whom Violet, in her spare moments, had been writing, returned on leave from duty in France. He was with the Royal Horse Guards and would soon be awarded the Military Cross. Vita likened him 'to a race-horse, to a Crusader, to a grey-hound, to an ascetic in search of the Holy Grail'. They liked one another and Vita could see that he was 'a rare, sensitive, proud idealist' – a 'tragic person'.[1] Denys did not at the time appear to her as a threat.

For the whole of that summer, mad and irresponsible as it was, Violet was entirely hers, and she was as happy during those warm, scented months as Harold was sad. 'Little one,' he wrote to her in early September, 'I wish Violet were dead. She has poisoned one of the most sunny things that ever happened. She is like some fierce orchid – glimmering and stinking in the recesses of life.'[2]

Some time in the early autumn, Vita, who indeed took conventional respectability seriously, did one of the most daring things in her life: she began cross-dressing in public places. One such occasion is described in her 'confession': dressed as a man, she left her house in Ebury Street and drove in a taxi with Violet as far as Hyde Park Corner. There she alighted and, with a cigarette dangling from defiant lips, swaggered all the way to Bond Street, where she rendezvoused with Violet and took her in another taxi to Charing Cross.

> Nobody, even in the glare of the station, glanced at me twice. ... I took Violet as far as Orpington by train, and there we found a lodging house where we could get a room. The landlady was very benevolent and I said Violet was my wife. Next day of course I had to put on the same clothes ... but again nobody took the slightest notice. We went to Knole!, which was, I think, brave. Here I slipped into the stables, and emerged as myself.[3]

These two well-known young women were indeed tempting providence.

The affair had spiralled into a giant firework. Twice they had escaped

<hr />

[1] Glendinning, p. 94.   [2] Nicolson, p. 110.   [3] Ibid., p. 111.

together, leaving behind them law and order and morality. But these escapades were not enough. Violet wanted more. She wanted Vita entirely for herself – and for ever. So much effort had been required to gain this much ground; more would be needed to persuade Vita to flee with her for good. She began by taunting Vita: by ridiculing Harold, her domesticity, her life at Long Barn as a married woman. 'Go back to your simpering little Harold if you like. I don't care,' she wrote from Clovelly in late August. 'Only yesterday somebody said what a pipsqueak he was. I'm afraid I only like real men, not *des femmes manquées*. . . . Rest assured that as long as I live I will never deteriorate to the level of a housefleur, a nice domestic creature who orders lunch and keeps accounts, a mere instrument of procreation, a matron, a housekeeper – pah! Each year a child. Your husband – this yearly horror complacently. Merciful Heavens! What a life!' And later: 'For him you sacrificed *everything*. You married someone who hadn't a penny, who had no "worldly qualifications". . . . And you bore him three children in pain and anguish.'

Violet did not relent in her abuse: she only varied her menu of taunts. Soon she insisted that Vita cease all intimate relations with Harold. She wanted total fidelity – a strange request for one so scornful of conventional morality. But she insisted all the same: 'Mitya, you will remember your promise to me . . . won't you? I shall never know a moment's peace if I think there is any danger of its being abolished.' Vita would very soon inform Harold that the physical side of their marriage no longer existed. Even with this pledge, however, Violet felt tortured by anything that appeared to jeopardize the 'Great Adventure' they had planned – to leave England at the end of November.

There was now also Major Denys Trefusis to contend with. As long as he was in France, he presented no problem, but soon he would be returning to England permanently, and would expect to become engaged to the notorious Miss Keppel. Violet had already more than an inkling of his humourless determination, and began exerting even more pressure on Vita, who now began to see Denys as a genuine threat. 'Our going away and abroad,' wrote Violet, 'is positively the *only* thing that can save me from an otherwise CERTAIN FATE.' She meant her engagement to Denys.

With the Armistice near at hand, it was difficult to secure passports to leave the country, but ironically it was Harold himself, with his influence in the Foreign Office, who obtained the necessary papers which got the women to France. They were leaving, he thought, for a two- or three-week holiday in Paris. As it turned out, they remained abroad for four months: from 16 November 1918 to 15 March of the next year.

The holiday began in Paris, where they lived for a week at the playwright Edward Knoblock's flat in the Palais Royal, dining a few times with Denys, who was still stationed in France. When they were blissfully alone, however, Vita abandoned her female finery and, rigged up as a man in suit and tie, she roamed the streets of Paris with Violet tripping beside her. Now they were Julian and Lushka, dining in cafés, dancing in nightclubs, strolling the boulevards, arm-in-arm, deep into the night. Here was Julian in all his glory (sometimes with his head bandaged), dragging on a cigarette, his arm round the waist of his short, plump girlfriend. 'It was all incredible – like a fairytale,' Vita would later write.

From Paris they went to Monte Carlo, where Violet again worked her magic, persuading Vita (who was expected home for Christmas) to stay on indefinitely. 'The weather was perfect, Monte Carlo was perfect,' and, indeed, 'Violet was perfect.'[1] There were some peppery moments, to be sure, but Vita loved her freedom and Violet loved her Julian. Together they worked on *Challenge* during those four 'wild and radiant months', when they were not walking in the hills, sipping wine, dreaming aloud or dancing in the evenings. Their most reckless moments were at the tables in the Casino, however, where they gambled wildly, lost heavily, and were soon penniless.

By mid-December they moved to a cheaper hotel and jointly pawned their jewels to pay for their rooms. Still, night after night, they remained glued to the tables. By late December Vita had almost ceased writing to Harold. He spent Christmas at Knole, alone with the two little boys.

In the letters of late December, his patience yielded for the first time to downright anger. Vita was being not only cruel but irresponsible, 'and I put it all down to that swine Violet who seems to addle your brain'.[2] In the New Year, Harold went to Paris to work at the Peace Conference. Installed in the luxurious Majestic Hotel on 3 January, he spent the next week looking for a small flat, where he hoped Vita would shortly join him. Some of her belongings, evidently left behind at Knoblock's flat, were delivered in a box to his office. Among its contents were 'some intimately messy things of Violet – some dead lip-salve tubes, a bit of dirty ribbon,

[1] James Lees-Milne, *Harold Nicolson: A Biography*, Vol. I (1981), p. 106.
[2] Ibid., p. 110.

one shoe, the whole thing so grubby and beastly I felt physically sick at their being muddled up with your dear clean intimate possessions'.[1] Such was his letter to Vita and his feeling for her Lushka. By 10 January, he was longing for Vita to return. Wouldn't she leave her 'dirty little friend'[2] for him? But the plea was ignored, and Vita continued to gallivant round Monte Carlo with Violet.

Disturbing rumours then reached Harold of their reckless gambling, and of their dancing together – Vita dressed as a man – in the Café de Paris. Word also reached him that 'all Paris was talking'.[3] And with Lady Sackville's tactless assistance, all London was soon buzzing with gossip of the two runaways. Violet Keppel, according to Lady Sackville's daily broadcast, was a 'sexual pervert' who had bewitched her virtuous daughter. As the notoriety mounted, Harold's humiliation deepened. 'Good God, how this Violet business has poisoned our life.'[4] But, still, Vita remained silent.

At last she yielded and promised to return to Paris on 1 February. Harold packed his belongings and, happily expectant, got their flat ready, but once again Vita went back on her word. Violet was too ill and too miserable to be left alone. Harold was shattered. All the sun had gone out of Paris, 'and it was dark & grim & horrible. I have never been so disappointed in my life. ... Little one, don't think I am angry or sad about *you*. I always dissociate these things from you – especially when you tell me frankly what has happened.'[5]

Another six weeks passed before Vita pried herself loose and went back to England by way of Paris. This was 15 March. She remained with Harold until the 19th and then returned to Brighton, depressed and suicidal, to the huge empty house Lady Sackville would be moving into in May, when she left Knole and her husband for good. Vita was scolded by her mother, comforted by Harold and flooded with letters from Violet.

Under Alice Keppel's swift managerial hand – 'a demon of a woman'[6] Vita called her – Violet's engagement to Denys Trefusis was announced on 26 March. With Violet's record of broken engagements, Mrs Keppel was anxious to have her securely yoked in matrimony. In Brighton, Vita read the announcement in the

---

[1] Loc. cit.   [2] Ibid., p. 127.   [3] Ibid., p. 126.   [4] Loc. cit.
[5] Nicolson, p. 111.   [6] Ibid., p. 112.

newspaper and 'nearly fainted'.[7] Although Violet's marriage to Denys was on the condition that it should remain unconsummated (an odd condition for the prospective young groom to agree to), the engagement itself made a cruel tear in the membrane of Vita's inflated vanity. Up to this time, she had been repeatedly endorsed as the one and only Man-Hero-Lover in Violet's life. That image was now in serious danger.

Violet, moreover, lost no time in using her engagement as a means of persuading Vita once more to leave England with her permanently. When Vita threatened to return to Paris with Harold, Violet threatened back: 'If you go to Paris, you will never see me again.' Vita went all the same and Violet's letters flew after her like ravenous birds – letters of love, letters of despair, letters threatening suicide and, worst of all, letters that struck Vita where she was most sensitive: hateful reminders that as a married woman she had no identity of her own. 'Do you think ... that *I* want you to become great and famous as the wife of Harold Nicolson? Don't you think you're sufficiently famous as that already? The beautiful and accomplished wife of Mr Nicolson, the lovely and talented wife of one of our promising young diplomats.'

Then there were letters that pandered to Vita's most cherished fantasies:

> You are made for passion, your perfectly proportioned body, your heavy lidded brooding eyes, your frankly sensual mouth. ... These are the best years of your life. ... You who might have been, who might still be! one of the greatest figures of your century – a George Sand, a Catherine of Russia, a Helen of Troy, Sappho! ... Cast aside the drab garments of respectability and convention, my beautiful Bird of Paradise. ... Otherwise, Mitya, you'll be a failure – you, who might be among the greatest, the most scintillating and romantic figures of all time, you'll be 'Mrs Nicolson, who has written some charming verse. She is daughter of the ————? Lord Sackville (forgive my ignorance), and often appears in charity matinées.'

On 30 March Violet repeated the conditions of her marriage: 'He gave his word of honour as a *gentleman, never* to do anything that should displease me – you know in what sense I mean.' Vita was

[1] Loc. cit.

unmoved. She remained in Paris. Violet persisted. 'I have given you my body time after time to treat as you pleased, to tear in pieces if such had been your will. ... You are my lover and I am your mistress, and kingdoms and empires and governments have tottered and succumbed before now to that mighty combination.' Still Vita wouldn't budge.

The wedding date was set for Monday, 16 June, and as the days passed, Violet grew more frenzied. In April she wrote one of her self-accusing letters intended to keep her Julian just slightly off balance: 'I am more odious and impossible than words can say. Put yourself in my place. ... I loathe myself, I *loathe* my selfish, jealous, suspicious, ungovernable character. I loathe my pettiness and mean-ness, my exorbitant disposition.' Violet was honest in her appraisal. She knew her defect. What was deceptive was the way she used them to gain her own ends, and this was what perplexed Vita.

By 7 May Violet was losing patience. 'If you can't, or rather won't, come back next Wednesday, darling, don't come back at all.' On the 8th: 'You are a rotter, Mitya. No wonder I trust Loge [Denys], and I don't trust you. Pat [Dansey] said yesterday, you would come sooner if it suited you. ... Oh God, how I despise you!' Then on the 9th: 'O Mitya, my life, my love, come back. You *must* come back. Sometimes, before going to sleep, by dint of desiring you, I end by feeling your body stretched out by my side, all the warmth of quivering flesh, the kisses of your mouth, and the caresses of your fingers, and I feel faint, and I'm on the point of dying.'

Violet knew every string on the harp of love, and she plucked them all, major and minor. Vita returned to London for the pub-lication of *Heritage*, and to Violet. The novel was a success. So was Violet. She induced Vita to elope with her on the eve of her wedding day – 'not sooner because we thought we should be overtaken and brought back',[1] Vita was to write later. But as May turned into June, the tension mounted and, with the calendar moving closer to 16 June, Vita grew daily more anxious. To Harold, she wrote on 1 June: 'Oh Hadji [the pet name his father used], if you knew how it would amuse me to scandalize the whole of London! It's so secure, so fatuous, conventional, so hypocritical. ...'[2]

Harold wrote back, urging her to come to Paris at once, and chided her mildly for attributing the 'muddle' she had got herself

---

[1] Lees-Milne, p. 130.   [2] Ibid., p. 131.

into to 'the conventionality of the world'. Vita had become a 'hard fierce woman', he wrote on 7 June, 'where there used to be so gentle and so tender a soul'.[1] He was vulnerable, defenceless. She was breaking his heart. Of course Vita knew this, but she also knew her susceptibility to Violet's enchantments. If she came to Paris earlier, she would be tempted to return to London to stop the wedding. There was no doubt about that. Violet thought that Vita would 'save her from this bloody marriage,' she wrote on the 9th. How astonished would Harold be if she did? 'I shouldn't be astonished in the least. It would be great fun, anyway.'[2]

Torn with doubt and misery as she was, Vita nevertheless responded to the steady stream of Harold's sane, imploring letters, and suddenly saw him as 'all sweet and gentle and dependent upon me'.[3] She yielded now to *his* vulnerability, to his recognition of her power over him, which, typically, she saw as just the reverse: 'You don't know your power over me.'[4] On Saturday, 14 June, she left by train for Folkestone. On the boat she changed her mind and tried to get off, but the gang-plank had been pulled away. It was too late. Harold met her at the Gare du Nord. They drove straight to Versailles, where he remained by her side all through Sunday.

In London, Violet was in a litter of emotion and uncertainty, believing to the very last minute that Vita would somehow manage to steal her away. But nothing of the sort happened. The elopement was off. On Monday, 16 June, the morning of the wedding, Violet wrote Vita one line from Grosvenor Street: 'You have broken my heart. Goodbye.'

Across the Channel, Vita, with Harold now back in his Paris office, sat in her room at Versailles 'holding my watch in my hand and watching the hands tick past the hour of Violet's wedding'.[5] First the organ would blare Purcell's 'Trumpet Voluntary'. Then the bride would arrive, pale and tear-stained. During the signing of the register, Dame Nellie Melba would sing Gounod's 'Ave Maria'. Then Denys and Violet would come down the aisle to the Wedding March from Wagner's *Lohengrin*, Violet still vaguely expecting some sort of miracle to happen.

But nothing happened. And a worse nightmare was to come in the next forty-eight hours

On Tuesday, Vita left Versailles and reserved a small hotel room for herself in Paris. That night, Violet and Denys arrived and

---

[1] Loc. cit. [2] Nicolson, p. 112. [3] Lees-Milne, p. 132.
[4] Nicolson, p. 113. [5] Ibid., p. 114.

checked into the Ritz. On Wednesday, now mad with pain and rage, Vita abducted Violet and took her to the hotel room where 'I treated her savagely, I made love to her, I had her, I didn't care, I only wanted to hurt Denys. . . .'[1]

On Thursday came the chilling interview with Denys. Violet told him of their plan to elope on the wedding day, adding that she cared nothing at all for him. He turned very white and they thought he was going to faint. That night, Vita, having by now lost all self-control, dined at the Ritz, where Violet looked on from her open window, with Denys behind her, weeping and hopeless.

In the waste and debris of these two days, two remarks in Vita's 'confession' reveal something about the nature of her relation to Violet. She wrote that Violet 'played me a mean trick over her marriage, and I wouldn't sacrifice Harold to someone whom I thought unworthy'. By what circuitous reasoning she arrived at this groundless conclusion, it is impossible to say. But the second item, also in her confession, suggests an explanation: Vita's sexual assault on Violet was 'to hurt Denys'. This indicates that it was Vita's own severely wounded image she was trying to repair, and the assault had nothing, or little, to do with Violet herself. It was an act of rage, not an act of lust. It was not even an act of jealousy. Violet's marriage had shorn all the splendour off Vita's ideal self, and this she appears to have interpreted as a 'mean trick'. The wedding represented to Vita Violet's symbolic abandonment of the swash-buckling Julian for the crusading Denys. Why otherwise would she want to 'hurt' him? For only by triumphing over this intruding male could Vita restore her own sense of masculine glory. Love played no part in this unholy trinity. And Harold, at this time, was certainly irrelevant.

The marriage brought violently to the surface Vita's hitherto buried self-contempt, lodged in her nature from childhood, which was both basic to and contradictory of the image she had of herself. The problem of how she could quest for glory and simultaneously feel self-hatred only makes sense when the former is seen as a consequence of the latter – that is, the quest for the glorified *ideal* as a means of temporarily obliterating the loathsome persistence of the *real*.

It was just prior to this period of turbulence that Vita told Harold that his essential goodness was the 'one thing left in which I

[1] Ibid., p. 145.

unshakably believe. . . . I simply cling and cling to the thought of you. You are my only anchor. I hate myself.'[1] Then on 8 June, eight days before the wedding: 'I know that I have hurt you, but I couldn't do anything to hurt you dreadfully and irrevocably. What a hold you have on my heart. . . . I love you more than myself, more than life, more than the things I love.'[2] There is no reason to question the authenticity of this statement, but had Harold read the two letters consecutively, he could not have failed to see 'I hate myself' pressed pitifully beside 'I love you more than myself'.

Vita spoke of her duality directly and intelligently. When she discovered that she was 'different', it was, however, an intellectual discovery. At this period in her life she had not yet learned, emotionally, to differentiate the *ideal* self she loved from the *real* self she despised. They co-existed within her in murderous combat. The violence she could not control in June 1919 would surface again, with even more devastating force, in the crisis that was destined to take place in Amiens on St Valentine's Day of 1920, just eight months away.

After the ordeal in Paris, Vita went briefly with Harold to Switzerland, and then returned to England, shattered and exhausted. The Trefusises proceeded to St Jean de Luz for three weeks, and from here Violet again showered Vita with letters demanding love, loyalty, fidelity and a great deal more.

For all Violet's cleverness, she was incapable of understanding that Vita loved Harold as a woman, and not with the masculine lust she felt for Violet; that she did not mind being a respectable, secure Mrs Harold Nicolson, arranging silver and crystal. And so Violet simply kept up her inexhaustible nagging: 'You moved to the Majestic *in order* to share his room. . . . What else might you have shared!' Harold was obviously her favourite dartboard. She did not know how thin was the ice she trod, how destructive her possessiveness had become. Julian wanted freedom with his Lushka, but Vita now often found herself harnessed to a shrill, unrelenting virago. Little wonder she sometimes altered the truth: there was no other way to gain a moment's peace. Instinctively, however, Violet knew when to stop, when to modify her strategy and rouse her fascinated Julian. It was as if a sixth sense told her when to change the tune with her 'Prince of Romance'.

[1] Ibid., p. 144.   [2] Glendinning, p. 106.

The newlyweds returned to England in late July and leased Possingworth Manor at Blackboys, Uckfield, Sussex, some twenty miles from Long Barn. With Harold in Paris and Denys in London much of the time, the women continued to see each other regularly throughout the summer months. Again, however, this was not enough. Violet wanted more. She craved 'Adventure veiled and elusive ... wanton and provocative. ... sly and surreptitious ... flippant and derisive. ... I want to dash my glove in the face of Convention. I want to fly and sing and dance. ... If you don't feel as I do, leave me alone!'

Vita unfortunately *did* feel as she did – and on 19 October she escaped once more with her 'vain, pleasure-loving' Violet to Paris and then on to Monte Carlo, where they remained until 18 December. Their intended destination was Greece, where they would gather 'copy' for *Challenge* (the novel was called 'Rebellion' at the time). Although it hurt him to do so, Harold made all the arrangements and was close to tears at their departure.

He had earlier begun an affair with the young, well-known fashion designer, Edward Molyneux. 'My sweet,' he wrote Vita, 'are you jealous? Do you mind?'[1] But Vita ignored the tease and deliberately avoided seeing Harold on her way through Paris. 'What a cruel contemptuous thing to do,'[2] wrote the ever-forgiving husband, but Vita was too busy arranging their way to Monte Carlo (as suitable to her as the Greek island of the novel's setting), where they resumed the carefree, irresponsible life they had led just seven months earlier. Once more Julian was deriving a perverse sort of pleasure in slouching at café tables, decked out as a man, puffing at a cigarette. 'I never appreciated anything so much as living like that with my tongue perpetually in my cheek, and in defiance of every policeman I passed.'[3]

In Brighton, where she now lived permanently, Lady Sackville, anxious to protect her daughter's reputation, again took up her pen in ignorance and wrote to all her friends that this 'viper' Violet Trefusis had once more lured her Vita away, and that poor Harold was perishing of a broken heart. Thus was Vita further sullied.

Lady Sackville was not just destructive, she was 'loony' as far as Harold could see.[4] He was upset that Vita had told her mother about their platonic marital relations. It was one thing if Vita chose to

---

[1] Lees-Milne, p. 141.   [2] Nicolson, p. 116.   [3] Lees-Milne, p. 140.
[4] Ibid., p. 141.

confide her own matters, 'but it is bad luck on me to tell her things about me, which are at once repeated to Ozzie [Dickinson] and via him *urbi et orbi*'.[1]

Affairs again came to a boil on 1 December when Harold promised to make a 'fearful row'[2] if Vita did not return to Paris within a week. On the 8th he wrote in desperation: Lady Sackville had descended upon Paris and was threatening to cut Vita from her will. Then Harold threatened divorce. Jolted back into reality by these dual threats, Vita deposited Violet in Cannes, promising to return shortly – and permanently – and, almost in the same breath, promised Harold permanent separation from Violet. The antagonistic tugs in Vita's divided self were beginning to fragment her judgment, her common sense and her values. She knew in some dark corner of her mind that one day soon she must leave Violet for good, but for the moment the fantasy of passion and glory was still overpowering.

Vita joined Harold in Paris on 18 December and found him in terrible pain (he had just been operated on for an abscess on the knee). For two weeks she remained with him and then went back to England. The Trefusises returned in early January 1920, and it was at this juncture that Vita, Denys and Violet 'met at a grotesque interview in London'. Denys was very business-like and 'looked like death'.[3] He wanted to know how much money Vita had to support Violet and herself if they went away together. In the same matter-of-fact way, he turned to Violet and asked if she wanted to renounce everything to live with Vita. Violet was frightened and asked for a week to decide. As Vita's biographer aptly observed, both women 'embraced the postures of rebels and outcasts, but backed off, consistently, when in danger of actually being cast out'.[4]

Shortly after the interview, Violet called Vita to say that Denys demanded that they leave England by 18 January or not at all. It is difficult to think of Denys's 'demanding' anything, but Vita, at any rate, believed her.

Harold returned to England on the 17th, walking on two sticks. Vita met him at Victoria Station and drove him to his parents' house in Cadogan Gardens. After dinner, she went up to his room and said she was leaving him for Violet and planned to depart on the

---

[1] Ibid., p. 141.   [2] Ibid., p. 143.   [3] Nicolson, p. 117.   [4] Glendinning, p. 107.

following day. 'He broke down and cried.'[1] Vita then left the Nicolsons and went to a hotel room she had booked in advance and spent the night writing letters. The next morning, 18 January, she returned to Cadogan Gardens and, after a great deal of pleading, was persuaded by Harold to remain with him at least during his two weeks' sick leave. If she still wanted to go after that time, he would do nothing to stop her. With that understanding they went down to Knole and remained there the whole time without once mentioning the impending separation. This sudden change of plan threw Violet into a panic, but Vita was too dazed to respond and Harold, as was his custom, turned away from confrontation and remained silent. From Violet came the message: 'Mitya, BE GOOD. I trust you. Don't relax, don't relent, don't sigh and soften: it's absurd, disloyal (to me), and useless. . . .'

By the time Harold left for Paris on 1 February, Vita was less sure of herself than she had ever been before. 'If I were you, and you were me,' she wrote to him, 'I would battle so hard to keep you – partly, I dare say, because I would not have the courage and the reserve to do like you and say nothing. . . . So I fish, and fish, and fish, and sometimes I catch a lovely little trout, but never the great salmon that lashes and fights and *convinces* me that it is fighting for its life. . . . You only say "Darling Mar!" and leave me to invent my own conviction out of your silence.'[2]

She was of course right. This was not the defiant Julian talking: it was the woman imploring the man she loved to protect her from herself, and this Harold could not bring himself to do. Nor, it appears, did he see that under all of Vita's expansiveness and aggression, there was a doubtful human being needing someone's signal of strength to keep her in line, and secure. This was precisely what Lady Sackville had and it was precisely this quality that Vita adored and respected. No matter how misguided, cruel, tactless or 'loony' she was, Victoria Sackville-West had a massive ruthless strength that protected what she loved. This is what Vita the woman *sought* and Vita the man *represented*. Harold saw the Julian side of Vita as 'bad', rather than different from the side he loved. Her brutal side stood for the sheer animal force that governs jungle ethics, and Harold was far too civilized to understand its nature and quality.

And so Vita went off with Violet, leaving behind a trail of evidence as to her whereabouts. She would look back on this

---

[1] Nicolson, p. 117.   [1] Lees-Milne, p. 146.

thoughtless escapade in the months to come as a terrible dream that left its victims bruised and speechless.

On 2 February, Vita left Knole and went to London with her luggage. Violet, who had been acting strangely, said she must spend the evening with Denys to settle some matters. It was agreed that they would leave the next day for Lincoln. When Vita got back to Knole later that day, she had a frantic call from Violet at a hotel in Trafalgar Square, saying that on no account would she return to Denys that night. Vita induced her to go back to him, however, only recalling, when it was too late, that Violet had been hinting for days that Denys had been threatening to break his 'promise'.

The next day, Tuesday 3 February, they left for Lincoln, which Vita was writing about in a book called *A Dragon in Shallow Waters*, and remained there until Sunday, the 8th. When they returned to London, Violet summoned Denys to a hotel in Liverpool Street and told him she was leaving England and him permanently on the next day. In their rooms later, Vita recalls doing 'the only thing I am in the very least proud of: I said I would give her up if she would go back to him.'[1] Violet refused, and on the next day they travelled down to Dover, where Vita remained overnight, so that Violet, to squelch further gossip and presumably to appease Lady Sackville, crossed the Channel alone. Her destination was Amiens, where Vita would shortly join her. From the Dover hotel that evening, Vita wrote to Harold: 'I swear to you by all I hold sacred . . . I used every argument, threat and persuasion to make her go back to Denys.'[2]

The following day, Tuesday 10 February, Denys turned up at Dover too, and a strange scenario took shape: together, he and Vita set off for France in a fierce gale, to join their beloved Violet and 'give her the choice between us'.[3] It was a 'symbolic' crossing. At first grim with one another, they were helped by the storm to drop their reserve and eventually become cordial. By the time they reached Calais, Denys had invited Vita to lunch with him in the buffet. Here was the courageous Crusader amicably munching chicken and drinking champagne with the glorious Julian, both crossing the Channel in the wildest of tempests, each to win the heart of the same woman! The scene would have been comic, had not the next few days held in store for them so much horror.

---

[1] Nicolson, p. 119.   [2] Lees-Milne, p. 147.   [3] Nicolson, p. 120.

They found Violet ill and trembling, and in a state very near hysteria. Her two suitors secured a hotel, got her into bed, fetched hot-water bottles and a doctor, ordered dinner and sat by her side, each feeling greatly relieved. The next morning, Wednesday the 11th, all three of them drove from Calais to Boulogne, still avoiding the subject that lay in their minds like a deadly explosive. After lunch in Boulogne they took a train to Amiens, where it was decided that 'the discussion' must, finally, take place. In the train, however, amidst their jokes, Denys suddenly wrote a message on a slip of paper – much like Levin's note to Kitty in *Anna Karenina*.[1] Only Denys's note, unlike Levin's declaration of love, was one of resignation and despair: he knew that Violet's mind was made up in Vita's favour, he wrote, and he would leave them at Amiens to return alone to England. In an instant, everything suddenly became tragic. They were still two hours away from Amiens. Vita removed herself to an unoccupied compartment. Denys wept quietly throughout the remainder of the journey.

The women went to their rooms in the Hôtel du Rhin, Vita oppressed, Violet indifferent. Calls had to be made and wires sent. Vita did both: she called to see if Denys was all right and telegraphed 'Harold where I was in case he should be anxious'[2] – an odd thing to do in her circumstances. Throughout the past several days, she had been writing to Harold in Paris, where she rightfully thought he was, but by the time this last wire was sent, Harold had returned to England and was searching for her there. They had crossed the Channel in the same gale, only in opposite directions.

After dinner on Wednesday evening, Colonel George Keppel made an appearance at their hotel. To Vita he was 'theatrical and unimpressive'[3] – almost inconsequential. They did their best to keep from laughing in his face. Despite the icy reception, the Colonel loitered at their hotel for the next two days as the women went about Amiens, exploring the devastations of war and visiting the Cathedral of Nôtre Dame. They had planned to drive back to Paris and from there take a train to Sicily, but because Violet had still not fully recovered, they decided to remain for a while longer in the ancient city. The next day, Friday the 13th, was their last day of uncertain peace and wavering hope. Everything would be different when they woke the next morning.

On Saturday, Denys and Harold flew from England to Amiens

---

[1] Part IV, Chapter XIII.　　[2] Nicolson, p. 124.　　[3] Ibid., p. 125.

in a rented, two-seater airplane. Lady Sackville had helped to engineer the plan; the daughter of the hot-blooded Pepita was feeling a wicked excitement in all this – 'quite like a sensational novel',[1] she wrote in her diary. Two distraught husbands descended from the sky to reclaim their wayward and recalcitrant wives.

At first the women refused to budge. They 'defied first Harold and then Denys, and then both together'.[2] Vita shot a volley of 'undignified and noisy' things at Harold; Violet assaulted Deny with undiluted hatred. He looked to Vita like a saint in a stained-glass window, very 'pale and frail', standing there staring and silent. Then, alone in Vita's room, Harold asked her: 'Are you sure Violet is as faithful to you as she makes you believe? Because Denys has told your mother quite a different story.'[3] Vita suddenly thought she would go mad.

Rushing to Violet's room, she met Denys on the stairs and asked him the humiliating question. He refused to answer. 'If you tell me you have, I swear to you I will never set eyes on Violet again.'[4] He remained silent. She then charged into Violet's room for confirmation – and got it. 'When?' shouted Vita. 'The night before we went to Lincoln,'[5] stammered Violet, gripped in terror, clutching frantically at Vita's arm. Insane with rage, Vita thrust her aside and rushed to her room, while Denys held Violet down. 'I packed my things, blind with passion and pain ... only thinking that I must get away at all costs.'[6]

Vita felt what all betrayed lovers feel. As with the wedding, however, only now very much worse, her brutal love-making, her masculine heroics, her reckless courage – all the aspects of the image so carefully groomed by Violet were now no longer valid. Vita was reduced once more to the timid, awkward girl, the self she loathed. With Violet's 'violation', the glorious Vita came crashing to earth. Her most cherished self had been slain by the allegation of one simple sexual act. The extent to which Vita suffered reflects the extent to which she depended upon Violet to keep that idealized self alive. Now nothing Violet could say, nothing Denys could do, would repair the wound they had jointly inflicted on her. Vita's glorification had suddenly become irrelevant, a thing of scorn and shame. She returned to Paris with Harold, broken and seething with self-contempt.

---

[1] Lees-Milne, p. 148.   [2] Nicolson, p. 125.   [3] Loc. cit.   [4] Ibid., p. 126.
[5] Loc. cit.   [6] Loc. cit.

The Trefusises travelled to the South of France. On the way, Violet fired another round of desperate letters and telegrams. From Gien: 'If you left me for ever, you would have killed us both.' From Vichy: 'My pity for Denys is dead. . . . Only disgust remains.' From Le Puy: 'O my love, I *hate* him so . . . with his tears and his servility.' From Nîmes: 'Denys doesn't want to see me again as long as I care for you.' From Toulon: 'Ah Julian Julian.'

Alice Keppel, who had been footing the bill for this bizarre adventure, was now on the scene. She had had enough. The truant daughter and ailing son-in-law (Denys had become very ill during all this) were ordered to go on a trip around the world, a journey that would take at least a year. If Violet did not agree to this, her mother would cut her off financially and never again would she be allowed to set foot in the Keppel house. The favourite daughter literally went down on her knees, but Mrs Keppel was adamant, she was 'inhuman'. Sonia had become engaged to Roland Cubitt, whose very proper family were against the match, and Mrs Keppel was doubly determined, at whatever cost – and cost was always the first item on her agenda – that this ludicrous affair with Vita be stopped at once. Vicious rumours were already rampant, and to allow the affair to continue would certainly jeopardize Sonia's imminent marriage and future happiness.

In desperation, Violet begged to have the marriage annulled, but then quickly recoiled: there would be the humiliation of a medical examination, Mrs Keppel reminded her wayward daughter; all annulments involved this procedure. Then Denys threatened her with divorce, naming Vita as co-respondent. 'I am trapped, trapped, trapped in every side,' cried Violet in late February.

Alice Keppel relented, however: instead of a trip around the world, the couple could go to Algiers for two months – or perhaps to Ragusa, if Denys found that more agreeable. Penniless as he was, Denys was now in the shaky position of temporary power. But whatever they chose, Mrs Keppel would not permit a divorce; the famous Alice Keppel would not tolerate the ridicule such an eventuality would incur. The marriage had indeed been 'a hideous mistake'. At one point in the matrimonial brawl, Violet tried to jump from her window, but 'even that didn't make her say I needn't go with Denys'. Alice Keppel might be a celebrated Edwardian hostess, but she had a will of iron and a heart of stone.

After many tears, much pleading and some fury, it was agreed that Violet could remain in the South of France, as long as Denys remained with her. His chief inducement for staying was Nancy Cunard, who was also in Monte Carlo. Violet agreed because it meant escaping to Bordighera, to stay with Pat Dansey and her friend Joan in the spacious Villa Primavera, close enough to Denys to quell Mrs Keppel's suspicions.

Matters were, however, far from settled: in fact, they grew steadily worse. Feeling caged and beaten, Violet once more began gambling wildly and losing heavily. Her quarrels with Denys were bitter and endless. The local people were treating her rudely and some of her own contemporaries were beginning to say they would not be seen with her in public. By the middle of March, in a frenzy of anger, she burned the manuscript of Denys's book on Pushkin.

In England, Lady Sackville had by now read the manuscript of *Challenge* and, scandalized, persuaded Vita to abandon plans for its publication. Vita agreed more 'as an act of renunciation [of Violet] ... than of contrition'.[1] There was no danger of this, however, for although the Nicolsons now blandly appeared in public – at theatres and dinner parties, as if unconscious of the inferno they had lately been through – Violet was still very much on Vita's mind. On 20 March, she once more joined Violet, this time in Avignon. They drove back to Bordighera, collected Pat Dansey and Joan, and went on to Venice. Vita did not return to England until 10 April.

But the expedition was so much irritation, with no promise of a pearl. On 23 March she wrote in her diary: 'Lushka horrible to me all day, and makes me very miserable and exasperated.'[2] Violet had been badgering her night and day to stay on indefinitely. When Vita succumbed, paradise was restored. In Venice, though, on the 28th, 'everything is black again'. Vita knew she must soon return to England and to her family but for the moment the 'slime and floating onions'[3] of the Grand Canal looked appealing compared to the misery she suffered with her Lushka. Everything was black indeed. Violet, ill and yellow with jaundice, was daily abusing Vita for abandoning her, insisting on remaining abroad alone, threatening suicide and generally adding more each day to an atmosphere already saturated with bitterness and disappointment.

The situation was not much better in England. Mrs Keppel was barely on speaking terms with her daughter, who, as far as she could see, was now no more than an ignominious appendage to her family.

[1] Nicolson, p. 177.   [2] Loc. cit.   [3] Loc. cit.

She wanted Violet out of London immediately, and proceeded quickly and quietly to install her and Denys in the Dower House at Sonning-on-Thames. Violet hated the house and the 'grey and sunless country'. It was like being in prison, with only Denys for company, and that only when he was not in London. Violet wanted Vita by her side, hermetically sealed in her own private void. She could endure any privation so long as she had that. There was very little else: she had lost the support of her family, the love of her husband and the respect of her friends; but even the last stronghold that Vita represented was now noticeably eroding.

Their meetings during the summer months – in hotel lobbies, in picture galleries, sometimes at Pat Dansey's London flat – were filled with tension, and their partings an increasing source of despair. When Violet went to Long Barn, she saw too much to remind her that Vita had a family, a home, and that Violet had no moral right to remain there for longer than conventional courtesy allowed. Worst of all, it was now becoming obvious that Vita simply could not see Violet's point of view: 'You think I am wicked and immoral and selfish – so I am, according to *your* standards, but not according to my own. According to my own, I am singularly pure, uncontaminated, and high principled. You will laugh, *but it is true*. And you can laugh all your life, but it will still be true.'

A curious new relationship emerged at about this time. Pat Dansey began writing notes to Vita that cast Violet in a highly equivocal light. 'All through those scenes and storms at Bordighera and Venice,' she wrote, 'I was working entirely on your side! ... Oh, Vita, think sometimes of your own happiness – not only of Violet's. ... She must prove herself stable, faithful and loyal before she can demand you to throw all away.'

In the middle of May, exhausted and depressed, Vita went sailing off Falmouth with her father – later joined by Harold – on his yacht *Sumerun*. Violet's letters pursued her: 'I can't bear to think of you in a boat in the sea with Harold. If you don't come back on Monday 31st [May] I shall have Raquel Meller [the great screen beauty] to stay with me.' A few days later came another letter calculated to unsettle its recipient: Sir Basil Zaharoff, one of the richest men in Europe, 'has asked me to become his mistress with a house in Paris, a house in the country, and unlimited credit in every bank in Europe – ' wrote the daughter of Alice Keppel.

The letters continued through June – inconsolable, urgent, queru-
lous letters. The Dower House in Sonning was driving her mad.
The noise of children was grating on her nerves. And finally on
2 June came 'the most serious letter I have ever written to you in
my life'. Violet was tired of being 'selfish and spiteful and malicious –
above all, I am tired of being jealous. . . . You will say it is selfish
of me to want you to give up everybody for me.' Since this was
true, there could be no other recourse but for Violet to abdicate her
claims and wish Vita well. This appeared, then, to be a solemn note
of farewell: 'I shall love you till I die, whatever you do. God bless
you and make you happy, and Harold too. . . .'

But five days later, Violet learned from her doctor that she needed
a complete rest: her heart was strained. 'Are you going to take me
to Evian?' she asked Vita, ignoring the noble sentiments of a few
days earlier. Clearly, Violet wanted at least to have her suffering
acknowledged. There was no one now to whom she could turn,
whereas Vita was surrounded by people who saw to her comfort,
worried about her well-being, were by her side through good times
and bad.

It was a fateful July. Matters were rapidly deteriorating: Denys
had struck Violet with a violence he had never shown before. '*He
likes hurting me*, Mitya. It made me feel suddenly cold and sick when
he twisted my wrist. . . . He smiled all the time – his eyes were two
glittering slits, and his mouth a thin, hard straight line.' A week
later, all of Vita's letters disappeared from the drawer of Violet's
writing table, 'so I suppose he has taken them. . . . I always tore up
the indiscreet ones, thank goodness.' Denys had burned all the
letters.

Vita was by now worn out and her love was drifting into still
waters. She confided the truth only to her diary: 'Oh Christ, how I
long for peace at Long Barn! But she is in such distress of mind and
so seedy that I must give way to her.' Lady Sackville opposed her
daughter's sympathy. To her, Violet was playing a 'wicked game'
and Vita blindly believed everything she said.

In August the two women drove to Hindhead and Rye, and were
happy for five days, but otherwise there was only 'wretchedness and
jealousy and turmoil'.[3] If it was true that Vita believed in Violet, as
Lady Sackville claimed, it was also true that Vita wanted her lover

---

[1] Glendinning, p. 110.   [2] Ibid., p. 111.   [3] Nicolson, p. 132.

to fight for her, like the doomed salmon. She missed that fight in Harold, but found it in abundance in Violet.

Pat Dansey at this time felt it her duty to inform Violet that the current scandal had reached such a pitch that shortly no decent person would have her inside their house. 'She also said that if I lived alone, withdrawn from the protection of my family, no one would come near me. O God! how awful it all is.' To complicate matters further, Denys once more introduced the threat of separation: immediately after Sonia's wedding in November, he would dissolve the marriage 'with the fullest publicity'. Alice Keppel threatened Violet too: if she refused to live with Denys, she would be cut off from the family completely and her allowance would be barely adequate – 'just enough to prevent me from starving'.

Violet gathered some information from Denys's doctor that suggested psychological impotence as the source of Denys's problem. There was no verification of this claim either then or now, but Violet appears to have used it to strike once more at her husband's precarious manhood. 'Yesterday morning,' she wrote to Vita on 2 August, 'I'm afraid I said some dreadful things to Denys in connection with what the doctor told me about him.' In this letter she also enclosed a fragment of one her mother had just written: 'I fear the scandal would be very great, and you would be the laughing stock of the country becoming Miss Keppel again.' Alice Keppel was not so much concerned about her daughter's emotional state as she evidently was about what Mrs Grundy would say. Whatever happened, however, Violet, by her mother's orders, would be forced to stay abroad for at least five or six years, to 'live it down'. As Violet's world was falling apart and her only hope was Vita, her lover, on 23 July 1920, was sitting in a field at Long Barn, confessing on paper their bitter story.

Late in August, Violet was taken to Scotland by her mother, to Duntreath Castle. Here she revisited old memories – and cooled down a little. So did Mrs Keppel. 'Mama is a remote, sometimes gracious, always stately and beautiful figure in my life,' she wrote to Vita on the 23rd. 'Yesterday men chinday [my mother], instead of being hard and inquisitorial and menacing, was kind and humorous and gay. ... She says she has been so happy here away from everybody.' The peace did not last long, however.

Having decided to get up a house party as she had done before the war, Mrs Keppel took Violet and Sonia and their husbands to

Holland with her, to Clingendaal. Denys, absorbed in his lingering illness, only came to the house for meals: the remainder of the time he spent in the 'bachelor's hut' tucked away in the spacious grounds. And Alice Keppel once again resumed her harsh treatment of Violet, 'saying unkind and spiteful things' to her and being so outrageously rude as to make the other guests squirm with embarrassment.

In such an atmosphere, Violet naturally tilted once more into a mood of escape, and began imploring Vita to 'take me away'. Whenever Vita wavered for a moment, Violet touched her most vulnerable spots: her Mitya was weak, superficial, shallow. 'It is my nightmare, your shallowness. And though you won't admit it, you haven't got the capacity for love that I have ... you are in pastel what I am in oils.' Vita must have winced. Violet had only one object in mind, however, and that was to flee somewhere with her lover, for ever. Denys's deepening illness in Holland was little more than a passing comment in her letters. She thought only of enticing her 'gypsy' to 'come away!' Aware of what her daughter was up to, Mrs Keppel did not relax for a moment. 'Her undisguised hatred of me is a terrible thing,' Violet wrote. 'She watches my pain and smiles cruelly.'

By October, even mild, even-tempered Sonia despised Violet – 'I have no one to turn to in my loneliness. ... I have never been so much alone as I have been here. ... I love nothing in the world but you.' This was no shallow seduction. Violet might be spoiled and pampered, she might like appearing helpless, she might instinctively thrive on chaos, but her tenacity was not fictitious: Vita was her lifelong lover, and whatever claims love made, Violet would obey and honour. She was in fact more possessive than she was jealous, and that possessiveness was uncompromising: it made her tell lies, behave disgracefully, exaggerate shamelessly. It made her at times appear to encourage abuse. But Violet's unreasonable – indeed, irrational – love was not to be toyed with. It was like a stick of dynamite which, even dampened by tears, could blast the lives of four people sky high.

As 1920 wore to an end, Violet made a calmer appeal: 'O Mitya, what are you making of four lives? ... Are you happy? Is Harold happy? Am I happy? Is Loge happy? Instead of four utterly miserable people, you could have two flawlessly happy ones.' Was Julian dead? Gone for ever? Where was his violence, his courage? Soon it would be Christmas. Vita would be sitting before silver and candles and china. That was fitting for the civilized Mrs Nicolson, but Violet's

Julian should be eating a stolen chicken in a field over flaming sticks, his eyes burning with acrid smoke and his gold earring glinting in the fire-light.

Whatever her fantasy, though, in actuality Violet spent that Christmas of 1920 alone, 'severed from everyone I care for'. Vita sent her a fur coat. It was her only present. 'I have never been so bereft, so utterly forlorn and friendless. ... Won't you help me?' The Julian in Vita responded with a 'final resurgence of passion',[1] and once more – for the very last time – she swept Violet off to the South of France. From the middle of January to 9 March, they lived in Hyères and Carcassone.

Harold returned to England on 1 February and once again found the nest empty. At the end of his tether, he shot angry letters off to Vita: she was selfish, she was weak, she must return immediately. Vita responded blandly that she must stay on 'for a bit' – she really disliked 'the squalor of dates'[2] and really it was 'indecent' for her to write when she was with Violet. 'You are to be back in England on Friday, February the 25th,' wrote Harold, now goaded beyond endurance. 'Don't misunderstand me. I shall really cut adrift if you don't. It is a generous date; it is longer than you promised; but it is a *fixed* date, and you must keep it.'[3] But Vita's persistent need of Violet could not be so easily set aside, and perhaps too some guilt and pity for Violet's situation got mixed up with her deeper feeling.

'My own beloved Harold,' she replied, 'I am so dreadfully unhappy ... about Violet being deserted and about my feeling responsible. You see, I *am* responsible. But I only love *you*. ...'[4] Whether or not Harold was calmed by this, he must have felt some panic upon receiving from the exhausted and ailing Denys a letter to say that he was going to dissolve his marriage. With Denys out of the way, there was no telling what Vita, who was like a 'cocaine addict' where Violet was concerned, might do. No one could now be sure of anything.

The 'fixed date', 25 February, arrived, but Vita did not. 'Certainly one of the worst days of my life,' wrote Harold in his diary that night. 'No home. No affection. No money. No happiness. Oh Viti, Viti, what have you to answer for ...'[5] he wrote on the 28th, *not* to

[1] Phillipe Jullian and John Phillips, *Violet Trefusis: A Biography* (1976, 1984), p. 58.　　[2] Lees-Milne, p. 159.　　[3] Loc. cit.　　[4] Ibid., p. 160.　Ibid., p. 161.

Vita, but again to his diary. Only one thing was certain: Vita was terrified of scandal, and this more than anything else brought her to her senses. As England's future novelist and poet, she could not smear her name with scandal of this kind. However much she needed Violet, however much she loved adventure and however daring her social transgressions, Vita had always been and would always remain a slave to convention and respectability.

On 9 March, Vita's twenty-ninth birthday, the two women returned: Violet to a fuming mother and to a husband who was not beyond caring, and Vita to the open arms of a grateful Harold. On 28 March, Vita wrote the final instalment of her confession: 'It is possible that I may never see Violet again. ...' If she chose not to live, it would be 'owing to me, while I remain safe, secure and undamaged save in my heart'.[1] While Vita wrote this, she could not have failed to hear ringing in her ears Violet's words: 'You have had to choose between me and your family, and you have chosen them. ... I do not blame you. If, one day soon, I seek for what escape I can find, you must not blame me.'

The letters begin to taper off here, but there was some further humiliation and betrayal before the Great Adventure was over. A terrible scene with Denys's mother came first. Violet had driven to the Trefusis house in Devon one evening to deliver a letter to Denys, who had said he would never see her again, a letter containing all the humiliating terms of surrender. About a mile from the house, Denys's mother, carrying a red lantern, sprang out of the bushes and ordered the car to a halt. She then abused Violet roundly in the presence of a tittering chauffeur, and ordered her to go back where she came from.

Another humiliation followed in the form of Hélène Claissac, Violet's childhood governess, whom Mrs Keppel had enlisted to stand guard over her daughter, now exiled to Italy. Violet was not to be let out of her sight for even a minute. Alice Keppel had reached the end of her tether too. A jailor was now needed.

Then came Pat Dansey's betrayal. By the spring of 1921, Pat was acting as go-between, relaying Violet's letters from Italy to Vita, and at some point she began inserting treacherous messages of her own: 'The thing *must* end for both of your families' sake. ... Vita, give Violet no promises and exact none from her.' This was on 14

[1] Nicolson, p. 132.

April. On 1 May, from Violet to Pat: 'O Misskins, I think you are the only person who loves me in the world. God bless you for it. But I am not with you. It seems so odd to have lost Vita and Denys, my freedom, my house, my money, all at one fell swoop. . . . Mama made me cry last night. She said if she had been in my shoes she would have killed herself long ago!'

Violet kept her faith in Pat as the one person she thought she could trust: 'Do you know,' she wrote, 'you have never let me down over anything? Bless you for it.' 'Julian doesn't write, and I can't, except through you. . . . My life is empty and futile and wasted.' The treachery begun by Pat in April had, by June, developed into a habit. She was now regularly slipping some subterfuge of her own into most of the letters from Violet to Vita: 'Sometimes I wonder if Violet could ever be happy in *being* happy. Do you know what I mean?' 'I am nervous at moments as to what madness she may commit. . . . I am afraid in September there will be trouble if she comes back to England.' 'I feel grey hairs springing out all over my head whenever I see her handwriting.'

By July, Violet had been transported to Clingendaal, with the Baroness de Brienen acting now as sentinel. Her pathetic letters to Pat continued: 'The one thing that keeps me going is that I feel I am still cared for.' In August: 'I see only too clearly that it would be impossible for me to live in England. I cannot bear being snubbed and mortified.' Pat saw only too clearly Violet's wretchedness, but lost no opportunity of reminding Vita of the impropriety of it all, well aware that scandal was Vita's darkest fear. 'As long as there is any connection between you two,' Pat admonished, 'the world will never allow the scandal to be forgotten.' In September: 'You mustn't be under the impression any-one is forcing Violet to go back to Denys. It is *entirely her own suggestion.* . . . If Violet did not claim my friendship, I think I might save you a lot of unnecessary pain.' In November: 'Oh Vita, she *is* hopeless. I hate the way she tricks and deceives people who have done everything for her.'

Pat Dansey was undermining Violet in the hope of replacing her in Vita's affections. With how much success her duplicity was met is not known, nor did it any longer matter, for infrequent as the letters had been, by the middle of November 1921, they ceased altogether. The great passion had cooled. Many months later, when *Challenge* was published in America, Violet received a copy, and the parts she marked 'reassured her that she had been the object of an incomparable love'.[1] One passage in particular stands out. It speaks of Julian's need for Eve:

> ... he asked from her, weakness to fling his strength into relief; submission to entice his tyranny; yet at the same time, passion to match his passion, and mettle to exalt his conquest in his own eyes; she must be nothing less than the whole grace and rarity of life for his pleasure; flattery, in short, at once subtle and blatant, supreme and meticulous, was what he demanded, and what she was, he knew, so instinctively ready to accord.[2]

But where did this 'incomparable' – and incredible – love come from? What was its source, its substance, its motive? Did Violet love Vita because she needed her? to ask Erich Fromm's question.[3] Or did she need her because she loved her? For there is an old psychological truth, where Violet is concerned, that people who carry within them a sense of emptiness urgently need to fill the void with something – love preferably, if it is available and the circumstances auspicious. When love is not possible, the emptiness becomes ravaging and they try to fill it with material things – food, possessions, luxuries – often beyond reason. Those unfortunate enough to harbour such a void seek out love in the way starving people search for food: they will do anything to satisfy their hunger. They feel, almost without exception or interruption or relief, the terrible need to please others, to succumb to their wishes, to inflate their love objects with their own dreams and to part with their own identity, if necessary, in return for love, in whatever form it is offered. They would give up their soul if they could. Hopelessly, they will lie, cheat, steal, pervert and corrupt themselves to unimaginable lengths in order to try to satisfy this insatiable hunger. Sometimes they become pitifully childlike in their quest, and so set on filling the emptiness that they lose their sense of reality and wander through life armed with only their fantasies, feeling for ever hungry and unwanted.

It is clear from the little surviving evidence we have that Violet was her mother's favourite, but Alice Keppel, as these letters amply testify, was a woman with an extraordinary need to control, possess and manipulate. The flashes we get of her from King Edward's

[1] Jullian and Phillips, p. 61.   [2] *Challenge* (1974), p. 230.
[3] *The Art of Loving* (1956), p. 41.

biographers are too sweet-scented to be wholly realistic. She could not have exerted so great an influence by means of charm and discretion alone. To have acquired so considerable a fortune required a determination equalled only by singleness of purpose – and that purpose was to captivate the King and keep him in her thrall.

Much as she cared for Violet in her own maternally restricted way, Alice Keppel's frugal offerings of the heart would never be adequate to so precocious a child and, in the complicated chemistry of that childhood, Violet developed a strong ambivalence towards her mother that expressed itself, on the one hand, by emulating her and, on the other, by resisting with all her childish might everything the woman stood for. And it is from these dichotomous tendencies that the Violet we see in these letters appears so inconsistent, contradictory and ultimately confusing. Fear of abandonment helped to keep Violet in her earliest years from open dispute with her mother. It was only when this gifted child was old enough to mimic her mother – or alternatively resist her – did the contest manifest itself in all its self-defeating determination.

Thus, if Alice defied convention as the King's mistress, Violet defied convention as mistress of the Honourable Vita Sackville-West. If the desirable Alice could charm the opposite sex, the flirtatious Violet could leave behind her a trail of broken engagements and broken hearts. If Alice loved material things, Violet loved them too – objects of beauty, she called them. If Alice loved the carefree epicurean King, Violet loved her careless gypsy prince. Conversely, if Alice respected law and order, Violet courted scandal and chaos. If Alice respected social restraint, Violet spat in society's face. If Alice gained her ends by muscular force, Violet gained hers by going 'limp and passive'. The list goes on.

The similarities (or their opposites) between mother and daughter are so symmetrical that it is almost as if Alice Keppel had imprinted upon Violet her own iron-clad strategies and tacitly bade her daughter to act them out in a way that made Violet in a sense her mother's emotional vehicle. For regardless of their surface differences, they had much in common. If there is any truth to this supposition, then certainly Violet would be her mother's favourite; certainly she submitted to her mother's need to control and responded to her need for homage. And just as certainly would Violet adore her mother for as long as she lived.

To be the receptacle of Alice Keppel's deepest impulses, however, implied on Violet's part a certain unquestioned submissiveness and denial of feeling. Moreover, it implied an emptiness of all ambition, direction and achievement, for achievement and submission are incompatible. Working towards some worthwhile goal – becoming a writer or a painter, for example – was in Violet's eyes an act of assertion, and assertion meant risking what little love her mother gave. Most unfortunate of all, however, the 'pact' or whatever we wish to call it, because it had been wordlessly and largely unconsciously communicated from mother to daughter, could never be brought into the open and examined.

In consequence, whatever anger, sorrow or emptiness Violet felt, it must remain always bottled up and unexpressed. She must suffer in silence and solitude, and moreover, in ignorance of the very source of her suffering. As long as the pact remained intact and functional, as long as Violet complied with its conditions, Alice Keppel could feel dimly justified in her treatment of her daughter and Violet would always feel dimly unfulfilled, unhappy and unloved. We have only to turn to her letters to see how they brim with these emotions. 'I have never achieved anything – and never shall.' 'I am lazy – nothing ever gets finished.' 'I'm so stupid.' 'I have only the weakest grasp of reality.' 'My life has been a waste.' 'I felt ... I had never loved or been loved.' 'You are my master – I am your puppet.' 'I want you hungrily, frenziedly. ... I am starving for you.' These are not simple turns of phrase. They are authentic expressions of the Violet no one knew – except perhaps Vita – and they represent, in a way no other single body of evidence has, Violet's reckless search for fulfilment – or 'happiness', in her romantic terminology.

Under Alice Keppel's counterfeit maternity, Violet was forever to remain dependent on others for emotional nourishment. Never understanding her mother's artifice, she would remain the eternal mimic of other people, with no core of her own. The feelings of anxiety connected vaguely with a sense of persistent uselessness that she felt as a child would transform themselves in her adult years to feelings of helplessness and self-disparagement. What was so remarkable in all this, however, was her consistent willingness to forgive, even exalt, her mother in spite of her terrible mismanagement of Violet's life.

Into this penumbral world Vita appeared, and with her, Violet would satisfy, for three years at least, the hunger that Vita was willing to appease in the form of ideal friend, protective mother and reckless lover. The friend went with her in search of freedom. The mother looked after her. The lover quickened her fantasies to life.

Violet learned very early that she was safest in an aura of romance and it did not take her long, even in adolescence, to discover Vita's preoccupation with domination or her dreams of glory. For Vita, especially, the muscular world of courage and conquest had pride of place. What differentiated the women in this realm of make-believe was that Violet curtsied to Love and Vita bowed to Lust. On the surface, to the casual observer, they seemed in pursuit of the same end, but in reality they complemented one another. Violet relied on sex to gain intimacy, and Vita used intimacy to achieve sex. This difference also coloured the way they regarded their adored mothers. Violet emulated Mrs Keppel: Vita courted Lady Sackville.

'I adore the unparalleled romance of her life,' Violet once said of her mother. 'I wonder if I shall ever squeeze as much romance into my life as she has had in hers. Anyhow I mean to have a jolly good try! *A tout prendre, je n'ai pas trop mal débuté.* ...' In many ways the feminine Violet and the masculine Vita might have been a perfect match. Violet recognized her lover's nature from the start. Vita needed constant affirmation of her own self-estimate. Violet provided that. Vita must appear ruthless, aggressive, indifferent to the puny claims of weaklings. Violet satisfied that too. Vita wanted no one to question her wisdom, her infallibility. Violet did her best, but did not always succeed. Vita needed to be depended upon for protection, understanding, affection, to be always in demand. Violet complied here too. What Vita needed, in short, was to glorify herself to match the masculine ideal of her fantasy.

We have only to glance at a couple of letters to see with what extraordinary perceptiveness Violet fulfilled her office. She was writing in 1910, aged sixteen: 'I love you, Vita, because you have never yielded to anything. ... I love you because you have the air of doubting nothing!' Ten years later, in 1920: 'If you desired it, I would have humiliated my flesh for you. I'd have submitted to what seems to me the supreme horror − I'd have had a child to give you pleasure.'

Glorification of the lover, self-effacement for the beloved: this was the pattern that won Julian's heart. What Vita hated in herself − compliance, subordination, dependency − she loved in Violet, who longed to be cradled, who shunned ambition and achievement, who so often felt helpless and unshielded.

What the letters dramatize so eloquently is that whenever Violet came close to realizing some goal or succeeding in some pursuit, almost without exception she did something to sabotage her efforts. It became almost a reflex. Success would have denied her the privilege of making extravagant claims on others, Vita especially. Further, when she failed, she suffered and suffering increased the intensity of her claims. If she went through such torments, should not Vita look after her? Love her for ever? So convinced was Violet of her martyrdom that she was sometimes cruel even to those who did care for her, who did take time and trouble on her behalf. It was easy to behave in this way if she saw the benevolence of others as something to which she was unconditionally entitled, and for such behaviour Violet was often harshly misjudged. But even this she unwittingly put to use. She could now feel self-pity, feel even more unworthy and badly treated than ever. She was a pawn, a victim. She had nothing, and Vita had everything.

All her suffering, however, encouraged her to feel a little superior to her victimizers and, as such, freed her to impose still further and greater claims. After all, had she not paid dearly for the little she got in return? Did not her suffering exonerate her, entitle her to the happiness she demanded? What Violet did not understand was that all this pain ultimately provided her with an alibi for not seeing that she was her own worst enemy, and thus further liberated her from the need to accomplish anything constructive with her own very conspicuous talents.

Violet's search for love became a way of life. Indeed, her self-worth was estimated by the degree to which she felt herself desired, sought after, prized. In this light it is easy to see how essential it was for her to establish intimacies, to be constantly surrounded by people, to feel menaced when left alone. This also explains in large measure her notorious reputation for making and breaking engagements. The ritual itself became a periodic means of gauging her own value. To be without a suitor was to be trapped in a void of nameless terror, so much was that value linked to someone else's estimate.

The consequence of Violet's dependency was the need to dissolve herself in Vita – to surrender and merge herself completely with the grand Prince of Romance. It was to Violet her surest means of survival: to live through another in the name of love. It was the worst means she could have chosen, however, and shows how fundamentally blind she was to her own self-destroying parasitism. She simply could not see the consequences of Vita's other life – the conventional life of home, husband and children – and without that vision nothing would convince her that romance and reality could not and would not mix. It took the horrifying scene at Amiens to prove it. That Violet had 'gone limp and passive' with another man, even though alleged and eventually disproved, was enough to paralyse Vita's heart and kill the illusion they had both constructed. It was not that Vita had lost Violet. It was that she had lost her self – her most treasured self: the Julian that Vita craved and Violet provided. 'I want you to rule, conquer, shatter, demolish,'[1] the extravagant Eve had said. All that was now a lie, a mockery. That day at Amiens, for Vita, was like the end of the world. Julian was dead.

Thus 14 February 1920 marked the beginning of the end. Vita grew reticent. Violet grew vindictive. The flood of passion dried up to a trickle of nostalgia and despair. Only a few faded letters of those final months preserve their anguish. Vita was thirty and Violet was twenty-eight.

At Long Barn, Vita eventually settled down to work and to her family. It was finally Harold's extraordinary patience and understanding that saved a marriage which was to endure successfully until Vita's death in 1962. Violet and Denys set up house together in Paris in a small flat in Rue Fourcroy. Theirs was one of those marriages that 'begin badly and end well'.[2] Denys died in the summer of 1929, before reaching his fortieth birthday.

Violet never married again. Then in 1940, with German bombs tearing France and England into a surface of craters, Violet escaped to England and the letters began again. There are not many of them, but it is clear from the few that have survived just how enduring each was to the other.

In an undated letter, written probably about 1941, Vita said:

> We simply could not have this nice, simple, naif, childish connexion without its turning into a passionate love-affair again. . . .
> You are an unexploded bomb to me.
> I don't want you to explode.
> I don't want you to disrupt my life. . . .
> This letter will anger you. I do not care if it does, since

---

[1] *Challenge*, p. 99.   [2] Trefusis, p. 77.

I know that no anger or irritation will ever destroy the love that exists between us.

And if you really want me, I will come to you, always, anywhere.

And from among the last preserved letters, dated 3 September 1950, Vita wrote:

I think we have got something indestructible between us, haven't we? ... a bond of childhood and subsequent passion, such as neither of us will ever share with anyone else.

It has been a very strange relationship, ours; unhappy at times, happy at others; but unique in its way, and infinitely precious to me and (may I say?) to you....

Time seems to make no difference. This is a sort of love letter I suppose. Odd that I should be writing you a love letter after so many years – when we have written so many to each other....

Oh, you sent me a book about Elizabeth Barrett Browning. Thank you, darling generous Lushka and you gave me a coal-black briquet ... which always burns in my heart whenever I think of you. You said it would last for three months, but our love has lasted for forty years and more.

The Letters

1910 to 1914

The first letter from Violet found in Vita's hoard at Sissinghurst is dated 11 September 1910, when Violet was sixteen and Vita eighteen, although there were no doubt earlier letters. After the two girls, both attending Miss Wolff's school, had first met in 1904, there had been visits to each other's homes, and in 1908 Violet had been on a trip to Italy with Vita. The increasingly ardent friendship between Vita and Rosamund over the next four years did not deter Violet from pursuing Vita, although the two met intermittently.

In September 1910 Violet was on the family's annual holiday in Scotland, where Vita visited her at Duntreath Castle, Alice Keppel's ancestral home. The death of Edward VII four months before had had immediate effects for the Keppel family and although Violet never refers directly in her letters to the relationship between the King and her mother, it was to shadow the whole of her life. The Keppels moved from Portman Square to a grand new residence at 16 Grosvenor Street and Alice Keppel, with her celebrated 'tact', decided on a prolonged stay abroad. In November 1910 the family left for Ceylon, where Sir Thomas Lipton had invited them to use the luxurious bungalow on his tea plantation. They stayed there for three months, giving Violet an opportunity to let her exotic imagination flower in letters to Vita.

In February 1911, George and Alice Keppel travelled on to China, while Violet and her sister Sonia were sent back to Europe 'to complete' their education in Munich. *En route* Violet saw Vita briefly in San Remo and from Germany, where she remained over the next year, she wrote provocative letters to Vita, by now a fashionable debutante. During 1911 Harold Nicolson was becoming increasingly important in Vita's life, although she and Rosamund Grosvenor remained in love.

In April 1912, Violet was back in London for her coming out

season and saw Vita again at Knole. There are almost no letters for this and the following year but Vita noted in her diary: 'This jealousy between R[osamund] and V[iolet] will end badly' and 'She [Violet] is mad; she kissed me as she usually does not, and told me she loved me.' In May 1913 Vita joined the Keppel family during their visit to Ravello, where they stayed with Lord Grimthorpe (who was possibly Violet's father). That summer Violet became very briefly engaged to Lord Gerald Wellesley, later the 7th Duke of Wellington, and was pursued by the dashing Julian Grenfell, gifted poet and athlete who, according to Sonia Keppel, looked like a Roman gladiator; there was a slight scandal when the two of them were caught in a housemaid's cupboard. Her circle of friends included Osbert Sitwell, whom she considered marrying, Gerald Berners and Nancy Cunard.

Vita became officially engaged to Harold Nicolson in August 1913. They were married in the chapel at Knole on 1 October, with Rosamund as maid of honour. Violet did not attend. The Nicolsons afterwards went to live in Constantinople, where Harold had his Foreign Office posting.

11 September 1910

I have to thank you for your entertaining epistle, my correspondent. It caused me, needless to say, a good deal of innocent amusement, which is obviously reciprocated.

Now you know how nice I can be when I like....

No, amiga, you will not have the opportunity of seeing me in November as the boat sails, I think, on the 2nd or 3rd of the month, and then, what with vaccination, clothing deemed suitable for the inconsequences of tropical climes, visits (here I groan!) to the doctor and dentist, touching farewell scenes with all my friends, I doubt whether I should find time for anything of a more absorbing nature.... As it is, my imagination soars into latitudes hitherto unheard of; indeed, they surpass in extravagance anything I have anticipated, ce qui n'est, certes, pas peu dire ...[1] Yet one of my lesser intuitions is, on my return to London, to purchase a small, but deadly revolver which I shall wear concealed about my person night and day, presumably to have a chance shot at unwary leopards

[1] which, certainly, is not to say little.

and elephants sagacious in their nocturnal wanderings round the bungalow in quest of food (30 likely!).

If you are very good and we are not all drowned in the Red Sea, devoured by mosquitoes or carried off by monkeys (like 'Mowgli' in the *Jungle Book*)[1] I will bring you back some sapphires, pearls and rubies (which they say are to be obtained for almost nothing!) to have made into something for your outward adornment. There! Isn't that nice of me? Didn't I tell you I could be etc., etc. You, on your part, must bring me some lion skins, dates and beads, or else I should inevitably expose myself to one of the deadly (almost, thank goodness! extinct) virtues, namely le désinteressement, chose qui m'a horripilié depuis ma plus tendre enfance.[2]

I have not yet received your play, which I shall gulp, whatever its failings or its merits. Please tell me plus en detail[3] your exact destination and how long you propose to remain there. It is more than possible that next year you will not see me in England at all. Would it not strike you as supremely humorous if this correspondence were kept up?

Now listen attentively and answer my questions: how much are you allowed to do et comment vous sentez-vous?[4]

We shall be at Duntreath all by ourselves till the end of this month. ... Yet another question: are you confined to a bath chair and bread and milk – If so, such things are procurable in the neighbourhood of Blanefield. However, all I require are nicely reasoned arguments to oppose all possible further suggestions on my part, which if the least in the world plausible would be duly accepted and docketed without delay.

V.

I go to Duntreath tomorrow. How do you approve of this condensed form of my handwriting (Can't find envelope to match – Have just found one!)

---

[1] By Rudyard Kipling.   [2] disinterestedness, a thing that has exasperated me since my earliest childhood.   [3] in more detail.   [4] and how do you feel? (Vita had not been well.)

Duntreath Castle[1], Blanefield, N.B.
16 September 1910

(Begun Tuesday morning, finished Wed. night.)

I arrived here yesterday. I have also arrived at the conclusion that I love this place almost – but not quite – better than anywhere else. The first time I set foot in this establishment I was exactly two months old. So you see it has every right to a place in my affections.

Every year I find it unchanged – the same stone for stone as it was 50 years ago, which is so comforting in a world of metamorphoses atmospheric and every conceivable otherwise – That, I feel sure is precisely the sensation you experience re-entering Knole after an absence of several months, or more, as the case may be. I suppose it is the same with everyone, who can boast the least thing in the way of ancestral abodes.

Yesterday a benignant fairy released me from a spell – oh yes! you may think! – which she cast upon me – or rather the part of me usually called one's memory – in a fit of exasperation about 18 months ago. You can imagine how grateful I feel for its complete restoration and rejuvenescence – I can't think of another word just at present, tho' two r's one on top t'other sound full of murderous intentions, even to my untutored ear. . . .

Do you remember the peacocks stalking round the house in the small hours of the morning uttering penetrating but unmusical cries the while, the gorgeous flaming sunsets that set the hills a-kindling for all the world like cabochon rubies? Do you remember the staid and stolid girl – a remote connection of mine – whose birthday we celebrated at a place called Lennox Castle? Don't you remember the enforced exercise à travers pluie et tempête[2] which I considered it my duty to afflict upon you? And the secret staircase and Sonia's[3] threats to accompany us, in spite of the fact that she had no clothing to speak of? And Willie's[4] violent infatuation which he really thought incurable at the time? And the haunted room and the Dumb Laird[5] behind the dining room screen? And the 'Viper of Milan',[6] and the deluge of Devotion which invariably and effectually inundated us both – whenever we set foot out of doors?

---

[1] The ancestral home of the Edmonstone family, in Stirlingshire, near Loch Lomond, dating to the fifteenth century and owned by Alice Keppel's brother, Sir Archibald Edmonstone, 'Uncle Archie'.　　[2] through rain and storm.　　[3] Sonia Keppel, Violet's sister.　　[4] Willie Edmonstone, Violet's cousin.　　[5] Celebrated ghost at Duntreath.　　[6] A play by Vita.

And my carefully thought out Scottish get-up to meet you at the station??

And poor Emily's justifiable perplexity when she saw herself confronted with no less than six different taps from which to achieve your bath? (I laugh even now when I think of it) and your − er − very natural reluctance to account for dear Margaret's absence in terms sufficiently edifying for my eager consummation? Don't you remember the purposeless, incessant tick-tick of pigeon-feet upon the roof, and the jackdaws flying from turret to turret?

... Surely you remember them? (This is what you novelists would call 'a flood of irresistible retrospection', is it not?) I prefer to call it the primary, inevitable speculations − evolutions − call it what you will − of a disinterred memory − which must re-establish its existence by remembering something or else go unadmitted. ...

Muchísimàs gracias, amada,[1] for your play, received this morning (yesterday) − I read it with the greatest interest, but I must read it over several times, before I can form an opinion either one way or the other. Parts of it struck me as being excellent, but I will tell you ma pensée en détail[2] in my next letter. ... I want an answer to my last effusion which, I trust, was read in the spirit in which it was written. This may strike you as a somewhat cryptic remark, but such, in reality, is far from being the case, I can assure you. Ya anochece, el sol se pone.[3]

Adiós

Si tu peux, viens. Pour toi rien n'est impossible, et tu le sais. Tu n'auras jamais lieu de t'en repentir.[4]

Duntreath Castle, Blanefield, N.B.
21 September [1910]

... Thanks for an amusing letter. Allow me to felicitate my correspondent on her decision − worthy in every respect of a rapid and reliable intuition, which my susdite correspondante[5] may well count among her proudest possessions.

---

[1] The greatest thanks, dear.   [2] my thoughts in detail.   [3] Night is coming, the sun sets.   [4] If you can, come. For you nothing is impossible, and you know it. You will never have reason to repent it.   [5] aforesaid correspondent.

As she most opportunely remarked in her last letter, it is a great and rare thing de se comprendre à demi-mot.[1] It is also one of the Latin traits which abound in my correspondent's character.

You will be at Kinross at precisely the same time as Mamma who arrives there on Saturday.

I do not know how long she proposes to stay. You will also see your old friend, my aunt, Mrs Winnington-Ingram, in whose company I trudged one stifling afternoon up to tea to see you in Florence.

... Stracchini[2] is greatly looking forward to seeing you again, so you will have to be very nice to her, and be surtout[3] very careful what you say about me as she is one of few enlightened, superior beings whose paragon of all virtues I am. Now you know why I — But no matter! This will keep as well as a great many other things. ...

I insist upon your writing a longer answer to this letter.
[16 Grosvenor Street, London]
8 October 1910[4]

Thank you for your letter, received this morning. I'll straight-forwardly avow to you that I worried unduly about this letter: it's that, you understand, I was waiting for it for quite a while ... (3 days, think of it! an eternity!) And I just about racked out my brains saying to myself: pray that nothing has happened to Vita — she who catches cold at the slightest breeze? the letter did not arrive. This morning on constating that my napkin was sheltered under a bluish envelope, something that strongly resembled a détente took place in the depths of my being. ... Just in case you don't know it, I am primitive in my joy as in my suffering. I've an unheard of difficulty to hold back sometimes my frolics of a happy child, sometimes my tears of a disillusioned one. ...

I've so much to do that to tell you the truth I no longer know in which direction to turn my head. From morning until night I do nothing but try on dresses (marvels! I want you to come to Ceylon, if only to see them! (O, Vanity Thy Name is Violet.')) ...

This house is more calm than ever, no noise except a distant

[1] to understand each other in every detail. lodge-keeper at Duntreath. [3] above all. in French. [2] Mrs Strachen, the wife of the [4] The original of this letter is

sound of horse carriages that does not traverse these walls two centuries thick. Certainly this is very little when I think of the Renaissance columns of Knole, the medieval staircase of Duntreath, the Elizabethan ceilings of Quidenham, of Melbury, and a thousand other places, but in London one must content oneself with little, and when I find myself alone at the end of this great elaborate salon, I feel myself to be suddenly transported two centuries in the past, and I see the beautiful ladies of the 18th century, with the powdered wigs, corseted in whalebone, leaning from the bow window while a Grosvenor Street fop ogles them with a lustful eye. . . .

I am in the act of asking myself if I ought to reply to your question? A question furthermore most indiscreet and which merits a sharp reprimand. Reply, don't reply, reply! Oh to the devil with discretion!

Well, you ask me pointblank why I love you. . . . I love you, Vita, because I've fought so hard to win you. . . . I love you, Vita, because you never gave me back my ring. I love you because you have never yielded in anything; I love you because you never capitulate. I love you for your wonderful intelligence, for your literary aspirations, for your unconscious (?) coquetry. I love you because you have the air of doubting nothing! I love in you what is also in me: imagination, the gift for languages, taste, intuition and a host of other things. . . .

I love you, Vita, because I've seen your soul. . . .

Saturday, 15 October 1910[1]

Thank you with all my heart, dear correspondent, for your charming dissertation on the mountains of Scotland and the delights that they offer at this moment of the year. I have to ask myself again if this letter is really from you? Vainly I force myself to look for a symbolic sense, a sequel. . . . But although I surrender myself to all possible and imaginable queries, my spirit remains in the dark. . . .

It is the first time in my life that I hear you pity the fate of those who have no shelter when the great winds blow. And – sad to say, but I must let you know – compassion, regard for, consideration for your fellow creatures doesn't suit you, my dear, no, not at all!

It will not brook my sense of the natural, inevitable, logical *fitness*

[1] The original of this letter is in French.

61

of things, which is one of the – if not *the* – foundation stone of Art and the very essence of the stuff artists are made of.

Ha! ... You see that I've drawn my sword and I won't refrain from expressing to you all my sentiments. Let's hope that this pleases you. ...

Let's see, where are we?

Ecco: let us hope that your séjour in Scotland will not be prolonged indefinitely, because, from your letter of yesterday, I fear that it might be fatal to your intellectual well being. What is this unbridled love of liberty, of every creature, exempt from social ties, free of conventions?

And those great wild promenades that you undertake across mountains and valleys with a mastiff for your only company? Will you unravel all of that for me! (Oh, but it's too soon to rejoice, I'm not finished; I've still enough for a page! You know when I get going . . .)

And those reveries beneath a glowing sky? And those crumbling old walls under which you sheltered yourself? And this bottomless contempt for the mean little human spirit (note, Mademoiselle, that I'm quoting you!) which, according to you, has no other function than to be surmounted which serves us for nothing but to accuse ourselves.

What is most amusing about all of this is that I entirely share your opinions, but I don't think that it is wise to thus formulate projects of 'renunciation' of the world and its 'pomps' which sooner or later you will find yourself constrained to transgress, not that I give this the least consequence. Four months ago at the most, it was only a question of balls, of cotillons, of parties, and what else? for your pleasure and you appeared (I say 'appeared' – women are so 'deep') to be delighted. And now for what I call to 'tempt Providence', and it's for your good that I exert myself in this manner. Listen to me and I will tell you what will ensue, if you persist in deviating from the path that the world by general accord (and by the 'world' I mean all those that are worth knowing) is pleased to allot you. You will become the wife of a gentleman – Oh, a fine one! I don't say the contrary, a most affable gentleman, one who could not be more hospitable, who would adore to entertain, and he would commit all the abuses – abuses of expense, naturally – in order to make himself agreeable to society. But I pray that my prediction will not be realized. You would be too unhappy, but not an unhappiness that would profit you. There is, if you wish to believe it, a very different sort of unhappiness which would exercise the most happy influence on your character and on your habits but to reveal to you its nature, its nuance, its state of being would appear to me the height of indiscretion, so I do not dream of doing so. You will have nothing to fear from this direction, I guarantee it.

So you are able to divine it (Oh, but I forget: you are no earthly good at guesswork. That is essentially my business, is it not?) I write to you from my brocaded bed in a perfect twilight, strangled by compresses, by cataplasmes, surrounded by mouth-wash, by ointments, by mint lozenges and other frights, but I'll spare you the enumeration.

It is necessary to add that once again I have my monthly and invariable sore throat? You might well write me a nice letter, although, upon my word, this is not a case of diphtheria, and in eight days it will be over, but do remember – Oh, alas! What have I said? And only five minutes ago I was telling you that sympathy was not to be expected from the likes of you and now I am deliberately asking that some of it may be expended on me and my tiresome sore throat! Ma non importa! We other women, we're all more harebrained, one and all, and believe me, it's you who take the prize. . . .

You will get this letter by Monday night or Tuesday morning at the very latest. Let me have your answer by Thursday morning. And – please spare me the weather! . . .

16, Grosvenor Street
23 October 1910[1]

O natural Coquette! It's all over with you! Your letter says much – too much – about your puerilities which are already innumerable. Is there, for instance, anything more deceiving than appearances? I tell you that nothing is more fascinating than a flaunted modesty which doesn't fool anyone! . . .

Ah, I had not realized that the quiet sea (translating 'me' – Heavens, what presumption . . .) could become rough.

Ah, I had not realized that music exerted upon you the same influence as upon _____ but shut up, no indiscretion.

Ah, I had never seen you depart from that beautiful calm that you so carefully maintain in your relationship with me.

[1] The original of this letter is in French.

But who do you take me for? Not the person that I am, that's certain. You do ramble on, or do you like receiving infuriated letters; really, do understand, you exasperate me when you make yourself so – dumb! – excuse the epithet. You are then so very boring (I tell you straight out) with all your pointless corrections (no other word comes to mind) that you think you can demand from me – by what right, good God, I wonder....

If you hadn't written me this awful letter, wild horses wouldn't have made me see you, but upon reflection, I've changed my mind. Yes, if you wish, come and see me again. Listen to what I propose: tea on Thursday (not on Friday, on Friday I couldn't see you). 16 Grosvenor Street and then dinner with me and my little papa,[1] and that's all.... Would you send me word, Miss, if you like my suggestion and as soon as possible, for needless to say I am positively done up, I haven't a single moment left for myself.

Now for your information, I leave London on the thirty-first of this month, that is to say Monday in a week. That suits you? My address from about the 23rd or 24th is Dambatenne, Haputele, Ceylon.

16, Grosvenor Street
31 October 1910[2]

Tonight I am crazy. ... I want to hurt someone: if you were here I should make you sit down. I should put my two hands on your shoulders and press. ... I should dig my nails into your flesh, my hands would contract, I should crush your sleeves, your bones. ... I should like to tear you up, to mutilate you, to make you unrecognizable. ... But since you are not with me, I shall be content with little. ... You have come, haven't you, with the clear intent of making me appreciate at all costs the dangers to which I should expose myself if I break faith with you?

And while listening to you I seemed to be attentive, didn't I?

It is obvious from my quiet behaviour that your speech impressed me profoundly and that consequently new resolutions began to dawn in my mind. Certainly you could see it sufficiently! And if only your imagination could take it in, you were holding, so to speak, my soul in your hand, you could mould it any way you liked.

[1] George Keppel. [2] The original of this letter is in French.

64

But — there's always a 'but' on such occasions — as you were contemplating it with a triumphant eye — it slipped through your fingers — to be buried in an old nook where nobody could follow it. ... God! How wrong you were, Vita! Judge rather: after your departure, I laughed till the tears came, then roared: what a debacle!

Understand, Miss, that I am not afraid of you (only the Unforeseen frightens me) and if I resist the temptation to deceive you as you have never been deceived in your life, it is because I am delighted, simply delighted that there remain so many things for you to discover that you have ignored until now.

What! You didn't know that I have my moments of madness, that I also occasionally love to venture on a territory almost totally unknown, a territory where one can only grope in dim light, that I also have my pride, that I am also a Woman?

What! You didn't know that to forbid me such and such a thing was a spur to my vanity, the more obstacles placed in my way, the more I am enticed. My God! How blind you are. The spirit of contradiction, you say? Well, that's me, the Spirit of contradiction — personified! My curiosity, on the other hand, is so great that I would let myself go to the extreme just to see how you would arrange to kill me? Would it be a stiletto thrust between the shoulder blades by a traitor at midnight or a poisoned cup by daylight?

Do tell me so that I know where I stand.

But first of all: do you know this yourself? Do you know this, Vita? Are you really certain, Chevreuse? ...[1]

Colombo, Ceylon
[December 1910][2]

... I write to you beneath a bewildering swaying of gigantic bamboo trees, at the far end of a garden which ought to belong to the *Thousand and One Nights*, or, if you prefer, this resembles El Dorado.

Do you like orchids? I adore them.

You would have the same feelings if you could see them as I do at this moment: meaning, in clusters, purpled, narcotic, with here and there some shameful misalliance as is suitable for plebeian orchids.

[1] A reference to the Duchesse de Chevreuse in Alexandre Dumas's *The Three Musketeers.* [2] This and the next two letters were written on different days but all three were enclosed in the same envelope. The originals are in French.

Haven't I a talent for descriptions, darling?...

Beneath a blazing tropical midday sky, the road to Maradane is reduced to powder: ... on each side arises the unexpected; foliage in turn sombre, sparkling, or brilliant. The heat is such that the slightest movement is exhausting. At a distance in a cloud of dust, one perceives the great weary oxen with their bloodshot eyes and backs slashed by blows. Alongside, gleaming black, the ox drivers.

Everywhere reflections, everywhere light, and then, from time to time, a coconut falls, slowly, with a dull sound on the brown earth.

A land of an absolute repose, of an absolute beauty, a rich land, an unbelievable land, bursting forth with all fruits and spices – the purity of a vermilion land, enamoured of light, drunk by sunshine. POSTSCRIPT: What do you say about my oriental style? As for me, I am stunned by it! *I flatter myself I am the possessor of one of the most adaptable natures in existence.*

Dambatenne at 5000 feet, 200 feet from the sun.
4 December 1910

I am giddy, the dizziness of heights.

I feel so tiny ... you have no idea. ... All the surrounding mountains conspire to crush me with their weight. Immense shaggy rocks are heaped up pell-mell around the house. The view is superb. 2000 feet below us smiling hills with delicate sylvan slopes can be perceived.

You see it, the stump of Adam's Peak[1] in the distant haze. Nearby it's the jungle, then, the sea. Here and there the lagoons – girded by banana trees, pomegranate, cactus, camphor trees, eucalyptus, and nutmeg trees – smoke in the sun like enormous tubs.

Unnecessary to tell you that I am of a sovereign laziness and that nothing less than a monsoon would make me abandon my divan....

Now for the little matter-of-fact information you love: we will be going perhaps to spend several days towards the end of this month at Nuwara Eliya, but you can write to me here and it will be forwarded.

I had all sorts of adventures on the steamer that I should like to be able to tell you about in person. ... Enough to say that the lady

[1] The most remarkable mountain of Ceylon (7,360 feet), a striking pyramid on whose rocky summit is a depression shaped like a huge footprint, claimed variously as that of Buddha, Shiva, and Saint Thomas the Apostle.

Violetta amused herself madly at the expense of others. Which is perhaps not altogether a good thing, but one pardons youth for many things, especially at 16 1/2. These are what you call puerilities. I call them simply imprudences – which amounts to about the same thing.

Do try not to get married before I return.

Dambatenne
12 December 1910

In vain one looks for some coherence, some telltale blade of grass in the inextricable labyrinth which is your last letter – a labyrinth, alas, which lacks an Ariadne to provide the conducting thread. . . .

In attentively re-reading, suddenly a sort of heavy anguish which I can only qualify as apprehension has just made my heart beat rapidly and makes my hand tremble as I write to you. . . .

It's trembling and it's sad.

For the first time your extra two years seem to me very real, arrogant, sinister. . . .

After all, I'm only a girl. I ought to have foreseen that perhaps at your age a masculine liaison would come about.[1] I would be wise to accept this. I feel that I'm about to say improper things. You won't laugh, promise that you won't laugh. For a long time I've asked nothing of you, so grant me this. It would hurt so.

Tomorrow we're going to Nuwara Eliya. We plan to spend most of this week in the jungle where these gentlemen-hunters are going to hunt alligators.

I hope terribly that they won't force me to participate. These enormous beasts all bleeding – pouah! It makes one shudder. Then we will go to see buried cities, beginning with Anuradhapura.[2] The jungle makes me tremble. I pray to return intact.

Violetta

[1] Vita had in fact met Harold Nicolson in June and he was now invited to Monte Carlo where Lady Sackville and Vita were spending the winter.
[2] Anuradhapura, founded in 437 BC, was abandoned as a royal residence in the ninth century; it and Polonnaruwa, the Singhalese capital from the tenth to twelfth centuries, had been buried by the jungle and were now famous ruins.

Dambatenne, Ceylon
2 January 1911[1]

... I have had every conceivable thing in the way of adventures these last two years. Shall I disclose some of the more thrilling for your benefit? You ask for nothing better, do you? And it's precisely because I understand your curiosity – quite natural really – that I'm determined not to tell.

I have more memories than if I were a thousand years old. A great chest whose drawers are crammed with balance sheets, verses, love letters, with law suits, novels, with locks of hair rolled up amid the receipts – hides fewer memories than my sad brain. It's a pyramid, an immense vault containing more dead than the ordinary grave. I am a cemetery detested by the moon where, as with remorse, drag out long verses, which fasten themselves to my most sacred deaths. ...[2]

I could go on reciting for half an hour if this would help to solace my spleen. Your last letter told me much about your present state. Shall I admit it, not hiding anything, that I've been given much cord to twist again. What a bitch you are! Excuse my language. I use it on certain occasions to bury my feelings which are apt to prove too much for me at times.

Well here's something that I think will make you laugh: imagine, chère amie, that I've brought back an alligator from my jungle expedition – an enormous one such as no longer exists today, enormous as the step of a staircase!

This really takes your breath away for once!

I killed it with my little rifle and if you are very good (as you would say), you shall have a purse made out of it for your birthday present![3]

Do you know that you have ceased to be a reality for me? ... You are a mirage that recedes to the degree that one approaches it. Speaking of mirages, I saw a very beautiful one in the Suez Canal at the mouth of the Red Sea. I was gazing with distracted eyes at the desert which stretches to infinity, the intense implacable sun gleaming as a furnace, a camel marching with great unequal steps towards the south – when suddenly I recall letting out a loud cry: 'See over there, the trees, the water!'

One looks: it seems then that a lake encircled by date trees and

---

[1] The original of this letter is in French.   [2] From Baudelaire.   [3] Vita's birthday was on 9 March.

leafy shrubs, incredibly blue and seductive, had passed unobserved. Immediately we rush to the maps, snatch up the spectacles, then all together to the Captain who, high up in his cabin, is stretched out in a sultry position. 'What is that lake which glitters in the distance, so blue, so solitary?'

The Captain descends, grumbling, aims his telescope towards the Egyptian shore: 'That, ladies, that is quite simply a mirage!' and he returns to his quarters, still shaking with his habitual healthy and vulgar laughter. . . .

Hotel Savoy, San Remo
9 February 1911

As it happens I shall be at San Remo some little time. My telegram was a trifle startling, was it not? I tried repeatedly to speak to you on the telephone, but alas and alack I was informed that the connection did not extend beyond the frontier. On second thoughts, however, I regretfully admitted t'were better so, as the sound of a voice you thought at least 5 hundred thousand miles away might prove somewhat disconcerting, to say the very least of it. Also, Mademoiselle a, dit on, le coeur faible. . . .[1] Would it suit you if I came Monday or Tuesday inevitably chaperoned by Mlle Claissac?[2] Alas, Papa will have departed by then, and my next German maid is awaiting discovery in Munich, whither I go soi-disant[3] to 'complete my education!?' . . .

Hotel Savoy, San Remo
12 February 1911

My dear Vita, what arrant nonsense! Why should I have been in London of all places? It was not *very* probable that I should go straight back to London fogs and mists, after tropical sunshine and the scantiest possible attire, was it? Of course if Mama and various friends and relations had wished to bring my young life to a premature end, they could not have chosen a better expedient. . . . Also,

---

[1] has, it is said, a weak heart.   [2] Hélène Claissac ('Moiselle'), Violet's governess.   [3] so to speak.

for argument's sake, let us suppose I had gone somewhere – oh, anywhere else – Cannes or Bordighera on the Riviera, I think, don't you, that after your very cordial invitation to stay with you from a week to a fortnight – I should have let you know my whereabouts? So I think I feel justified that, all things taken into consideration, you are, if anything, a shade more 'impossible' than I am. And as you seem particularly to want me to put les points sur les i,[1] how long is it you desire my presence? For one day or several? This, I am aware, is a severe breach of délicatesse on my part, but I have already given you no less than three opportunities in which to state the length of time you would like me to be with you, and you have failed to take advantage of any of them. I could perhaps come and see you – somehow Thursday but you must arrange all this yourself....

Munich
Easter 1911[2]

I would like to tear you away from your Italy, give you a great slap across both cheeks and take you away with me on a delightful journey, far, quite far away from everything that has a narcotic effect on a nature which appears from your last letters to be half asleep.

My God, my God, how can I snap you out of this detestable Olympian calm which contrasts so dreadfully with my purple and scarlet memories....

Then ... we will descend on Spain, you as my pupil, I your cicerone. I will show you Fuenterrabia (the French say 'Fontarabie') with its filthy streets and fanatical cohorts. Irun, shadowed by the Pyrénées with its beautiful cruel girls, Pamplona, flanked by eroded mountains, Burgos, wise and archaic. Follow me and I will show you the matadors parading on Sunday afternoon, the filthy disgusting priests, the ragged beggars who spit insults in your face because they are contemptuous of you for having yielded to their supplication; follow me everywhere; I will show you eyes of black velvet which, all by themselves, bandy indecent proposals, the sevillana, the fandango, undulating bodies, throbbing castanets, the magpies strutting between the olive trees, the sad countryside, the fluttering mantilla, the unfolding fan.

[1] dots on the i's.   [2] The original of this letter is in French.

Follow me, follow me! I will force you to see the hand swift to murder, blood spilt in secret, the calculated vendetta that is pitiless and has never heard of the word 'pardon', which waits to strike the fatal blow, never missing, each to kill in his turn. Shrink from crime? What are you thinking of? This is the order of things, this will be done – cursed be anyone who dares to intervene!

Oh, I will show you treason, infamy! Women without scruples, without shame, who act according to principles that are largely perverted, not to say disgusting, who say: 'Get out of the way' to the World and its Apostles, who meddle and criticize them.

I will show you the mad woman, Vita, the mad woman, do you understand, who snaps her fingers to call back her lover who was disembowelled before her very eyes last Sunday in the bull-ring!

[1911]¹

Oh Vita, I get so sad when I think how like we are to two gamblers, both greedy to win, neither of whom will risk throwing a card unless the other throws his at the same time! You won't tell me you love me, because you fear (wrongly, most of the time) that I will not make the same declaration to you at the same moment!

Bavaria
16 June 1911

If you are not already engaged (my business transactions, you will observe, are invariably carried out in English²) you might perhaps care to spend a fortnight of the month of August somewhere in the Austrian Tyrol with Mamma and myself, as she suggested my asking somebody for myself besides her own friends. Where, ganz gestimmt,³ I cannot yet say, but you can regard this as an invitation from my mother as well as from myself.

I quite appreciate the whirl of excitements and otherwise in which you find yourself at the present moment, but nevertheless expect an

---

¹ The original of this letter is in French. ² Unlike most letters from Violet to Vita at this time, which were written in French. ³ quite surely.

answer as I repeat this is from my mother as well as myself, and if the answer be 'No' I must immediately set myself the task of finding someone else.

The great music festival is in full swing here – or rather will be by the middle of next week. I would not miss it for the whole London season – and many other things besides. So you are at liberty to set me down as a musical fanatic. . . .

In the course of the next few weeks you may receive a photograph of me; I warn you as it is highly probable you will not have the remotest idea 'who the lady is'. . . .

Grand Hotel, Heidelberg
15 March 1912

My dear, This is absurd! What on earth possessed either you or your parents to think of tearing off to Spain at this time of year!? You will probably freeze to death, there is not a thing out in the way of trees or plants – Nothing begins till after Easter; – why not go *then*? Then you get all the good corridas,[1] whereas if you went now, I don't think you could get one.

In any case, you cannot travel direct to Cordova – you always stop in Paris on the way south. My arguments are feeble, but I can't help it. I shall most certainly suffocate with rage if I don't see you in Paris – all my plans were arranged to a nicety and I do so *detest* having them upset, as you *must* come to Spain, stop in Paris, buy clothes, and incidentally see *me*, on the way –

Ecris moi:[2]Princess Hotel, Rue de Presbourg, à partir de demain.[3]

[1] bullfights.   [2] Write to me.   [3] as of tomorrow.

1914 to Spring 1918

For most of the first three years of the war, Violet saw very little of Vita and there are no surviving letters until April 1917. In the summer of 1914, Alice Keppel borrowed Clingendaal, the house in Holland of her friend, the Baroness Daisy de Brienen, where the party of guests included the 'dazzling' Lady Diana Manners (later Lady Diana Cooper) and her mother, the Duchess of Rutland, and, in Violet's subsequent words in *Don't Look Round*, many of 'the brilliant doomed young men the war was to annihilate'. With the outbreak of war, George Keppel rejoined his regiment and Mrs Keppel went to work in a Field Hospital in France. Violet worked briefly in a soldiers' canteen and by 1917 was escaping from loneliness in London by visits to Margaret – Pat – Dansey at Berkeley Castle, the home of Pat Dansey's uncle, Lord Fitzhardinge.

During this time Vita remained happily married. She had returned to England in June 1914 and on 6 August gave birth to her first son, Benedict. Violet, 'at her own sarcastic request', was one of the godmothers. Harold was transferred to the Foreign Office in London for the war years and in 1915 the couple bought Long Barn, not far from Knole in Kent; in 1916 they also bought a house in Ebury Street, London. Their second son, Nigel, was born on 19 January 1917. That summer Violet and Vita saw more of each other, both in London and Kent, while Harold was increasingly occupied by his war work. Vita's friendship with Rosamund Grosvenor had faded over these years, while Violet's passion continued to smoulder, awaiting the opportune moment to erupt. This happened on 13 April 1918, when Violet went to visit Vita alone at Long Barn.

Royal Crown Hotel, Sevenoaks
18 April 1917

... We saw all over Knole, which seemed to me more beautiful than ever. How I adore that place! Had you been a man, I should most certainly have married you, as I think I am the only person who loves Knole as much as you do! – (I *do*, really) – I met Miss Cardnich (the adolescent one) on a bicycle. We waved effusively. She appeared not a little surprised to see me here – I don't know quite where I want to go next? There doesn't seem to be any place near here likely to suit my purpose!

Bless you and a million thanks –

Coker Court,[1] *Yeovil*
29 October 1917

Darling, I seize my pen for the first time during I don't know how many years to write you news of a casual kind, and *not*, for once! to implore your protection for either illicit interviews or clandestine correspondence. Soit dit en passant,[2] I shall be *furious* if you don't answer my letter, and I shall never write to you again! I'm told you desire to let Ebury Street for the winter, if so, we both belong to the old-fashioned coward category of women who would rather live in a suburb of Bristol than go near London at the present moment! On the other hand, I shall be very angry if it *is* true, as it means I shan't see you during the entire winter, which, believe me, would be equally deplorable for both of us. I simply can't get on without a periodical glimpse of radiant domesticity, and you will become smug to an intolerable degree if the vagabond – what Dorothy calls 'rackety' element – as supplied by me, is indefinitely withheld from you. We mustn't let it happen. We are absolutely essential to one another, at least in *my* eyes! ...

I have returned here in spite of – h'm – alien influences? – Dorothy[3] is as attractive as ever and I love her (nearly) as much as

---

[1] The home of Dorothy Heneage, partly Tudor and partly Georgian, one of Violet's favourite houses.   [2] By the way.   [3] Described by Violet in *Don't Look Round*: 'Dorothy Heneage came into my life when I was about seventeen. As regards age, she was midway between my mother and myself. ... she resembled a furry little animal out of one of La Fontaine's fables. ...'

you. I shall love her considerably *more* than you, if you don't instantly answer this letter. . . .

. . . I love this place. I always feel either that I am going to have the Romance of my life here, or that I've already had it!

I go tomorrow to Badminton (Glos.) for the full moon. I have a sudden craving for your society, that is why I have written to you – Sois gentille, réponds moi.[1]

V.

25 January 1918

Once upon a time, there lived an artist and a woman, and the artist and the woman were one. In the course of time the woman married; she married the prince of her dreams, and irrevocable, changeless contentment descended upon her. The artist was temporarily forgotten: wrapped in comfortable torpor, the artist slept, and the woman gloried in her womanhood and in the happiness she could give. . . .

One day the artist awoke to find the chamber of her slumbers shrunken and distorted, the windows had become so small, she could scarcely see out of them, the brocades were faded; damasks and satins hung like limp ghosts on limp nails. . . . Stricken with panic she rushed to her window; she saw a woman playing on a smooth lawn with a laughing child. Presently, they met; they confronted each other, the woman serene, loving, imperturbable, the artist defiant, jealous, irritated beyond endurance. And the artist stood and jeered at the woman. Poor artist: Dishevelled, irresponsible gypsy, it was more than she could bear – Now the woman belonged heart and soul to her husband and her children, but the artist belonged to no one, or rather to humanity. Fancy one, she roams the earth, here today, gone tomorrow – the world is stuck with the useless flowers of her favour. . . .

The combination of the woman and the artist had produced a species of mentality as rare as it is sublime; an artist whether it be in painting, in music or in literature, must necessarily belong to both sexes, his judgment is bisexual, it must be utterly impersonal, he must be able to put himself with impunity in the place of either sex.

[1] Be nice, reply to me.

The result of this intellectual equilibrium was to make you aware suddenly of the wisdom of the ages in the eyes of this woman; a woman of perfect truth, limpid, unmistakable, untouched by the instability of man – you realized that she had something of an eternal truth, of an eternal beauty in her, far, far beyond the reach of our puny comprehension. . . . Something as old as the mountains, as old as the world, yet forever young, forever unattainable. . . . Something divine, godlike, vertiginous, that sees even those least known to it from the plane of superlative understanding and commiseration. The singing lyre that is vouchsafed to a thousand inarticulates – the artist god, yes! The artist who should be fed each day with new intuitions, new conditions, new loves and new hatreds to be kept singing for humanity! The artist – the supreme luxury that the gods toss to the world when it feels it must either speak or die!

And the woman perchance will smile when she reads this, and her friends will say what an ideal wife and mother she makes, which is true, but the artist will shrink in horror from the imputation of smugness that these words cannot fail to convey –

God knows it is aesthetically incorrect that the artist should be hampered by domesticity, Pegasus harnessed to a governess-cart, Marysas playing the harmonium. I shut my eyes, I seem to see, despite the Demeter-like attributes with which the woman is undoubtedly crowned, not the woman, but the artist striding the mountain tops, silent, inspired and alone.

April 1918 to March 1919

From 28 April to 10 May 1918 the lovers went to Cornwall and stayed in Hugh Walpole's cottage on a cliff overlooking Polperro. On 14 May Vita, with Violet's help, began writing the novel that would finally be published as *Challenge, a roman à clef* set on a Greek island portraying Vita as Julian and Violet as Eve. During the spring and summer Violet wrote a flood of passionate, often frenzied letters to Vita as they made plans to leave England and live together. They borrowed Hugh Walpole's cottage again in July, and there were frequent meetings in London and Long Barn. That summer too, Violet became acquainted with Denys Trefusis, a handsome officer in the Royal Horse Guards. A grandson of the 19th Lord Clinton, he was described by Violet as 'an Elizabethan personage'; he had lived in Russia for four years, returning 'more Russian than English' in 1914, when at the age of nineteen he had enlisted in the 'Blues'. He served in France and Flanders, rising to the rank of major and receiving the Military Cross for bravery.

With the Armistice on 11 November 1918, the long awaited 'escape' became possible and, having enlisted Harold's help to gain passports, Violet and Vita left on 18 November for Paris where they stayed for an idyllic and reckless week in the flat of playwright friend Edward Knoblock; then, rather than return to England as their families expected, they went on to Monte Carlo, and remained there for the next three months. Harold spent Christmas at Knole with his sons and Vita's parents, who were now on the verge of separation. In response to his pleading letters from Paris, where he was on the staff of the British delegation to the Peace Conference, Vita promised to join him there on 1 February but she stayed on with Violet in Monte Carlo until 15 March 1919, when Vita finally left to visit Harold before returning to England.

[Spring 1918]

... How much longer am I to endure the farce of snatching a few hours at a time with someone who holds my life in their keeping? My sister is playing Prince Igor[1] – the part that is so like my Dmitri. ...

I shall take you to hear 'Khouantchine'[2] which is of all music the most sensuous, the most 'bariolé',[3] the most abandoned, and the most desolate. ... One day I shall write a book on the baleful influence music has had on my life. ...

[1918]

... I may be writing rubbish, but then I am drunk. Drunk with the beauty of my Mitya! All today I was incoherent. I tell you, there is a barbaric splendour about you that conquered not only me, but everyone who saw you. You are made to *conquer*, Mitya, not be conquered. You were *superb*. You could have the world at your feet. Even my mother, who is not easily impressed, shared my opinion. *You have also changed,* it appears? They said, this evening after you had gone, that you were like a dazzling Gypsy. My sister's words, not mine. A Gypsy potentate, a sovereign – what you will, but still a Gypsy.

They also said they noticed a new exuberance in you, something akin to sheer animal spirits – that never was there before. You may love me, Mitya, but anyone would be *proud* to be loved by you, even if they were to be thrown aside and forgotten – for somebody new. ...

---

[1] Opera by Borodin, first produced in St Petersburg in 1890; here being played on the piano by Sonia. Violet was identifying the passionate voluptuous music with Vita, 'my Dmitri'.   [2] Unfinished opera by Moussorgsky, first produced in St Petersburg, 1886, then in Paris and in London, 1913, in a version altered by Stravinsky and Ravel.   [3] multicoloured.

5 June 1918

Mer Dmitri, I adored the letter you wrote me 'from the woods' – the only long letter I have ever had from you. Don't you think you might make a *habit* of such letters? I treasured it up till yesterday afternoon, then 'degusté'[1] it, slowly and voluptuously.

The description of Julian I thought most adequate.[2] You say it's not like you! It *is* you, word for word, trait for trait. I laughed long and uproariously over the part where you said, all people worshipped him *without his* being conscious. Signiferait-il que tu commences à t'apprécier?[3] Let me think you do, at all events, and I shall not have lived in vain.

I must say I should like either a more *detailed* description of Julian's appearance whereas hitherto you have confined yourself more to the impression it produced on other people. 'Julian was tall,' let us say, and 'flawlessly proportioned. The perfect height of the Greek athlete is alleged to have been 5 ft 10 in, but Julian surpassed this by at least two inches. Julian's hair was black and silky. Eve found herself wondering what it would feel like to stroke, and promptly did so; she was amazed to feel a sensation akin to pain shoot up her fingers and lodge itself definitely in the region of her heart. However she was determined to analyse Julian's beauty, feature by feature, and as he lay stretched full-length in the grass, thinking – what! We wondered uneasily – here was an opportunity not to be neglected.

'How graceful he was, how young, how strong! Eve studied the recumbent figure with eyes in which lay something like a grudging caress. Yet she hated herself for finding him beautiful, for beautiful he undoubtedly was. How resentfully she probed those heavy-lidded eyes, green in repose, black in anger, ever smouldering with some fettered impulse. She wondered: will Julian ever let himself go? Will he ever fling all reticence to the winds? Will he ever know what it is to experience the soul-scarring emotions of love and hatred? Then, abruptly, her gaze fastened itself on his mouth. She was conscious of a slight tremor: – his mouth, nothing if not classical – with its rather full underlip, was not the mouth of austerity, of abstention. No, it was a sensual mouth, and its sensuality was enhanced, not diminished, by the strongly moulded chin, with its cleft in it.

---

[1] tasted.   [2] In the novel Vita was writing.   [3] Does this signify that you are beginning to appreciate yourself?

'Eve, often to tease Julian, told him he looked like a Gypsy, but she was later to admit that his wonderful "apricot" colouring was one of his chief merits. How like a young Hermes he was, pagan, impersonal, indifferent ... and a wave of unaccountable despondency swept over her. She felt suddenly very futile and inexperienced.'

How will that do? I haven't written carefully, but it's more or less what I want to convey. I'll write it over again properly, if you like. It's too wonderful writing about you. I can't tell you how much I enjoy it. Of course you must remember that this description is intended (when re-written) for 'before'. Darling, 'after' the Hermes turns into Bacchus – you must let me do that, will you? Oh HURRAH! I can describe you in your leopard skin – tell me when you're ready for that. ... Darling, I adore you – you're getting too conceited for words....

your Alushka

30 June 1918

Men tilich, it was Hell leaving you today. God how I adore you and want you. You can't know how much. ... Last night was perfection. ... I am so proud of you, my sweet, I revel in your beauty, your beauty of form and feature. I exult in my surrender, today, not always though. Darling, had your novel been in French, it must inevitably have been christened 'Domptée'.[1]

Mitya, I miss you so – I don't care what I say – I love belonging to you – I glory in it, that you alone ... have bent me to your will, shattered my self-possession, robbed me of my mystery, made me yours, *yours,* so that away from you I am nothing but a useless puppet! an empty husk. Alushka need not have been ashamed of being Dmitri's mistress ... on the contrary! ...

What do I care what I say to you? I have, if anything, added a few 'curtains' to my manners for other people's benefit, but for you there are no curtains, not even gossamer ones! I exult in the knowledge of how little we have in common with the world....

Your Lushka

BURN THIS! Promise.

[1] 'Mastered' i.e. subdued.

Not to be shown to the community or anyone, for that matter!!

It amuses me to continue my indiscreet correspondence with you! Tho' to be accurate, it is not so much indiscreet as speculative and analytical. Still, I don't see why it should be a one-sided affair – in other words, why you should not answer the letters I write to you, when I *should* be writing others most imperatively concerning my personal welfare? But then, as you know, I have few scruples, and (thank God) no responsibilities!

In the generous empire of my affections, you must, and surely have! allotted me one tiny province – say not larger than the republic of San Marino, over which I hold sovereign undisputed sway, untrammelled by any brow-beating constitution – where I can have my tiny say in the affairs of your empire, and a tiny voice in the thunder of your parliament?

You play a very strange and important role in my life. You have grown up with me. We have been children together: consequently you are always there. You have always been 'there'. You are as immutable as the mountains, as reliable as the seasons!

Sometimes I feel with you a wild and wanton child, born none-theless with an ineradicable reverence for your superior wisdom: a fond and foolish child rifling the world for new and wondrous toys to lay at your feet. A boastful, reckless child, forever on its mettle, because it is being 'dared' to accomplish the impossible, to climb the notchless trees, to jump the 7 foot hurdle. I come to you and say: 'See what I've done? . . .'

The only real beauty is to be found in the simplest things. Nothing elaborate can ever be beautiful. God forbid that real beauty should ever pass me unrecognized. I was thinking yesterday at the Slade[1] that here was real beauty: dozens of minds all intent on the pursuit of art, all striving to the utmost of their ability to ensnare beauty, and the pursuit of art, however unsuccessful, is always beautiful. Then I saw people in their true perspective and they all seemed vulgar and uninspired and the meanest drawing there was worth more than all their thoughts and endeavours.

The only two things that matter are love and beauty – beauty of character as well. There are some exceedingly *un*beautiful things in

---

[1] Violet was taking lessons at the Slade School of Fine Arts. Founded in 1871 and named after the art collector and patron, Felix Slade (1790–1868), the school gave courses in sculpture, painting and drawing.

my character: lies and deceits which are as morally ugly as a squint and a hunchback – just as unsymmetrical and disfiguring. So is gossip, and snobbishness and bigotry. They are equivalent to a crooked nose, a harelip, and a retreating chin! No, the beautiful, free, godlike things are passion and enterprise, courage and impatience, generosity and forgiveness! Heaven preserve us from all the sleek and dowdy virtues such as punctuality, conscientiousness, fidelity and smugness!

What great man was ever constant? What great queen was ever faithful? Novelty is the very essence of genius, and always will be. If I were to die tomorrow think how I should have lived! With this last Swinburnian transport, I must end this letter. Don't you think it is entitled to an answer? If not this will be the last of the series!

'Ah, one thing worth beginning,
One thread in life worth spinning,
Ah sweet, one sin worth sinning
    With all the whole soul's will;
To lull you till one stilled you,
To kiss you till one killed you,
To feed you till one filled you,
    Sweet lips, if love could fill;

To feel the strong soul, stricken
Through fleshly pulses, quicken
Beneath swift sighs that thicken,
    Soft hands and lips that smite;
Lips that no love can tire,
With hands that sting like fire,
Weaving the web Desire
    To snare the bird Delight.

So hath it been, so be it;
For who shall live and flee it?
But look that no man see it
    Or hear it unaware;
Lest all who love and choose him
See love, and so refuse him;
For all who find him lose him,
    But all have found him fair.'

[1] From Swinburne's 'Before Dawn'.

This afternoon I steeped myself in music pour revivre,[1] and to forget (a contradiction in terms). The medium was a pianola, but one excused that, it was so well played. ... O my dear, there is nothing in this world equal to music: 'la raison est trop faible, et trop pauvres les mots'[2] alas! for her sister arts – they are nowhere in comparison.

I listened to Grieg, elflike, mischievous, imaginative, romantic – so Latin sometimes despite his Norwegian blood. ... You would love Grieg. You would love the saccadé[3] rhythm of Anitra's dances, and the grotesque horror of 'In the Halle des Bergkonigs'. In the fairyland of music, Grieg plays gnome to Debussy's magician....

Then I listened to Debussy, and almost reeled to hear the beauty of *La Mer* (so like Irkutsk) and his *Petite Suite* – which is the epitome of XVIII Century gallantry, joyousness and impudence. O my darling, I could make you love Debussy as much as I do *myself,* only it would take time. Then with an epicureanism worthy of Marius,[4] I selected Brahms, the wild, the 'exultant' the free – *your* musician, par excellence. Indeed I played *you* into everything, or almost everything I heard....

17 July 1918

... Mitya, your letter was not altogether satisfactory. Primo, compared to mine, it was short; secundo, it sounded reconciled (more or less) to this horror which has come upon us. It didn't batter the doors and smite the knobs with bleeding fingers as much as it ought to have. If you knew how I lingered and doubted, doubted and lingered, you would make your letters as long and as convincing as it is possible for you to make them....

Ozzie [Dickinson][5] and I have already discussed you at great length. Ozzie saying how much you had 'improved' recently, how much 'entrain'[6] you had, how you at last seemed to treat people as if they were human beings – Then, the sublime comment: 'It will

---

[1] to live again. [2] 'reason is too weak and words too poor'. [3] abrupt, jerky. [4] Walter Pater, *Marius the Epicurean* (1885). [5] Oswald Dickinson (1869–1954), the bachelor brother of Violet Dickinson, Virginia Woolf's intimate friend in adolescence. [6] gaiety.

be a terrible day' when you at length 'wake up'. He suspects infinite depths of passion and 'abandon' in you, which he says that up till now have lain more or less dormant. Rather good, what? I mean perspicacious. I said I ardently hoped that that day was nigh – He said how nice someone was but scarcely 'emballant'.[1] (I discreetly held my peace). 'So domestic,' I heartily acquiesced, 'so constant and contented'. Yes, yes, all that. 'But not in the least thrilling, not your (my) type – ' No, most emphatically not. O my God, Mitya – and you *can't* know what I feel about + + +[2] being with you when I want you so terribly. Darling, can't you write oftener than once a day?? *Please*. . . .

22 July 1918

. . . For 16 nights I have listened expectantly for the opening of my door, for the whispered 'Lushka' as you entered my room, and tonight I am alone. What shall I do? How can I sleep? . . . I don't want to sleep, for fear of waking up, thinking you near by my side, and stretching out my arms to clasp – emptiness!

Mitya, do you remember this?

> All that I know of love I learned of you,
> And I know all that lovers can know,
> Since passionately loving to be loved
> The subtlety of your wise body moved
> My senses to a curiosity
> And your wise heart adorned itself for me.
> Did you not teach me how to love you, how
> To win you, how to suffer for you now
> Since you have made, as long as life endures,
> My very nerves, my very senses, yours?
> I suffer for you now with that same skill
> Of self-consuming ecstasy, whose thrill
> (May Death some day the thought of it remove!)
> You gathered from the very hands of Love.

. . . I think you now do realize that this can't go on, that we must once and for all take our courage in both hands, and go away together. What sort of a life can we lead now? Yours, an infamous

[1] overwhelming.   [2] Harold Nicolson.

and degrading lie to the world, officially bound to someone you don't care for, perpetually with that someone, that in itself constitutes an outrage to me, being constantly watched and questioned, watched to see if the expected reaction is not taking place, questioned to make quite sure there is no one else!

I, not caring a damn for anyone but you, utterly lost, miserably incomplete, condemned to leading a futile, purposeless existence, which no longer holds the smallest attraction for me....

A cheery picture, isn't it? And you know how true it is. At all events, I implore you to run the H.N.[1] fiction to death. It is the only thing that can save us, the only thing that will ensure peace for both of us.

En attendant,[2] I think 'there is a lot to be said for being (temporarily) dead'. Mitya, what stabs me like a knife is to remember you here in this room watching the last things being packed preparatory to going away with you, a fortnight ago. When I think of that and you waiting for me on the stairs, I feel quite faint from the pain of it all. My God, how exultant we were! And now, 'la vie est devenue cendre dans son fruit'.[3] There is nothing to look forward to, nothing.

I never thought I would (or could) love like this....

14 August 1918

Bacco mio! After I had left you I went to John St. Its châtelaine was out; so I took advantage of her absence to play the pianola. I played Daphnis et Chloe, very suitable for Bacco, and so lovely! ... Then suddenly, whilst I was playing it, I found my ideal! You've no idea how exciting it was. My ideal is this, Mitya: to live far, far away in Greece for preference, Sicily, failing Greece – to live in the woods, on the mountain slopes, by streams and by rivers – never to see anyone, save perhaps an occasional shepherd, and to live there with Mitya, in the spring, only it would have to be always spring! Mitya in his convolvulus wreath – or, no, Mitya with a faun-skin thrown over his shoulders, with little gilded hoofs, its head clothing Mitya's head within – Bacchus 'sweet upon the mountains'. I quote Euripides....

[1] Harold Nicolson.   [2] In the meantime.   [3] 'life now has ashes in the fruit'.

Oh, Mitya, come away, let's fly, Mitya darling – if ever there were two entirely primitive people, they are surely us: let's go away and forget the world and all its squalor – let's forget such things as trains, and trams, and servants, and streets, and shops, and money, and cares and responsibilities. Oh God! how I hate it all – you and I, Mitya, were born 2000 years too late, or 2000 years too soon.

14 August 1918, 1 o'clock

My adored beloved, I have come as near to breaking my heart to-day, as ever I have. ... When you said on the telephone that you couldn't come, nay, worse, that you had hurt yourself badly, everything went quite black, and I felt suddenly sick. I wanted more than I have ever wanted anything before to take the next train down to Sevenoaks. . . .

. . . I went to Pat's[1] for lunch, still wondering unsociably whether I wouldn't chuck everything and come by the afternoon train. By the time I had finished lunch I had made up my mind to do this, and was going to have told you so on the telephone, when Lily[2] informed me you had gone to Knole, which so enraged me, that I immediately changed my mind – (Pat did *not* try to deter me from coming, on the contrary).

I haven't told you the worst, Mitya. I was so utterly miserable when I got to Pat's before lunch, about 12.30, that I broke down and sobbed my heart out and told her I couldn't bear going away and why. Darling, you know how generous she is. She was genuinely sorry for me and tried to help me about getting to you. Then when you said you hadn't really been to Knole, I was again determined to get to you, côute que côute.[3] I knew that it was folly and that it would inevitably be found out, but I didn't care, I resolved to give myself a chance, not a very good one, but just a chance of catching the train. I felt I would give the whole of my life to see you for five minutes. I found a taxi and told him to drive to Charing X; Mitya, I missed the train by two minutes. I don't think if I could have got to you I would ever have left you again. Mitya, how can I tell you what I am suffering? . . .

I want to see you. I want to hear your voice. I want to put my

---

[1] Pat Dansey's.   [2] Vita's maid.   [3] cost what it will.

hand on your shoulder and cry my heart out. Mitya, Mitya, I have never told you the whole truth. You shall have it now: I have loved you all my life, a long time without knowing, 5 years knowing it as irrevocably as I know it now, loved you as my ideal. . . .

And the supreme truth is this: *I can never be happy without you*. I would be quite content to live on terms of purely platonic friendship with you – provided we were *alone* and *together* – for the rest of my days. Now you know everything. You are the *grande passion* of my life. How gladly would I sacrifice *everything* to you – family, friends, fortune, *EVERYTHING*. . . .

20 August 1918

Mer Dmitri, It was charming of you to send me the eau de toilette, also the seal, which I *loved*: Monseigneur est plein de bontés pour moi.[1] I will try not to get really suspicious until you send me either a diamond dog-collar or a tiara. . . . Darling, you see the grades, I'll translate:

Eau de toilette ⎫ soap ⎪ handkerchiefs! ⎪ stockings! ⎬ chocolate ⎪ flowers ⎭	slight flirtation *Küss die Hand*.[2] (I would prefer not to plead the sublime 'I love it')
Cigarette cases ⎫ lingerie!! ⎪ Fabergé trifles ⎬ hats ⎪ parasols ⎪ dressing table things ⎭	in danger of becoming serious
Red + Diamond „ „	Le Déluge: Pearls (je déguerpis)[3]

Dmitri was quite right. I ought never to have left him. Tout de même, c'est un peu fort, tu sais:[4]

---

[1] My lord is full of kindness for me.   [2] I salute you.   [3] I'm lost.   [4] All the same, it's pretty hard, you know!

... One thing is quite obvious, and I mean it *seriously*. You do not miss me one half as much as I miss you – mais nous allons changer tout cela, mon petit Mitya. C'est idiot[1] ....

I've just had a thrilling conversation with Ozzie [Dickinson], who made the amazing statement that you must be 'temperamental' if your character was in keeping with your looks! 'You could have knocked me down with a feather!' – He said you were too dazzlingly beautiful and that you ought to have a marvellous life!

This is padlock, mind. Swear not to mention it. He said that M. un Tel[2] had 'not improved with age', that he'd developed a middle aged point of view and was condescending and cocksure, but Mitya, he thinks you too wonderful and so you are! He said you had never been as beautiful as this year, that you were so much admired and – 'coveted'!!

What an awful ass M. un Tel is! ... Everyone is censorius about his colossal self-conceit – and Why? we ask ourselves....

You could have the whole world at your feet. I'm a prize ass for telling you this, I know – But, unlike M. un Tel, I do not under-estimate your worth, and the attraction you have for others or *they* have for you!

Darling, there is an almost lovely (illegitimate) girl here, aged 16. Neither of her parents will have anything to do with her, isn't it monstrous? She *is* pretty. Last night Ozzie and I went up to her room (she was in bed) and played 'consequences' with her for hours. She looked too delicious in blue pyjamas. (May I have pyjamas?) Dmitri would have bestowed on her his awful connoisseur's look!! (God, how Lushka adores Dmitri.)

[1918]

Who said I had no friends in America? What do you think of the enclosed – and from a famous prima donna too, God bless her![3] She was being 'very well' with my father in Munich, no wonder she calls him a 'charmeur'! O God, how I long for that sort of life again. It's the only sort worth living ... Damn 'ladies' and 'gentlemen' and respectability.

Au fond, what do you know of la vie de Bohème?[4] Nothing,

---

[1] but we'll change all that, my little Mitya. This is mad.   [2] Mr So-and-so (i.e. Harold Nicolson).   [3] Dame Nellie Melba.   [4] Bohemian life.

nothing. You think by knowing a few artists of the elite, and occasionally visiting a studio – officially or unofficially – and going to picture galleries and being au courant with the latest 'trouvailles'[1] that it entitles you to a place en Bohème?

But have you ever *belonged* to these people yourself? Have you ever worked all day in a filthy, ill-ventilated studio with only a schinken-brötchen[2] for your lunch? Have you sat night after night in the poulailler[3] of an opera house with the score in your hand, and your head so full of music that you swayed like a drunken person when you emerged from this ether? Have you mixed with all sorts and conditions of people – not stars, the 'arrived', but all the dozens who will never be stars, who will never arrive? Have you sat for hours with would-be opera singers, sobbing and heartbroken because they have been refused a part which spelt bread and butter for them?

No, Mitya, you know *nothing*, nothing at all, and one day I will return to these people whom I love, I will belong to them irrevocably, and you, you will live rich, 'received', respected, and you will ask me to your parties, and people will say how nice of you it is, and how broad-minded you have always been: 'In fact, I believe they were great friends once,' et toi, tu feras l'article pour moi.[4] You will say: 'Oh, you must meet her, she is unlike anyone else,' as though I were a curious animal, and you will get a few 'Bohemian' friends to meet me, in order that I should not feel like a fish out of water. Do you think I would come? Not I!

> You came and croaked beside me in the wood,
> You said: 'The days are dreary' and you said
> 'The view from here is very good.'
> By God, I wished that you were dead!

And what is so killing is that you will probably have become a celebrated poet/novelist and I shall have achieved nothing but disreputability! (Is there such a word?)

O God, I feel bitter, bitter. . . .

O my God, Mitya, some demoniacal force is at work on me, you fool! I shall have you before you have time to do anything, and you deliberately blind yourself to these things. One day the storm must burst and you will be swept away with everything else.

---

[1] discoveries; 'hits'.   [2] ham roll.   [3] gallery.   [4] you will make compliments about me.

Clovelly
25 August 1918

... My days are consumed by this impotent longing for you, and my nights are riddled with insufferable dreams. ... I want you. I want you hungrily, frenziedly, passionately. I am starving for you, if you must know it. Not only the physical you, but your fellowship, your sympathy, the innumerable points of view we share. I can't exist without you, you are my affinity, the intellectual 'pendent' to me, my twin spirit. I can't help it! no more can you! ... Nous nous completons.[1]. ...

Mitya, we *must*. God knows we have waited long enough! Something will go 'snap' in my brain if we wait any longer and I shall tell everyone I know that we are going away and why. Do you think I'm going to waste any more of my precious youth waiting for you to screw up sufficient courage to make a bolt? Not I! ...

I want you for my own, I want to go away with you. I must and will and damn the world and damn the consequences and anyone had better look out for themselves who dares to become an obstacle in my path.

Clovelly
26 August 1918

... What fun your having a pony! I wonder if I could ride him? Darling, it's so essential that Dmitri should ride – he really ought to hunt? When we're abroad we must have horses, and I'll ride with you till I break my neck, which is quite certain to occur, if good horsemanship becomes an obsession with me! What an equestrian letter! It really ought to go like this: Dear old thing, hear you've picked up a bargain at Tattersall's.[2] You always were a one for sniffing out a good thing. You take my tip and keep tight hold of it. My two-year-olds are turning out rather bad – never get decent grub nowadays, this war's playing old Harry with my stud. They've nabbed my second horseman too, damn their cheek! Believe I shall have to collar my lady as whipper-in: – not but what she couldn't round hounds slip-up, if she wanted to! Well, so long old thing, if you care to put in a few days later on at the old place, you know you're always welcome. P.S. Bring your hunting kit.

[1] We complete each other. ...   [2] Race-horse dealers.

I've been reading Thomas Hardy's poems, Mitya. I don't like them: they are ponderous and wordy. The post has come, and with it a letter from Denys T. which will make you mad – I can't help it, darling, I can't control his letters from here. It begins 'My fairest Fialka!!' Shall I quote? ... 'My company won the boxing competition, thank you. Tomorrow I am jumping in another horse show. I can see this must interest you.

'Oh my Fialka – just came back from the second horse show, having won the jumping again – a very pleasant silver cup withal. I had the devil of a struggle with another horse and we had to go round the ring four times before they could judge between us. After this I have to compete for the Army show. I think you must have brought me luck in many ways, my mascot!'

Dmitri, I have greatly dared, and now I am terrified. But admit, it's not my fault. I was not there to see what he wrote. ... God! If you knew how poignantly true is all I wrote you last night. You would realize the futility of making plans for 'after the war'.

Clovelly
27 August 1918

I cannot conceive why you didn't see fit to answer either of my telegrams yesterday. Perhaps you were too frightened of Harold – really, it's too absurd....

Your letters are full of Prof. Ross.[1] I should *not* have taken any part in your discussion on the Art of Life. My views thereon are a dead secret, and are not known by any more than 2 people, yourself being one. Do you realize how frightfully little I discuss things with people? – I mean, things like religion, Epicureanism, ethics, and so forth. I never, *never,* discuss them....

I am more jealous of my own secrecy than of anything in this world. I *hate* discussing topics that might furnish people with clues about me. I do not want people to get to know me; rather than this should happen, I will build an extra fortress of reserve round myself, I will treble the guard at the gate, Cerberus himself would be less furious than the 'spadassius',[2] ready to transfix any intruder!

---

[1] Sir (Edward) Denison Ross (1871–1940), orientalist and counsellor of the British Embassy in Turkey, Director of School of Oriental Studies (London Institution) and Professor of Persian; a prolific writer.   [2] Unidentified.

I resent even *your* knowing me more than words can say. I mean the real 'me'. . . .

I wrote to your mother yesterday but made (purposely) no mention of you. Chinday[1] has been so marvellously 'witful' here that I could forgive her anything. She *is* a clever woman: I do admire her. I adore the unparalleled romance of her life. My dear: our respective mothers take 'some' beating! I wonder if I shall ever squeeze as much romance into my life as she has had in hers; anyhow I mean to have a jolly good try! À tout prendre, je n'ai pas trop mal débuté. . . .[2]

Clovelly
29 August 1918

Mer Dmitri, Yesterday was great fun: I thoroughly enjoyed myself. You know how Lushka occasionally *enjoys steeping* herself in a thoroughly 'raste'[3] atmosphere: well, she did yesterday. The place was fairly teeming with illicit entanglements! Our hostess was living with a gentleman who was not her husband. Another gentleman was staying there with a lady who was not his wife. A charming American of almost international disrepute came to tea with a ravishingly pretty daughter who was not the daughter of her husband, and so on, ad. lib. I imagine you know almost everybody there, but Lushka is being dis-creet!

They had an extraordinarily continental whitewashed villa by the sea, filled with orchids and photographs of Russian Grand Dukes and a shameless Rumplemeyer tea with madeleines, petits fours, and chocolate eclairs en veux-tu en voilà.[4] With very little effort Lushka imagined herself to be back at Biarritz, an illusion that was further facilitated by listening to the conversation of these people! Dmitri would have been in his element! How I wish he had been there!

Mind you, Lushka only enjoys this sort of thing once in a while, because she has really no taste for sordid intrigue, except if it happens to be really picturesque and then she's all for it.

My dear, I have just got your letters. You didn't really answer about

---

[1] Mother, i.e. Mrs Keppel.   [2] In any case, I haven't had too bad a start. . . .
[3] A special word in the Violet/Vita vocabulary, possibly 'fast' i.e. 'sexually exciting'.   [4] whatever you desire.

the vital thing I asked you. Go back to your simpering little Harold if you like. I don't care. Only yesterday somebody said what a little pipsqueak he was. I'm afraid I only like real men, not des femmes manquées.[1] God! How angry I am! My dear, soyez sans crainte, je trouverai moyen de me consoler,[2] be it now or later on, does it very much matter? I'm not one of those idiots who think that it is possible to devote the whole of their life to one person, You know perfectly well I won't. 'Pourquoi le mot "toujours" sur des lèvres mortelles?' Non, il faut varier le menu.[3] Rest assured that as long as I live I will never deteriorate to the level of a housefleur, a nice domestic creature who orders lunch and keeps accounts, a mere instrument of procreation, a matron, a housekeeper – pah!

Each year a child. Your husband – this yearly horror complacently. Merciful Heavens! What a life! May I be preserved from it! ...

I would have refused you nothing, Mitya. No one has existed for me except you for the past 5 months, BUT I refuse to go on. I will have you all to myself or not at all, so you can choose.

In the train
15 September 1918

... My beautiful, romantic Mitya, our scruples are not worthy of our temperaments. Think of the life we could have together exclusively devoted to the pursuit of Beauty. Oh, Mitya, chepescar![4] What have we to do with the vulgar, prattling, sordid life of today? What care we for the practical little soigné[5] occupations of our contemporaries? You *know* we're different – Gypsies in a world of 'landed gentry'.

You, my poor Mitya, they've taken you and they've burnt your caravan. They've thrown away your pots and pans and your half-mended wicker chairs. They've pulled down your sleeves and buttoned up your collar! They've forced you to sleep beneath a self-respecting roof with no chinks to let the stars through – but I, Mitya, they haven't caught *me* yet. I snap my fingers in their faces. Come away, Mitya, come away, when they're all asleep in their snug white beds ... I'll wait for you at the crossroads. ... Ah, Beloved!

[1] effeminate men.   [2] never fear, I'll find a way to console myself.   [3] 'Why the word "forever" on mortal lips?' No, one must vary the menu.   [4] escape! (gypsy).   [5] carefully executed.

Appley Hall, Ryde, Isle of Wight
15 September 1918

Men tiliche, What a journey! I feel terribly exhausted d'autant plus[1] as I was unaccountably ill today.... The boat was crowded: dank and depressing to a degree. Squalling children and loquacious sailors: I bound myself round a coil of rope, closed my eyes, and tried to pretend that I was crossing to France. Presently, I heard an insidious lisp at my elbow: 'Oh, Darling, how I with we were going abroath!' It was heaven.

At these words the Wanderlust of four starved years rose up and nearly choked me! That it should be voiced by name struck me as nothing short of sublime, somehow. Voice continued: 'If only we were going to Theylon or Algieth, or Egypt – ' She had a wealth of yearning in her lisp – I swooned. O Mitya, get away we *must*. It is an obsession with me. To see the much vaunted cliffs of Dover retreating in the mist, the intoxicating swish of the waves becoming more emancipated, less dogmatic, every moment! The bustle and the chaos and the grating of deck chairs – 'C'est y là bas, la France, dis, Papa?'[2] A little boy ... asks a hairdresser who is smoking a rank cigar and spitting with great precision and punctuality on a pile of tartan rugs ... 'Tais toi, tu m'ennuies.'[3] Then to his wife, who is as yellow as a lemon, and looks as though she might be sick at any moment, 'Si on allait manger, ah bien?'[4] Then a would-be boisterous voice: 'Looks as if we're in for a bit of tossing, what?' Then the blasé cosmopolitan says, 'Say, the "Lapin Agile" isn't nearly as much as it was,' and the anxious old lady muttering: 'I can't think where I put my wothersill?'

O Mitya, come away with me! Let's go to Paris, the Riviera, anywhere. What do I care, so long as we are out of England!...

Most beloved, I had an extraordinarily vivid dream about you last night, vivid in the sense that I saw you as clearly as though you were in the room, and, Mitya, you were dressed as the Count d'Orsay,[5] for some inexplicable reason: I can see you in a high fluffy 'taupe' coloured top-hat, a blue coat, an infinitesimal yellow waistcoat, skin-tight flesh-coloured breeches, high jack boots, and you carried a black cane with an ivory knob. I have never seen you so vividly in any dream, and, Mitya, you looked too irresistible!...

[1] all the more.   [2] 'There it is, France, yes Papa?'   [3] 'Shut up, you annoy me.'   [4] 'How about going to eat, all right?'   [5] Alfred-Guillaume Gabriel, Comte d'Orsay (1801–1852), a famous dandy.

Appley Hall, Ryde,
Isle of Wight
20 September 1918

I'm so sorry, I wrote you the most frenzied letter, but you are a fool to play these tricks on me: tu sais que ca tourne toujours mal.[1]

I don't in the least mind your knowing Pat [Dansey], only I'm damned if I were – say, Charles II, if I would assiduously cultivate the friendship of Louis XIV, knowing that Louise de Kerouaille[2] had been, etc. etc. A somewhat far-fetched simile, but still – si ca t'amuse?[3]

I shall do something desperate the next time I am in the mood I was in yesterday, so you had better look out. Are you aware you wrote me a page and a half about the physical endowments of your parlour maid? Poor thing, I suppose Dmitri would have thought nothing of seducing a parlour maid! (You had better not leave this letter about.)

Listen, Mitya, (this is NOT reprisals!) the young lady here, whose name I would rather not disclose, is not what I first thought her. How wrong first impressions invariably are! She is *not* stupid, and she is dreadfully attractive, and – worse still! – she is rather like a much prettier *me*! Not really like, but the 'same school'. Sometimes she is lovely. . . . She has long almond-shaped eyes, the aquamarine colour I'm so fond of, sometimes blue, sometimes green, with intensely black lashes and a nose which distinctly resembles mine, and quite the loveliest red mouth I have ever seen.

You would rave about her. I look *good* in comparison. She doesn't dislike me. I thought she did at first. She amuses me? . . . I shall buy her a present in Ryde this morning.

Why are women by far the loveliest things in the world? There's nothing to touch them, I suppose that's why I have such an innate admiration for my own sex. . . .

Later. Mitya darling, it's all bunkum about Mademoiselle 'une telle!'[4] – only done to annoy you. She *is* pretty but she's a conceited minx, and undeserving, as such, of any attention. Moreover, she has a vile figure and I hate people to have bad figures, baddish legs, and quite deplorable hands – rather like Sibyl Colefax.[5] . . .

[1] you know that this always goes badly.   [2] Charles II's mistress, created Duchess of Portsmouth, who had been sent from France by Louis XIV to fulfil this role. The daughter of her son by Charles II married William Anne Keppel, 2nd Earl of Albemarle.   [3] if this amuses you?   [4] Miss So-and-so.   [5] Sibyl, Lady Colefax (1874–1950), a famous London hostess, and friend of Vita and Harold Nicolson.

O Mitya, I'm glad you've told M. un tel,[1] but I wish you would let *me* tell him too. .... Will you stay with me till Thursday?

Appley Hall, Ryde,
Isle of Wight
23 September 1918

I'm so sorry to be so impossible: I know I am: chronically dissatisfied. But, Mitya, even you in your blindness were fully aware that your visit to Pat would not exactly fill me with rapture. You do these inevitably mischievous things, and then profess surprise at the result. ... However ... it's a hopeless business when all the joie de vivre has departed. Practically ever since I've been away, I have been overpowered by the supremely unsatisfactory aspect of our lives....

What *is* the good, Mitya? I get far more unhappiness out of love than happiness. Jealousy, immediately omnipotent, is at the root of all my misery. It is a disease, and will kill *our* love as surely and remorselessly as cancer gets its victim in the end.

You see it is *never* without something to feed on. The only time when I forget it temporarily is when I'm with you – when I'm away it rules supreme. You see, there is always the insurmountable Nicolson to deal with; if only I thought he would disappear some day, but he won't. I have almost ceased in a sense to be jealous of what he is to *you,* I am jealous of what he is to you in the eyes of the world....

It would be absurd for you to be jealous of *me,* because you know at the bottom of your heart that it is *impossible* for me to care for more than one person at a time – when I say care, I mean it is impossible for me to be even *fond* of anyone but you or merely superficially interested. Whereas you admittedly have affections, very deep ones ... for people who, God knows, are no concern of mine. The bargain is a one-sided one: you are all in all to me – and I am the dominating interest of several interests for you. I know you love me, but not at all in the same way as I love you. How can you help it? You have inevitably other affections, other resources – if I fail you, you have plenty of other people to fall back upon. If

[1] Mr So-and-so, i.e. Harold Nicolson.

you fail *me,* what have I got? Drink, morphia, prostitution, *what* then? Am I being funny? I don't feel funny.

I am becoming terribly Anna Karenin-ian, malgré moi.[1] Look at *facts*: Since we've loved each other, who has been the most light-hearted, the most optimistic, the most irresponsible? *YOU.* Which of us has become debonair, sociable, talkative, amusing? *YOU.* Which of us has gaily lived au jour de jour sans souci du lendemain?[2] *YOU, YOU, YOU!* ...

Hill Hall, Theydon Mount, Epping
1 October 1918

... I only received the letter you wrote me from Ebury Street. I liked seeing you go off by yourself yesterday. I only went in C. de L.'s motor[3] because it matched my mood – and my dress. How I wished you could have come to the concert, but you wouldn't have liked it. I haven't educated you (musically) quite up to its level. I only *just* got there myself – my legs were dangling over the edge all the time! Denys was ultra-technical, super-dissective, devastatingly biographical about each item in turn. I think, on the whole, I prefer going to concerts with (slightly) less Musical People.

Muriel Foster[4] was divine! Adequately 'corsetié'[5] for once! and austerely garbed in black velvet. ... And what a voice! My Lord, what couldn't one achieve with a voice like that: D. said she had the finest mezzo he had ever heard. We had to leave in the middle in order to catch our train.

I'm sorry to have to tell you that D.T. [Denys Trefusis] has been a succès fou.[6] Mrs Hunter has taken to him as a fish takes to water, and Phyllis enthuses boisterously and obtrusively about (1.) his appearance, (2.) his 'manliness', (3.) his sense of humour.

Mitya, I'm not saying this to make you jealous ... believe me once and for all. Remember the one occasion when I remained silent about somebody! Surely you prefer this artless prattle! ...

---

[1] in spite of myself.   [2] from day to day without a care for tomorrow.
[3] Not identified.   [4] Not identified.   [5] corseted.   [6] enormous success.

[1918]

... I have finished 'Jude the Obscure',[1] which I think quite
marvellous! – one of the finest works I have ever read in my
life. What an impression it leaves on one's mind! No wonder its
conception and execution together took 7 years! This is indeed a
tour de force.

If you have got it, read Phillotson's reasons for letting her go to
her lover. ... That is what I call magnanimity.

... You will never know or understand the *tortures* I am going
through at present; even I see that I am absolutely distracted. I try
spasmodically to cope with my book, but I find I can only write
intelligibly when my mind is at rest. ... Intanto,[2] will you send me
the letter I wrote you when you were at Knole recovering from
measles. Perhaps you had better send both for safety?

Please write me long letters, or you will find, one fine morning,
that the cage is open, and the bird has flown. ...

[October 1918]

I have just got your nonplussed telegram. I am so sorry, but I can't
write what the matter is, because I most emphatically don't want to
have a row with you. I am quite miserable enough as it is, and a
row would simply break me just at present, so please don't insist.

I am fool enough to love you as much as ever: that ought to
suffice. When we see each other, I hope we shall be able to put
things straight, as they are killing me. ... But I don't wish to allude
to them.

Je t'aime – bien plus que tu ne le mérites – et mon amour me
tue.[3] We must see each other next week.

O Mitya, il faut à tout prix que je te voie – le plus tôt possible[4] –
and whatever happens, we must not quarrel: it would be fatal now.
Is it any use imploring you to remember your promises to me with
regard to Harold?[5] It is so unspeakably awful for me to realize you
cannot be trusted a yard which I can prove to you only too well
when I see you and see you I MUST.

[1] By Thomas Hardy. [2] In the meantime. [3] I love you – much more
than you deserve – and my love is killing me. [4] I must see you at any
price – as soon as possible. [5] that Vita would not have any 'intimacy' with
Harold.

Ecoute, si tu l'aimes ainsi que moi, de grâce, dis le moi franchement. Tu me dois cela. Je ne t'ai jamais fait de mal; au contraire, je voulais te dédier toute ma vie.[1] I implore you – *to tell me the truth*! Don't spare me; it is not worse than the present state I am in. If you love him, really, let me go, darling. You will be much happier. I love you with all my bruised heart. That is why *you must tell me the truth*. . . .

[October 1918]

. . . O Mitya, you will remember your promise to me while you're at Brighton, won't you? I shall never know a moment's peace if I think there is any danger in its being abolished, and honestly, you *don't* know, you *can't* know what tortures I endure. Please – O *please* – don't break me on the wheel again, because that's what it feels like. You will never know how jealous I am of you till the Day of Judgment, when you will be told by a benignant angel in spectacles qui fait de la contrebande[2] in Cold Water for poor little *hot* Lushka!!

And he will shake his head pityingly and say: 'Yes, are you surprised now that it landed her There!'

Don't think I look upon it as being in the least *funny,* because I have permitted myself the above little humorous écart[3]: these jokes are torn from the depths of my soul and hurled inexorably at your feet, where they sit bravely smiling and bleeding!

O Mitya, let me trust you, let me trust you as much as if you were part of myself – Don't let anything distract you even *temporarily* from me and from the Great Adventure.[4] Don't let B.M.'s[5] thousand-and-one confetti-like grievances make tiny indentures on your beautiful smooth (the only time this word has been used in any but a derisive sense by me!) resolution. Don't let Comfort and Luxury and Peace stifle it in their feather-bed breasts. . . .

---

[1] Listen, if you love him more than me, for heaven's sake, tell me frankly. You owe me that. I have never done you harm; on the contrary, I wish to dedicate my whole life to you.   [2] who smuggles.   [3] side-step.
[4] giving up everything and going away together.   [5] 'Bonne Maman' – i.e., Vita's mother.

14 October 1918

... No one can doubt your having loved Harold. Surely there's sufficient proof of that to last you a lifetime. For him you sacrificed *everything*. You married someone who hadn't a penny, who had no 'worldly qualifications' – you could have married anyone. And you bore him three children[1] in pain and anguish. ... I write to you now as 'Mrs Harold Nicolson' – that's what I've got to put on your envelope – What claim have I on you? *None!*

... And even now in my agony, I mayn't claim you, Harold must not be told at any price that I am yours. What is your love worth, if you daren't claim me? You poor craven thing! I would *claim you* to anyone, scandal or no scandal! ...

18 October 1918

Thank you for your ejaculatory letter which for one terrible moment I thought was from Nancy Fairbairn![2] 'Drunk with amber cigarettes and gardenias! Dead drunk! ... Blind! ... St Dunstan's! ... Braille! ... your letters, darling! ... champagne! ... Shall tell you! ... We shall see! ... Everything's different! ... Jewelled world! ... Baby's found! ... Duchess of Marlborough! ... Eternal youth! ... Let's face it! ... Marvellous, darling! ... Golden! ... What your life is! ...'

Darling, I love teasing you. ... I think my letters are nicer than yours: for one thing, they are far more personal. The spirit of discretion in yours is more than I can bear! ...

Darling, remember you're young and I'm young, and middle-aged pastimes are not yet for the likes of us. That's why my whole being rose in revolt at the sight of you, young, not ill-favoured, infinitely and variously attractive, playing either bridge or poker with a lot of ancient fish-faces not so very long ago. You remember the occasion. This morning I received a parcel containing some magnolia buds which I not unnaturally thought were from Dmitri – but not at all! They were from Orsino,[3] wasn't it pathetic? Le chevalier sans peur et sans reproche[4]. ...

So I'm to be made into a Levantine am I? Couldn't we go to

---

[1] The Nicolsons' second son (b. November 1915) was stillborn. [2] Nancy Cunard, who married Sydney Fairbairn (November 1914), a marriage which lasted for twenty months. [3] Possibly Orsino Orsini, from an aristocratic Roman family. [4] The knight without fear and beyond reproach.

Ithaca, which is where I hail from?[1] You can make a very amusing 'raste' cosmopolitan background, full of poetry. . . .

Mitya! Be anxious: because I am meeting at luncheon a man called George of Serbie,[2] who has the reputation of being irresistible, very good looking, and quite unscrupulous! . . . George Karageorgevitch! It is positively delirious!

Alushka

21 October 1918

Best Beloved, you have no idea how difficult it is for me to write to you: I hate writing to you as I like pretending you have never gone away, and that I have only to raise my voice for you to come to me. . . .

All the frills and furbelows, conceits and coquetries have vanished utterly, leaving my love gloriously and brutally naked, to take or leave – as you will. For the moment, lies and prevarications, finesse and delicacy, wit and humour have deserted me completely. . . .

I want to meet you on similar ground – if you don't know what I mean, look at the difference between the last two letters you have written me, and the last two letters I have written you. Mind you, I am not finding fault with your letters, far from it, but they arrive – I'm alluding more specifically to the one I got tonight – they arrive curled and scented and bejewelled . . . they are very genuine, but they never lose control of themselves for one instant, they are eloquent, polished and conciliatory. To be met by what? My letters – scarcely letters – too débraillé[3] for that – protests, declarations, blasphemies, reeling, gasping, dishevelled, gross, red, unpardonable, mad!

How can any agreement ever be arrived at between these Bolsheviks and these punctilious politicians of the 'nicer régime'?

No! Down with your powder and patches, your shilly-shallying, and your half-measures. Tear off your clothes and your finery, and we will meet as equals, as rival candidates for romance and for Liberty!

[1] Violet's great-grandfather, an Edmonstone, when Governor of the Ionian Isles had married a Greek girl and Violet's grandmother was born in Ithaca.
[2] George Karageorgevitch (1881–1972), son of King Peter I of Serbia, who had renounced his rights to the throne in 1909.   [3] untidy.

22 October 1918

Once again, you have gone and left me. How often is this little ordeal going to repeat itself? These partings are as so many pinpricks – but they become a wound, a great gaping red wound, eventually. Brighton, hard, mechanical, vulgar Brighton and the joys of domesticity – la rentreé au bercail[1] – correct, comfortable. . . . Mitya, my wild free, devil-may-care Mitya no longer. Mitya ousted by someone gentle, affectionate, considerate, nice – someone inordinately fond of their mother, and their children . . . Aie! that hurt, but no matter. Why not face things as they are?

. . . I can see it all, humorously tender towards the foibles of your mother! Overjoyed at seeing Ben and Nigel.[2] Why not? Ben is a pretty child, and like you – painfully affectionate and full of solicitude for Monsieur un tel [Harold] . . . At dinner, you will have the eternal furniture – decoration conversation, interlarded with scraps of Roman reminiscences, and conjugal badinage.

God knows, I love and admire your mother but her frequent allusions to your happy married life I find infinitely galling. . . .

O my God, Mitya, and this is what I have to endure. It's the *incongruity* of the whole thing that I mind as much as anything. It is like playing the *Walkürenritt*[3] on a piccolo and a penny trumpet. It's so infinitely and tirelessly *belittling* – It's like hanging the *Nachtwacht*[4] in the housekeeper's room. It's like a panorama of the Dolomites painted on the back of a menu.

O God, and I can't make you see the hopelessness of it all! . . .

25 October 1918

. . . I infinitely prefer someone blatantly illiterate to a person who can talk 'a little' and just adequately on most things. Oh Heaven preserve me from 'littleness' – and 'pleasantness' and 'smoothness' – these three things clog the wheels of progress more than anything in the world, except our bugbear à tous deux,[5] security.

O Mitya, give me great glaring vices, and great glaring virtues, but preserve us from the neat little neutral faintly pink or faintly

---

[1] the return to the fold.   [2] The two sons of Vita and Harold Nicolson.
[3] Wagner's 'Ride of the Valkyries'.   [4] Rembrandt's 'Nightwatch'.
[5] to us both.

mauve ambiguities that trot between. If virtue is the fashion they dress in white, they dress their miserable little assimilative souls in white, and part their hair down the middle – if vice is the fashion, they dab rouge on their cheeks and smoke Nezain cigarettes.

Oh my God! I would like to denounce them from the tribunals of the world, the people who say neither yes nor no, but who wait until they hear the Verdict of their arbiter elegantism, before they dare express an opinion. . . .

Be wicked, be brave, be drunk, be reckless, be dissolute, be despotic, be an anarchist, be a religious fanatic, be a suffragette, be anything you like, but for pity's sake *be* it to the top of your bent – *Live* – live fully, live passionately, live disastrously au besoin.[1] Live the gamut of human experiences, build, destroy, build up again! Live, let's live, you and I – let's live as none ever lived before, let's explore, and investigate, let's tread fearlessly where even the most intrepid have faltered and held back! . . .

25 October 1918

Men tiliche, I didn't enjoy seeing you go off tonight at all. O Mitya, how hideously complicated life is becoming, but one thing is *certain*: man camelo tuti –[2]

Mitya, you could do anything with me, or rather *Julian* could. I love Julian, overwhelmingly, devastatingly, possessively, exorbitantly, submissively, incoherently, insatiably, passionately, despairingly. Also coquettishly, flirtatiously, and frivolously. Horrible thought! What friends Denys and Julian would be! . . .

Station, Bideford
[1918]

The most unforgivably cruel thing has happened: the village here is very like Polperro; in exactly the same way does it slant down to the sea; the little narrow streets . . . all paved with cobblestones and the green shuttered houses are almost identically huddled and untidy. To make things even more intolerable, Chinday was at her

---

[1] if necessary.   [2] I love you, I can't be without you (gypsy).

worst, at her snobbiest, at her unholiest, because I am here. The things she said hurt so much, that after a time I ceased to feel them. I just wondered dully what relation I was to this woman to whom all beauty was non-existent, and who only judged people on their material worth? . . .

Chinday, who hates music, never reads a line of poetry, or anything for that matter but the most trashy novels, who is not genuinely interested in art, and cares nothing for even one of the things that mean such a lot to me? It's impossible, it's intolerable, and always the note of slight condescension that obtrudes itself on everything she says to me, as though I were her social, moral and intellectual inferior. I may be the first two, but I swear I'm not the last.

Friday morning

How you would adore this place! It is certainly the most beautiful I have ever seen in my life. I have a marvellous view from my window – the house stands on a terrace 600 feet above the sea. The gardens are one mass of blue hydrangeas, and fuschias grow abundantly wild, as in Ireland. There are superimposed 'layers' of coastline, like the drop scene of a theatre . . . all wasted because you are not here to see it.

Thank God! Ozzie [Dickinson] comes here today, and I shall be able to talk to him about you. . . .

Later

I am determined to write to you now, as Chinday is not yet down, and there is no one to look over my shoulder. Darling, there is no one here who could inspire the smallest interest in me or I in them. Pamela and Barbara[1] I like very much, but oh! the innate 'bedintism'[2] of the McK's![3] They really ought to be sitting round a lamp looking at a photograph album covered with brass knobs! . . . Say a little prayer daily that I should not tell Ozzie about you! Never have I wanted to indulge in the Supreme Indiscretion as much as I do now. I feel like any Frenchwoman in any French play who says to any other

---

[1] unidentified. [2] A word invented by the Nicolson circle, originally from the German 'bedienen', 'to serve'; 'bedints' were servants, but used in this context the word suggests 'vulgar', 'genteel' or 'middle class'. [3] Possibly the McKenna family.

Frenchwoman: 'Figure-toi que j'ai un amant. . . .'[1] It's so simple. . . .

Damn Monsieur un tel – Damn him for being with you when I'm not, damn him for his smugness and complacency, his pinkness and his conceit. I dreamt about him last night. O Mitya, you can't blame me if I think bitter thoughts and occasionally have to speak them aloud. After all, he is (all unconsciously, I admit) the one inevitable obstacle to our happiness. ... If you knew what unhappiness is mine, ah, Mitya – chepescar,[2] we must, we must, and soon – before I lie 'five fathoms deep' at the bottom of the Sea ... with two twin pearls, where once were my eyes – [3]

31 October 1918

Men cheringue, I felt a pig for not coming to see you today but I have had 'schnupfen'[4] ever since last night, and you know what a frightful row I should get into if my mother discovered I had been. I spent the entire morning with her. ... Then I had to go and get photographed – not, as you may imagine, solely for Denys T., but for anyone else who cares to have one....

... Listen, as to going away, it must either be the 9th (a Saturday) or the 18th – for reasons which I have already defined. I must know by *Saturday* which it is to be, as Russell Cooke takes a week getting passports. You mustn't tell a soul you are going as he says it could get him into trouble and dish us, anyway. Personally, I think the sooner the better.

I am economizing strenuously in order not to arrive impecunious in Paris (if the gods will it). Nobody was ever more practical than I am at the present moment. But for mercy's sake, lie low about it until the very last moment.

[1] 'Just think, I have a lover ...'   [2] let's escape, let's run off together (gypsy).   [3] A reference to Shakespeare's *The Tempest*, I. ii. 394.
[4] a cold.

5 November 1918

Mitya, you must forgive me for not having come this afternoon. There are two true reasons. (1.) I should be so annoyed if I caught influenza, having escaped it hitherto. (2.) Je ne me sens pas dans mon assiette.[1] I think I ought to have 24 hours to recover. You've no conception how ill I felt this morning. You've no conception how much the whole thing has upset me. Perhaps I really have got a screw loose! I don't know.

I feel like having a dozen hot baths, with plenty of disinfectant, not because of catching influenza or because of any germs of a different nature that might have settled on me, but because I want to be of a cleanliness – mental and moral and physical – without parallel, without precedent. I want to come to you, my skin glowing – almost smarting! with health and cleanliness. Would that my mind and my soul could be equally clean! ...

Mitya, we will get to work, you and I, and together we must accomplish something beautiful and true and clean. We will eliminate the words lust and passion from our vocabulary. They are dirty, and hideous. Without very much difficulty I know I could re-conquer my pre-début frame of mind, which was the chastest thing I know, and I'm hanged if I don't achieve something yet!

O let's get away, Mitya, this atmosphere stifles me! No wonder I have always lived in a world of my own – or as much as possible, in a world of my own; no wonder I have always preferred fairy-tales to facts, fairies to people. O Mitya, let me tell you the secrets I have hoarded for years – I must, I must tell you, as I can never tell anyone else. It has been the strangest Barrie-esque, Debussy sort of worlds. ...

O Mitya, I can't tell you how intensely I hate ugliness, sordidness, practical and material things. They break off little pieces of my world, where I have always lived and played alone. The only person who ever suspected its existence was Pat [Dansey], and even she never penetrated beyond the threshold.

There grow all manner of tropical plants and creepers like tired blue tresses. ...

It is half magical, half mythological; there are leprechauns and hamadryads, centaurs and hobgoblins. There Clytie changes herself into a sunflower nine times a day, if I will it, and there Arethusa flies perpetually from Alphens, her bright hair streaming in the wind. ...

[1] I'm not in good form.

And always there is music – music of birds and flowing waters, music of trees and whispering reeds – and sometimes, in September, music of pounding hoofs, and clashing cymbals. ... Good night, most beautiful –

6 November 1918

My precious Mitya, that poor child [Sonia] is so bad with asthma; Mama has been up with her all night. I can't bear to see that poor little thing ill, struggling to get her breath. She is so good, and never complains. She was always having it when she was little. If she is not better when the doctor comes, I shan't go away. Mama is so marvellous when anyone is really ill. So cool and calm and competent. She has not been to bed all night.

I'm so thankful Denys is away. I hate his being mixed up with *us*. I want to say to him: 'What is my sister to you anyway? You don't belong here.' And should have probably said it, which would have been unnecessarily unkind.

Mama and Sonia and I are au fond a very compact trio. Darling, you would be so sorry if you could see that poor patient little white faced thing. She says she has never felt so ill, and I know she wouldn't say it if it weren't true....

9 November 1918

By this[1] you will see I have had to have recourse to the degrading expedient of ringing up Monsieur un tel and asking him what he can do about passports.

I don't think he took me seriously, so the rest is entirely in your hands. You will realize how exceedingly distasteful it was to me having to ask a favour of Monsieur un tel; if anyone else in the Foreign Office would do as well, I will lose no time in applying to them. You have only to tell me who they are....

---

[1] A letter which Violet enclosed from Sidney Russell Cooke, stating that before he could issue the permits necessary to visit Paris, he would first need passports for Miss Keppel and Mrs Nicolson, and that passports were obtained from the Foreign Office, where Harold Nicolson could arrange for them more easily than he could.

10 November 1918

... I have just been talking to you on the telephone. I am chilled by the profound indifference and nonchalance of your voice. Mitya, *can't* you, *won't* you understand that if we don't get away soon, we shall *never* get away. Our getting away and abroad is positively the *only* thing that can save me from an otherwise CERTAIN FATE?[1] Certain, because I am not sufficiently despicable to kill a person who is one out of a thousand, who was cheered and acclaimed three days ago by two regiments for his magnificent daring and skill? Mitya, I implore you not to misunderstand me, you know who it is I love – surely I have given you sufficient proof....

Now is not the time for irresolution and prevarication. C'est le plus fort qui l'emportera[2] – not because I don't know or am uncertain – alas! I know only too well which it is I love, but it's *the one who gets there first.*

Julian ... WORK! work day and night till you get those passports. I get so desperate because sometimes I feel I battle alone. I don't feel reinforced. You know as well as I do that two people who are absolutely *determined* to get their own way, at any cost, usually end by getting it. Tell Monsieur un tel that *I* want to get to Paris to get married, if he wonders why I'm so dead set on going – tell him *anything* – I don't care –

11 November 1918

Mitya, what a damnable shame you weren't here to witness the greatest display of emotion in the whole history of our race! (Please admire my perfect journalese, freshly inaugurated.) No, but seriously, you will never cease regretting you weren't in London this morning of all mornings. We knew at 9.15 a.m. Winston Churchill rang up[3]. ... I was out of the house like a flash to purchase flags! I tossed it with largesse to everyone I passed: 'Do you know the Armistice has been signed?' in almost every case to be met with a stare of complete abrutissement.[4]

In Selfridge's I bought armfuls of flags, flung down enough

---

[1] Marrying Denys Trefusis.   [2] It's the strongest who will win, (i.e. Vita or Denys).   [3] Winston Churchill's friendship with Alice Keppel dated from Churchill's youth and continued until after World War II.   [4] Stupefaction.

money to cover thrice the amount, and tore home again! Papa and I went out on the balcony to hang them out; no sooner had he hung the first flag than the maroons [sirens] went off! A gigantic and unforgettable 'A-h-h-h' went up from a thousand throats, and people began cheering as they only do in plays dealing with the French Revolution (when the hero harangues the Girondins). The last vestige of dignity fell from me – I tore up Bond Street, cheering at the pitch of my voice, rushed into Barbelline [?], dragged out the caissière[1] (who happened to be a friend of mine) and so ran hand in hand up Oxford Street to buy some French flags, which I looted from Selfridge's Bargain Basement. We then hailed a taxi, draped it in flags (also the chauffeur), picked up four wounded Tommies, and an old woman who sells flowers on Bond Street, and drove to Trafalgar Square, which was in a state of absolute delirium!

Thousands and thousands of people all cheering themselves hoarse, people piled like apples on every taxi, bus, and cart, screaming, weeping, singing, gesticulating. . . .

I've never seen a more impressive sight in the whole of my life. Why do you always miss every excitement? This only happens once in a lifetime, or rather, once every two or three hundred years! (You might read your mother this letter, as she wasn't here to see it all. I'm sure she would have gone mad with the rest of us.)

People were dancing farandoles all down Regent Street; in the restaurants they got up on the tables and sang God Save the King and the Marseillaise. O Mitya, Mitya, *why* weren't you here. . . .

[1] cashier

March to June 1919

Violet returned from Monte Carlo in March, distraught at the separation, and under pressure from her mother, who was determined to scotch the affair. She very unwillingly became engaged to Denys Trefusis on 26 March. The wedding was due to take place in June but Violet, desperate, pinned her hopes on Vita preventing it by eloping with her on the eve of the ceremony. Vita had gone to stay with her mother in Brighton – where Lady Sackville was setting up house after separating from her husband – and was in London that spring for the publication of her novel *Heritage*, while Violet kept up her passionate cries for escape.

At the last moment, Vita yielded to Harold's pleadings and, two days before the wedding, fled to Paris, avoiding the temptation to intervene. On 16 June, the ceremony took place at St George's, Hanover Square, with Dame Nellie Melba singing Gounod's 'Ave Maria'. Violet had evidently secured Denys's promise that the marriage would not be consummated, just as she insisted that there would be no intimacy between Harold and Vita.

The newly married couple left to spend their first nights at the Ritz in Paris, en route to the south-west of France. On 17 June, a distraught Vita turned up and made violent love to Violet. Terrible scenes with Denys followed over the next two days, in which Violet told Denys of the plans to elope.

16, Grosvenor Street
[March 1919]

Your letter has made the whole difference in the world to me. How we understand each other! You know that the love of liberty is the strongest, cleanest, purest thing in me. It is incorrigibly pure, incorruptibly chaste. I may be worthless, but the impulse to get away, to shun all petty restrictions and mundane mesquineries, to be frank and free and fearless is the *one* thing that is *not* worthless in me. . . .

Ah, Mitya, you are jealous of D.T. Shall I tell you why you are jealous of him? because *he is like you*, and that's what it is that makes *me like him*. That is gospel truth. In your heart of hearts, you know perfectly well that he is 'one of us' – that he belongs to the all too small confraternity of adventurers, the reckless, the enterprising, and the free – that instead of being an enemy, he is a compatriot – he speaks the same language as we do – All three of us are young, absolutely indifferent to the world's opinions, equally intolerant of treasured conventions.

For twopence we go search for the philosopher's stone, the Holy Grail, or the fourth dimension! We set out by ourselves to discover El Dorado, and to our dismay, we find somebody else trying to discover it too! Brother –

[March 1919]

. . . Tonight, I have made a decision. If you go to Paris, you will never see me again. Perhaps you will be pleased to read this. Perhaps it is what you have hoped for all along. I make this decision because I love you so dreadfully and for no other reason. . . . I'm sorry to have to say it, but I can't trust you. I am more miserable than you have any idea of – In giving you up, I am giving up my whole life. . . .

Today, in Westminster Abbey, I felt absolutely annihilated. All around me, there seemed to be nothing but old age and death – Old age weeping for those who were dead. And a voice seemed to whisper 'Qu'as tu fait, O toi, que voilà, de ta jeunesse?'[1] And I felt so tiny and helpless, and infinitely lonely.

One's only friend is God, and one scarcely dares turn to God when one has sinned. May I be forgiven for praying for you, but I can't help it. Is it so wrong what I ask? To be with someone I love with all my heart and soul – in poverty and obscurity. To cultivate what little talent I have, and to work incessantly, to share the few possessions I had with other people, to give any money I made to the poor, and to keep just what was necessary for me to live on, to encourage and sustain all the poor struggling blessed people that my heart goes out to and that I never knew so well. . . .

Is it so wrong?

[1] What have you done, oh you, with your youth?

21 March 1919

My most darling love, another dreadful day – will this nightmare ever end? and it has only just begun, and you have gone away....
It is so awful being constantly with someone who doesn't care two rows of pins about someone, incredibly grim and silent into the bargain, and who, I obscurely feel, only wants to marry me 'out of revenge'. We are not even on friendly terms – I only feel there is something implacable about him....

What's going to happen? Are you going to stand by and watch me marry this man? It's unheard of, inconceivable. I belong to you, body and soul.

You know how I loathe and abominate deceit and hypocrisy. To my mind it is the worst thing on earth and here I am putting it all into practice – all the things I have most loathed and denounced to you....

If we could go away, you and I, even for a few months, I would get out of it – but if I got out of it, and remained here alone and without you, my life would be unendurable.

Chinday would make everything hell for me. If I had to go off and live alone at this juncture, I should put an end to myself....

O my love, and this time last week we were still free and happy and – together, and all life seemed full of youth and spring and Romance.

Do you remember when we stood together and looked down over Monaco – at that moment I thought: Mitya will never leave me.

O Beloved, and that night we slept in each other's arms....

I feel it is so dreadfully wrong of us to attempt to conceal it, for me not to tell. There would never be a particle of happiness in my life (provided it continued?) away from you....

O Mitya, you must know how repugnant it is to me to tolerate this relationship. It is *absolutely contrary* to all my ideas of morals. I mayn't have many, but this absolutely does them in. I hover between indescribable self-loathing and plans of suicide....

Saturday, [March 1919]

I'm so glad you are enjoying yourself in Paris! I thought you would. It must be delightful going to all the sort of places we would go to together, Mitya. I'm glad your anguish is 'exquisite'. I wish I could say as much for my own. My God! Mitya! You don't *begin* to know what unhappiness means! It's 'weak' and 'undignified' to 'sit down under sorrow', is it? 'unclassical', and above all, why not *'defeat'*? So far as I can make out, it *is* defeat – it is defeat for *ME*.

My God, Mitya, it makes my blood boil! You can't alter the 'circumstances' of your life, can't you? Well, I'm going to damn well alter the circumstances of mine!

What do I care if people hear of you or not? You're not *mine*, you would only be bringing glory to someone else, to the person who *does* have the good fortune to own you! Do you think, are you misguided enough to think, that *I* want you to become great and famous as the wife of Harold Nicolson? Don't you think you're sufficiently famous as that already? The beautiful and accomplished wife of Mr Nicolson, the lovely and talented wife of one of our promising young diplomats. My God, Mitya, if I could kill you, I would.

... You write me literary, beautifully polished letters, with melodious, flawlessly turned sentences. Why don't you curse and rant and rave? Why don't you curse the blasted fate that's taken you from me? Why don't you curse the malignant fate that keeps me awake crying for you night after night? ...

I tried to make you like me, and failed. I tried to make myself happy, and failed. I tried to make my life a success – a permanent one – and failed again. My life – what is left of it – is just one raw, limitless bitterness. . . .

You will lead a happy, successful, uneventful brilliant life – probably ending up by being the wife of an Ambassador! Dazzling prospect! When you are old, you will look back upon your youth and think: Well, yes: I had one very strong temptation, but, Thank God! I was able to resist it! ...

In Paris you will be taken to see artists and artists' studios. You will associate with literary and artistic people. (Someone will see to it that you don't only have to go with bores.) You will talk art and poetry: people will say witty, brilliant things: a man called, I think, Jean Cocteau, notably.

You will think: How wrong Lushka was in imagining I lead the ordinary conventional life of a diplomat's wife! Look at me now, in a real Bohemian milieu! *Good God Alive*, Mitya! But a *real* studio in which *real* Bohemians lived – not merely les arrivés – would all put on clean clothes to receive the wife of a Peace Delegate! You can't have your cake and eat it! Either you would be 'pigging it' on two or three hundred a year in a rive gauche attic with me – perhaps not even that, uncertain as to where you were going to have your next meal – or else, you're the other thing, the wife of the Peace Delegate, beautiful, ambitious, prosperous, influential – but you can't be both!

Why do you write to me on British Delegation paper? Are your letters censored, that they are so cold? Have you promised someone that you would write me merely friendly letters? . . .

They have taken you away from me, Mitya. They have taken you back to your old life, you who are *so prone to take fakes for the genuine article*. You will think you are catching glimpses of our Bohemian life now.

My poor Mitya . . . It was Julian, not you, and Julian is dead.

Remember what I said. It's the truest thing I ever said about you. You *are* so prone to take fakes – faked people – for the genuine article. You don't *know* the genuine when you see it. You who are so critical, you have been taken in time after time – taken in by me. You think I'm clever and *I know I'm not*, but had you come to me, *I would have had genius*.

I am filled with a rage of self-destruction now, a sort of moral suicide. You could have made anything of me. I would have walked among the stars.

Sunday morning

It is a lovely day. I wonder what you will do. You're so far away, *so* far away. Figurative mountains, oceans and continents separate you from me. As it's Sunday, someone will get the day off, and will naturally spend it with you. You probably won't write to me today, because you won't have time, and you won't be alone.

You will wear your most becoming clothes and look lovely. You will probably go and sit in somebody's room, while he changes his clothes – like you did when I was in Paris – and he will say: 'My little Mar,'[1] and *kiss* the back of your neck.

[1] Mar was Harold's nickname for Vita.

Tu me fais horreur, Mitya, parfois tu me fais horreur.[1] The depths of duplicity in you make my hair stand on end....

28 March 1919

Mitya, I am so miserable and I realize miserably and despairingly how imperfect are all human relationships, even the most ideal – how incomplete and unsatisfying...

[1919]

Men tiliche, I have been talking all the evening about Paris – Paris when we first arrived there – Knoblock's flat[2] – O Mitya! It makes me drunk to remember it, and the hoard of days, weeks and months we had ahead of us.

I shall never forget the mad exhilaration of the nights I spent wandering about with Julian as long as I live! Even Monte Carlo was not better. As good but not better. It makes my brain reel to remember! The night we went to the Palais Royal and the night we went to 'La Femme et le Pantin'[3] were the happiest in my life. I was simply drunk with happiness. We were just Bohemians, Julian and I, with barely enough to pay for our dinner, free, without a care or a relation in the world. O God! I was happy! I thought it would never come to an end. I was madly, insatiably in love with you.

Julian was a poet sans sou ni maille:[4] I was Julian's mistress. One day Julian would write great poetry and make money – but, en attendant, we just had enough to live on. I worshipped Julian. The Paris of François Villon, *Louise*, *La Bohème*, Alfred de Musset, all jumbled up, lay at our feet: we were part of it, essentially.

As much part of it as the hairy concierge and the camelots who wear canvas shoes and race down the boulevards nasally screaming, 'La Patrie! La Presse!' and 'La Femme et le Pantin'. I lay back in an abandonment of happiness and gave myself up to your scandalously indiscreet caresses, in full view of the whole theatre!

Not ladylike perhaps! But then I had never known what it was like to be a lady!

[1] Sometimes you horrify me.   [2] Playwright Edward Knoblock, author of *Kismet*.   [3] *The Woman and the Puppet*, by Pierre Louys.   [4] without a penny.

Then we drove back in the dark taxi, and the chauffeur smiled knowingly and sympathetically at you. I'm sure he thought: 'C'est pas souvent qu'ils doivent se payer ça, pauvres petits....'[1] Then the flat, the deserted, unutterably romantic Palais Royal, Julian's impatience, Julian's roughness, Julian's clumsy, fumbling hands.... O God! I can't bear to think of it! ...

As Professor Ross said to me tonight, you are made for passion, your perfectly proportioned body, your heavy-lidded brooding eyes, your frankly sensual mouth and chin. You are made for it and so am I.

I said to Professor Ross that I thought you were one of the most moral people I knew. He spat with derision: 'Pah! With that mouth, with that chin. With those antecedents! Tell me another!' (Professor Ross cheered me up considerably while he was there.)

My beautiful, my lovely, I want you so.

These are the best years of your life. Soon you will be thirty. Youngish, but no longer young, then thirty-eight, forty, middle-aged.

What will you have to show for your lost youth, your fading beauty, no longer exuberant and magnetic, but hard and austere and expressionless? You who might have been, who still might be! one of the greatest figures of your century – a George Sand, a Catherine of Russia, a Helen of Troy, Sappho! ...

Cast aside the drab garments of respectability and convention, my beautiful Bird of Paradise, they become you not. Lead the life Nature intended you to lead. Otherwise, Mitya, you'll be a failure – you, who might be among the greatest, the most scintillating and romantic figures of all time, you'll be 'Mrs Nicolson, who has written some charming verse. She is daughter of the ―― ? Lord Sackville (forgive my ignorance), and often appears in charity matinées.'

30 March 1919

... Denys said he would *romandinae* [marry] me on any terms I choose to make, that he would consent to anything rather than that I should leave him. He said if I left him he would kill himself. He said I only had to tell him exactly what I wanted and it should be

[1] 'It's not often that they must pay this [taxi fare], poor kids....'

done. He gave me his word of honour as a *gentleman, never* to do anything that should displease me – you know in what sense I mean. What *am* I to do? What can I say? There is only one thing to be done, that is to run away without saying anything to anybody.

Wretched Loge![1] He cares for me drivellingly – his one *chic* was that I thought he didn't! ...

I have just got a letter from him confirming in writing all that he said yesterday. I will show it to you. Mitya, it is all so dreadful.

... Something burst suddenly and sickeningly, and I realize with a gasp of pain how happy I was, and worst of all, I see you, Mitya, beautiful and exuberant, glowing with youth and health and happiness....

'Lushi! *Lush*! Why don't you answer when I speak to you? Come and give me a kiss at once! No, not like that! ... A proper kiss! What do you *mean* by not kissing me when I tell you to?' And all the time a voice is singing – but so far away I can hardly catch the words.... Yes, I can ... just! ... And I think: Yes, that's all that remains of the four happiest months of my life.... a time....

[March 1919]

My own sweet love, I am writing this at 2 o'clock in the morning at the conclusion of the most cruelly ironical day I have spent in my life.

This evening I was taken to a ball of some good people. Chinday had previously told all her friends I was engaged so I was congratulated by everyone I knew there. I could have screamed aloud. Mitya, I can't face this existence. I shall see you once again on Monday and it depends on you whether we shall ever see each other again.

It is really wicked and horrible. I am losing every atom of self-respect I ever possessed. I *hate* myself. O Mitya, what *have* you done to me? O my darling, precious love, what is going to become of us?

I want you every second and every hour of the day, yet I am being slowly and inexorably tied to somebody else.... Sometimes I am flooded by an agony of physical longing for you ... a craving for your nearness and your touch. At other times I feel I should be

[1] Violet and Vita's name for Denys, after the fire god in Wagner's *Das Rheingold*.

quite content if I could only hear the sound of your voice. I try so hard to imagine your lips on mine. Never was there such a pitiful imagining.... Darling, whatever it may cost us, tiri chinday[1] won't be cross with you any more. I suppose this ridiculous engagement will set her mind at rest....

Nothing and no one in the world could kill the love I have for you. I have surrendered my whole individuality, the very essence of my being to you. I have given you my body time after time to treat as you pleased, to tear in pieces if such had been your will. All the hoardings of my imagination I have laid bare to you. There isn't a recess in my brain into which you haven't penetrated. I have clung to you and caressed you and slept with you and I would like to tell the whole world I clamour for you.... You are my lover and I am your mistress, and kingdoms and empires and governments have tottered and succumbed before now to that mighty combination – the most powerful in the world.

14 April 1919

Men cheringue, I had rather a trying evening with Loge. He was even more silent, inscrutable and indifferent than usual. When I entered the room, he made one remark: 'You look as though you had been very demonstrative?' He then took up a book and started to read....

I began to read too, but I was really wondering all the time what he was thinking about. He is a sphinx, that man. This is not done to intrigue you, it's just nonsense, not worth writing....

Mitya, fly, fly! I feel we are like people who have built their house at the foot of a volcano – like all the people whose houses cluster round the foot of Vesuvius. They have been so accustomed to talk of eruptions that they end by treating the volcano almost as an accomplice to protect them from eruptions! – until one fine day they awake to find its flanks streaming with lava, and the terrible cinders overtaking them by leaps and bounds!

That's why I say: Fly, Mitya, Fly! While there is yet time – and there's so little.... Why don't you assert yourself, your claims on me, before all the world? Why don't you smash this grotesque engagement? Why don't you say: Sachez qu'elle est à moi.[2] ...

---

[1] your mother, i.e. Lady Sackville.   [2] Understand that she is mine.

19 April 1919

You are gone and I am all alone – more alone than I have ever been in my life, I, who have plumbed the very depths of loneliness. All my life I have been lonely. I never knew what it was to have companionship till I met you. Why doesn't one just die automatically when left by the person one loves? You know I spoke the truth when I said je n'ai rien qui m'attache à la vie....[1]

Only a woman can abandon herself utterly to love. A man's life is never completely filled by it to the exclusion of his work and interests. Love to him is only a thing of leisure, a thing he can give himself up to when he isn't working. How can a man be as completely *dependent* upon a fellow being as I am on you?

Very few women could. Only women who have got no stamina, no powers of resistance, no fixed ideas of what is right and what is wrong, no affections or interests of any sort or kind.

Quand je donne, je donne à pleines mains.[2] I withhold nothing.

Who worse equipped for everyday life than I? You yourself have reproached me for my unreality! How can I help it? I have never had any truck with what I consider the sordid side of life; I know nothing, have contrived to know nothing about things which any girl of 15 could explain to me. I live in a world peopled entirely by my own imagination. I live with people who have nothing in common with ordinary mortals, a world that a half crazy trouvère[3] of the middle ages would have devised when drunk. I *hate* my world! What consolations are these flimsy fancies of mine when I'm half dead with crying and loneliness? ... Tu ne sais pas tout le mal que tu me fais.[4] I know you are not thinking of me! I know you were excited at the thought of seeing someone again, that their arrival by aeroplane appealed to you, that you thought it picturesque, that you and the two children rushed up to see it alight, that you pointed upwards and said: 'Look! There's Daddy up there!' or words to that effect.... That you were all agog to hear of someone's experiences.... That it's 'Hadji' this, and 'Hadji'[5] that, and you are strolling almost arm-in-arm....

And that I, I who love you fifty times more than life, am temporarily forgotten – set aside – no more thought of than the lumpy

---

[1] I have nothing that connects me to life.   [2] When I give, I give all.
[3] minstrel.   [4] You don't know all the harm you do to me.
[5] Nickname of Harold Nicolson, used by his father and Vita.

urchin who presses his nose against the window pane of some rich house, watching the people within laughing and eating. . . .

[April 1919]

I must say you excel in writing one strictly uncompromising letters – but why? Have I shown myself unworthy of your trust? Have your letters been read by a quartet of tittering housemaids? Has the dragon in shallow waters become a butt for shrimps?[1] ou quoi enfin?[2]

Caution is a quality I abominate and despise – especially when there is no need for it. If there were I should warn you. My letters are *never* tampered with and those I receive from you are instantly committed to the flames.

I got a letter from le V.E.[3] this morning which could fairly have made Dmitri sit up! (On such occasions slang is undoubtedly permissive.) As a matter of fact I am rather frightened of him. I'm not at all sure he doesn't mean to _____. Why doesn't Dmitri take better care of Alushka?

21 April 1919

I have read your letter once again – your letter written in the same handwriting as when you were fourteen, and I was twelve. . . . The same beloved handwriting that thrilled me even as a child. Almost blinded by tears, I seemed to see all the letters you had ever written me – those when you were fourteen, were shy and tender and confiding. At 16, alas! they had already begun to be indifferent, cautious, and undemonstrative: but there were one or two cherished exceptions which I knew by heart almost: at 18 and 19, they were no longer regular, your letters. They were few and far between, hurried and noncommittal, but with a stray sentence here and there which betrayed that malgré tout,[4] you had not forgotten. . . . They got less and less personal, finally when you were 21, they were social arrangements. Then they ceased. . . .

[1] A Chinese proverb, one of Violet's favourites. Vita used it as the title of her novel, *The Dragon in Shallow Waters* (1921).   [2] or what really?
[3] Unidentified.   [4] in spite of everything.

For four long years they ceased. . . .

A year ago they began again. The one you wrote me after we had returned from Polperro began: 'My darling' . . . I thanked God, and thought to die with gratitude. And since, ah, Mitya! . . . How wonderful they have been! They have been love letters, from *you*, from the same you whom I loved as a child, who wrote to me when you were fourteen – the same little neat, symmetrical writing. . . . Practically all my life I have known it: it has grown up with me, with me it went into long skirts and with me put its hair up, figuratively speaking. Familiar and adored.

My God, Mitya! How could I think of losing you forever? . . .

I remember your saying the first time I went to C. Malet,[1] 'We may be separated for a bit, even for a year, but all through our lives we will always come back to each other.'

And you threatened to leave me forever!

What have I done to you, Mitya, except love you? . . .

29 April 1919

My own Mitya, I got your second letter, written Sunday, this morning. It is about the only letter that sounded as if you *really* missed me since you went away. Of course I've written; I'm surprised you haven't received my letters. I wrote c/o The Foreign Office on all of them. I wish you wouldn't use that horrid Delegation Britannique paper – isn't this petty? . . . But little things seem to matter so dreadfully now – and yet, they don't, because sometimes I feel as though I had ceased to exist, as though I had just been emptied of all that was vital and that the envelope remains though all the sawdust has trickled out – A 'broken doll' – You'll be sorry someday you left behind a broken doll!

It is only a week tomorrow since you left – a week today since I said goodbye to you – it seems like years. . . . O Mitya, what *are* you doing with our lives? I feel sometimes you are my evil genius, and that you see the most appalling calamities gathering ahead and that you do nothing to avert them. Since you left, Pat [Dansey] has never ceased urging me to marry – all the strength of her extremely strong will is concentrated on that.

She doesn't want to take me away herself, that is partly why. She

[1] Château Malet, the villa near Monte Carlo leased by Lady Sackville.

says it is *your* duty, not hers, to get me out of this, and to take me away until it has blown over.

... If only you would come back – I don't see Pat very often, and hardly ever alone – Joan[1] and she are inseparable.

O darling, it *was* a waste of time, your being jealous of Pat. . . . Everything seems to conspire to throw me on the mercy of ——. You observe, my chronic misery, Pat being unavailable, Chinday's hardness and unkindness, the intolerable atmosphere of this house, my loneliness. . . .

Please write to me as often as you can, please, please. . . .

30 April 1919

... You don't know, you'll never know, the loneliness that I feel. You'll never know how unhappy I am. You'll never know how intolerably I miss you. . . .

I don't know where to send this, or if you'll ever get it. My heart is a stone inside me, Mitya. I feel too stricken even to cry. Just sick and stupid.

You who are so considerate, why didn't you tell me? It would have been so simple, the kindest thing to have done. Oh darling, Rupert Brooke always describes so exactly what I feel. There is something reassuring about it. If I could write beautifully, I should have said what he said. . . .

> 'Slip, when all is worst, the bands,
>   Hurry back, and duck beneath
> Time's old tyrannous groping hands,
>   Speed away with laughing truth
> Back to all I'll never know,
> Back to you, a year ago.
>
> Truant there from Time and Pain,
> What I had, I find again:
> Sunlight in the boughs above
>   Sunlight in your hair and dress,
> The Hands too proud for all but love
>   The Lips of utter kindliness
> The Heart of bravery swift and clean

[1] Pat's close friend, Joan Campbell.

Where the best was safe, I knew,
And laughter in the gold and green,
    And song and friends, and ever you
With smiling and familiar eyes,
    You – but friendly: you – but true.

And Innocence accounted wise,
    And Faith the fool, the pitiable.
Love so rare, one would swear
All of earth for every well –
Careless lips and flying hair,
    And little things I may not tell.
It does but double the heart-ache
When I wake, when I wake.'[1]

30 April 1919

No letter from you today, beyond what I got this morning. I have only had scraps from you today and yesterday. What are you doing? God knows. The letter I had yesterday was written on Hotel Majestic writing paper, so I suppose you spend most of your time there?

O Mitya, I've been dreaming such beastly dreams about you all night. I need hardly tell you they were jealous ones. I woke up very early and have been reading Rupert Brooke's letters ever since. They're so delicious, Mitya. I make this paragraph personal, from a letter of his to Violet Asquith: 'I suppose you're rushing from lunch party to lunch party, and dance to dance, and opera to political platform. Won't you come and learn how to make a hibiscus wreath for your hair, and sail a canoe, and swim two minutes under water catching turtles, and dive forty feet into a waterfall, and climb a coconut palm. It's more worth while.'

... Mitya, would you come to Spain with me, and meet me in Venice about the middle – say the 20th – of June? I *must* know this. The most awful thing has happened. I've raved so much about going to Spain that Denys says if you won't go with me, he *will*. So if you don't come, I shall go on to Spain with him from Venice. I can't say I don't love Spain any more, because I've told him I adored it. ... If you think he likes our going there almost immediately after

---

[1] Rupert Brooke, 'Sometimes Even Now' (1912).

man si romandinado,[1] you're quite mistaken. He is only making this sacrifice to please me, because, of course, it will make him look an awful fool, my leaving him so soon.

So you must come to a decision *at once* and let me know. I make no further comment. You won't fail me again, will you, Darling? . . .

1 May 1919

Men cheringue, I have been to the ballet which was divine – there were three: Petrouchka, Papillons, and the Good Humoured Ladies.[2] I *loved* Petrouchka – its animation and unreality. Do you remember the jostling, dancing, drunken fair? How I longed for you?

There were the most delicious women in it who waved their hands high above their heads (like I do sometimes!). I adored them. There was another woman who played the spinet during the Good Humoured Ladies. She was so pretty. Why is it that it always seems miraculous when a woman does anything well? If a man played a spinet adequately, no one would look at him. With a woman there is something so illusive, so skilful, so witty, so ironical, so fantastic, so primitive, so infinitely blessed, that you feel you would give ten years of your life for the music to repeat itself: Each word is a poem, each glance an intrigue, each gesture a romance!

There are only two completely divine things in this world: music and women! . . .

. . . I assure you that there is nothing on *earth* more beautiful than a beautiful woman. Personally, it fills me with such awe and reverence, that my hand shakes so much, I cannot attempt to draw. I feel it would be a sacrilege.

I used to feel I must faint, my head used to swim and I could scarcely walk. I would go a hundred miles to see one. . . . Old men, young men, boys. Pah! I hate them. They fill me with repulsion. There is nothing in the world more repellent to me, even small boys I think unutterably repellent.

[1] our wedding, marriage (gypsy). [2] Stravinsky's *Petrouchka* (1911) had been created with Serge Diaghilev's 'Ballets Russes' company, which occasionally rehearsed in the Keppels' house in Grosvenor Street. (The music from *Petrouchka* was Violet's favourite all of her life); *Le Papillon* (1860), a ballet pantomime, music by Offenbach; *Good Humoured Ladies*, a comic ballet based on the work of Scarlatti, with decor by Léon Bakst, first produced by Diaghilev in Rome in 1917.

2 May 1919

I've just been to 'Ivan'[1] with Loge's adamantine family. I *hate* them, Mitya. I came to that conclusion this evening. I hate their overbred appearances, their academic mind, their musical aloofness and superiority, their inflexible point of view, their incredible *pride*, their extreme reserve and insurmountable indifference, their lack of humour, and – let it be faced! – total absence of any outward manifestation of humanity!

My poor Mitya and it's what I reproach you for! Apparently, to be human is an extraordinarily rare thing. Being intensely, almost vulgarly human myself, I had never realized it! *They* think it indecent to display any enthusiasm about anything, except music, and then – Oh! Mitya! It's not *our* music! It's things we should never, never like, or understand.

I hate them. I would like to tweak their aristocratic noses. I would like to tear their immaculate clothes from off their backs. I would like to give them penny dreadfuls to read, and make them listen to *Helen of Troy* for 4 hours a day on the gramophone!

I'm trying to find the dominating adjective for them, because they're not exactly *bien*, or prigs – no, certainly not prigs – or old-fashioned – no! It's *aloofness*, that's what it is, sheer arctic aloofness. 'Yes, *you* love and hate, but good God! *we* would never dream of doing anything as common as that, and if we did we wouldn't show it for worlds!' That's why I hate them. They were unutterably disgusted because I cried at Ivan.

Oh my sweet, how I miss you. How I *longed* for you at the opera.

Do you know what would happen to me if I married one of them? I should dry up. I could never be natural, I could never be emotional, I could never confess I like sensuous things. He has already admitted he thinks my enthusiasms puerile and rather silly! And as they have their root in the innermost depths of my being, you know what it would cost me to suppress them, and to merely say I 'liked' a thing, when it filled me with rapture. I hate *them*, Mitya, and sometimes I hate *him*. I should be *miserable* with him. I feel trapped and desperate. This morning, in despair, I went to see Pat – she is going to try to find a way out. She wasn't in, so I followed her to the rooms of Mr Berkeley. I had to go up in a lift like the one at the Windsor Hotel[2] – with ropes. I felt suddenly sick

[1] A reference to Glinka's opera, *A Life for the Tsar*, about Ivan Susanin, a peasant who sacrifices his life to save the Tsar.   [2] At Monte Carlo.

when I remembered that the last time I went up in one was là-bas, tout là-bas, au beau pays bleu[1] – and how you loved working it yourself, and how when *I* went up alone, I always found you rather impatiently waiting on the third floor, generally in a hurry because you wanted to go to the Casino!

I have succeded in putting off the romandinado[2] for a fortnight – c'est toujours ça de gagne ... Tous les jours il se meurt quelque chose en moi.[3]

No letter at all today.

Later

I have had a letter from you enclosing your poem, which I suppose you have shown to H.N. considering it is about him. (I suppose you cried on his shoulder.) What a comfort it must be to you to think I have given up all hope of ever going away with you for ever. But *have I*? Shall I ever, as long as I live? Every day I get a little more jealous of H.N. And I can't do anything. I like the way in which you take my romandinado for granted – you needn't, my dear. There is, *believe me*, every chance of its never coming off. It will be 'indefinitely postponed'.

So if you stay away under the impression I am going to be romandinado either on the 11th of June, or later, you are making a great mistake – and the longer you stay away, the worse everything will become. Pat says it is high time you came back to attend to your affairs and mine.

You said you were going away for a fortnight. On the letter just received you say 'shall I stay away altogether?' – You make me feel absolutely *murderous* toward you – I suppose it has never entered your damned empty head that I am counting the days till you come back??? You make the mistake of your life if you think that 'having striven', I'm 'giving up the strife' – *I'm NOT* and I'm damned if I ever will. I'll battle for you as long as I've got breath left in my body – I don't care if you think it futile –

You damned silly fool. If I had given up all hope of ever being with you, don't you know I would have put a bullet through my brain long ago? You wait and see – It may take years, but you wait and see – If I can't have you, I'll have my revenge.

---

[1] There [Monte Carlo], over there, in the beautiful blue land. [2] marriage (gypsy). [3] It's always something gained. ... Every day something in me dies.

Later

My sweet, forgive me my truculent letter. I'm sorry. Come back, darling, and I will show you how different I can be.

O Mitya, it seems such *years* since you went.

Hugh [Walpole] was here to tea. He goes to Polperro tomorrow. This time last year we were there. We were so happy, Mitya, in newly-discovered freedom – Yes, and it was after our return that I discovered the letter you had written to H.N. God, Mitya, do you wonder I mistrust you? If you were capable of that, what *aren't* you capable of?

No, it was all perfect until we got away – and then: (How marvellous it must be to trust someone implicitly –) Mitya, you must think my letters dull, 'not up to my usual standard' but I can't write you treatises on the emotions, and theories about *The Way To Live* when I am in my present condition.

How often must I remind you that I am *not* intellectual and that I exult in the fact! May I quote Oscar Wilde without being intellectual? 'Where an intellectual expression begins, all beauty ceases' – not that there's any beauty in the stuff I write you – it's sheer undiluted mental anguish. That's what it is –

I love you so.

3 May 1919

When I got in just now, I found a parcel in the hall. I opened it and felt as though I had been struck: it was 'Heritage'.[1]

O Mitya, my darling, darling Mitya, I am writing this in floods of tears. I beg and implore you to come back. I have been crying almost uninterruptedly ever since I got your letter this morning. I got Pat to take me out to lunch, poor thing. She is at her wits' end to know what to do. Mitya, for the sake of your own future, you must come back....

What I pray for is an answer to my telegram. I am alone, alone.

How could you write those awful words in that letter? When you knew I could neither see you nor speak to you?

Men cheringue, I thank God for your telegram: I hope it also means you're coming back next Wednesday.... I am more odious and impossible than words can say. Put yourself in my place.... I

[1] Vita's novel, published in 1919.

loathe myself, I *loathe* my selfish, jealous, suspicious ungovernable character. I loathe my pettiness and meanness, my exorbitant disposition; I loathe my hardness and bitterness, cynicism and vindictiveness. Each day I miss you more; each day you seem to be withdrawing yourself still further from me. . . .

[Telegram]
4 May 1919

MARRIAGE REMIS JUSQUAU COMMENCEMENT JUILLET TE SUPPLIE TELEGRAPHIER DISANT QUE TU VAS BIENTOT REVENIR TELLEMENT MALHEUREUSE[1] — KEPPEL

5 May 1919

Men tiliche, there is an old blind Italian playing the fiddle in the street outside. I feel as though I must burst into tears, because it reminds me so of Emmanuel Zecchi. . . . Do you remember 'La Paloma' and 'La P'tite Dance du Métro'?

O my God, Mitya, we were happy! I defy any two human beings to be happier than we were! The whole of my coloured and eventful existence seems drab and lifeless compared to those four gorgeous months! . . . Mitya, it must happen again before we die; it must happen soon again, whilst we are young, and strong, and healthy. The luxury of those four months, the prodigality! . . .

It was sweet of you to wire about the poem – thank you so much. I have just started another; if it's any good, I'll send it you – but it is almost certain not to. How I wish I had worked enough at poetry for it to be a companion, instead of a very distant and grand acquaintance who more often than not cuts me dead when I bend double in the gutter for her coach to pass me!

As Loge rightly remarked the other day: 'For mercy's sake, be one thing or the other, but *don't be both*! – Either make up your mind you want to marry and settle down, and in the course of time have and bring up a family – *and leave art alone*. Or else if you have a talent or, in other words, the artistic temperament, give up your

[1] Marriage postponed until early July I beg you to telegraph saying that soon you will return – very unhappy.

whole life, and if need be, other people's, to the cultivation and perfection of that talent, which is of infinitely more importance to humanity than a satisfactory married life, but whatever you do, *don't attempt to run both*!' I quote verbatim. It's about the only point on which we are thoroughly in harmony. The human being who is in possession of a talent is worth a hundred times more to posterity than the ordinary average domestic human being built for the procreation of his species. Nearly all the people we know belong to that category. I'm hanged if *I* want to be!

The more I think of marriage, the further removed from it I feel! It is an institution that ought to be confined to temperamental old maids, weary prostitutes, and royalties!

O darling, darling, for one dazzling blinding minute I saw our love – Julian's and mine, as it would be! O God, the fun of it! I would let Julian propose to marry old maids he met! He should flirt to his heart's content. He could patronize every cocotte in the neighbourhood. He could lead honest women astray, or the pre-liminaries thereof – he could offer them hats and jewels (which he couldn't pay for anyway). He could take them to cafés de nuit, and dance with them half the night. He could be the most marvellous, irresistible, unscrupulous scoundrel on the face of this earth, and I should absolutely worship him ... and probably sell whatever jewels I had to give him a fresh buttonhole every day....

[Telegram]
5 May 1919

MARRIAGE POSTPONED LAST NIGHT TILL JULY SHATTERED BY YOUR LETTER IMPLORE MAKE ALLOWANCES FOR GREAT UNHAPPINESS AND DETESTABLE CHARACTER PLEASE WIRE ON RECEIPT OF THIS SAYING YOU'LL COME BACK NEXT WEEK DON'T READ MY LETTERS — KEPPEL

6 May 1919

... In the evening I read a book called *The Moon and Sixpence* by Somerset Maugham.... You must read it. I cut a critique of it out of a paper to send you, but I expect it to be lost – irretrievably, by now.

I won't tell you anything about it, except that it is my theory put into practice: namely, that if a man's a great artist, that it doesn't matter *how* he lives his private life, or how many lives he sacrifices to his own egoism, that it is wrong and unnatural to judge such a person by our own (yours, not mine) miserable standard of right and wrong. Such things simply don't exist for a person of that calibre. Darling, there are several conversations in that book that might be ours ... between the artist and a person who hasn't really, but tried to assume, the moral being – not that I wish to compare my despicable self with an artist, let alone a great one, but it is the artistic temperament qui y est pour quelque chose[1] – and I think I may lay claim to a fair share of that.

And the friend talks, and he talks, and he piles it on: 'Then, isn't it monstrous to leave her in this fashion after seventeen years of married life without a fault to find with her?'

'Monstrous,' says the artist benignly ...

Later

I mentioned casually that I had a poem in Country Life, when I couldn't think of anything to talk about. All Chinday said was: 'Really, how nice. How much are they paying you for it?' And later in the day, she remarked: 'Of course, it's no use writing poetry unless you get paid for it.' The point of view! I nearly shrieked aloud in my agony! I nearly said: 'It's not possible that you should be my mother. I won't, I can't, believe that we are any relations!'

I have got your letter, Mitya. I have shown it to Pat. It came just as I had had the worst row with Chinday I have ever had in my life. I nearly struck her. . . . But all the time, I thought, in three days I shall have Mitya, and your letter came, and I could see you didn't want to come back, that you would obviously infinitely prefer to return later. I rushed round with it to Pat, the tears streaming down my face. . . .

[1] which counts for something.

130

7 May 1919

I understand your letters less and less. When you left London, it was on the understanding that, if you went to Paris and for a fortnight, there would *be no question of your returning then*, that you would come back here when the fortnight was up, and stay at Long Barn until H.N. joined you there. Why this change of plans?

My God, do you suppose I would ever have altered the date of my romandinado if I thought you were going to play me this trick?

However, it can easily be changed back again to the 2nd. If you can't, or rather won't come back next Wednesday, darling, don't come back at all. . . .

8 May 1919

What do you mean by beginning your letter to me 'My darling Lushka'? It looked rather silly, your letter, because it arrived when I had just finished writing the most earnest appeal to Julian; however, when J. gets that letter, which I sent to his hotel, it will show far more clearly than anything else how unfounded are his suspicions.

As to your letter, let me deal with it as methodically (are you sure you weren't an office clerk in a previous existence?) as you do.

1. 'Last spring, when you came to stay you were thrilled,' etc. Admitted.
2. 'Last autumn before he got leave, you were thrilled.' Admitted.
3. 'The day he actually came you were excited,' etc. Admitted.
4. 'During his leave you told people you were in love,' etc. Admitted. I certainly told people that, and why? To camouflage our going away. . . . You yourself told Pat I was on the verge of falling in love, you admitted, for the same reason.
5. 'When he went back to France you cried and were miserable,' etc. Cried, yes. Miserable, no. Anxious, yes. But there is a vast gap between being 'anxious' and 'miserable' – I was anxious then. I am miserable for quite another reason *now*. All the difference in the world.
6. For Paris, *entirely* responsible, largely intended as camouflage, to give Chinday (who knew all about it) to her mind, excellent reason for going there.

7. 'You wrote saying you were in love with him.' Admitted: reason, *odorous*, and you *know* it. If I thought you had ceased to care for me, and that you cared for someone else, I would tell him so. . . . and act the part.

8. 'Several people who have seen you together, say that you were obviously in love.'
Drivel. Not worth answering.

9. How *D A R E* you doubt my word as to the meaning and purpose of the letter I showed you? My word is better than yours any day – why should I have been so triumphant at having secured that letter otherwise? I swear by nonero jeli,[1] by your life, by my own, strike me dead if I'm not speaking the truth, that that letter means *exactly* what I told you it meant, and the person who wrote it, wrote it in anguish, as the highest and most unassailable proof of their affection for me. That person has never given me the smallest cause to doubt their word, or mistrust them. Any promise, even quite trifling ones, has been most scrupulously kept. Why should I doubt that person, when they refrain from even kissing my hair, or taking my arm? Does someone show as much restraint with you? I bet they don't! Besides, you have probably never asked them to!

10. 'Whenever he has mentioned you to me, he has done so with absolute certainty and absence of self-consciousness . . . on the contrary, he evidently enjoys talking about her –' But merciful Heavens! Don't you realize even now that the person in question is as proud as Lucifer, and would deliberately do everything in his power to convince you (whom he accepts on trust) that everything was au mieux[2] between us? When we were away, you told me that someone had told you he heard from you every day. Well, it is exactly the same thing, don't you see that? Pride and resentment that anybody should know that things weren't going well. *I constantly tell him I am wretched, not in love with him, and that I don't want to marry either him or anyone else as long as I live.* Once I told him I *was not* going to marry him with the result that you know.

11. No, I have not told him I cared for someone else. He has said himself and I have agreed that I was fonder of you than of anybody.

12. It *was* me, you damned idiot, who put off the marriage – If you

[1] our love (gypsy).   [2] in the best way.

want to know how exactly, it was by a rabâche-ing[1] I couldn't be romandinada[2] when I wasn't well – also by saying that everyone would be out of London at the races. Damn it all, you might have guessed without my having to tell you.

13. I have about 8 bits of jewellery in the world and you know how much I love [*indecipherable*] I never tried to spoil your beastly [*indecipherable*]. I didn't see why you should *mine*.

14. I say quantities of beastly things about myself; you've heard me say them. But it offends my vanity that anyone else should. If you had one ounce of perspicacity, you might have guessed that too.

To summarize: He does *not* think I'm andre jeli[3]; he thinks I like him as a friend, and as a *friend to be trusted*, and I swear that is all. How can I prove to you the *absolute truth* of all this, save in one way? By 'Chapescando'.[4] You have but to say the word and I write three lines on a piece of paper (O God, how I long to –) . . .

I've just got another infuriating letter from you. What the devil do you mean by saying you 'don't think you will be able to get away before the 20th'? I notice you've given up stating why.

You are a 'rotter', Mitya. No wonder I trust Loge, and I don't trust you. As Pat said yesterday, you would come sooner if it *suited you*. . . . Oh God, how I despise you! Whose is the finer conception of jeli,[5] mine or yours? Yours is *rotten, rotten, rotten*, and each day the conviction sinks in a little deeper that I am a FOOL, and that you aren't worth it. Si tu tiens à moi,[40] don't you think you're rather silly to let this happen? I won't say any more.

9 May 1919

Men tiliche, I have been in the country all day looking at a house. I can't *can't* have one with anyone but tuti.[7] My whole nature rebelled à une telle trahison.[8]

I was with Pat, who was very kind and sympathetic. O men

---

[1] repeating the same old thing.   [2] married (gypsy).   [3] in love with him (gypsy)   [4] escaping, running off together (gypsy).   [5] love (gypsy).   [6] If I'm dear to you.   [7] you.   [8] at such treason.

tiliche, is there anything in the world so dead as un amour enseveli?[1] It is tragic. If it is the same sartuti,[2] I am indeed a fool to be jealous.

Men tiliche, in the train going there ... I felt suddenly faint. I want you so terribly. I want you in every sense, but I want you quite terribly. You know how. You've no idea what it is like with me. I tried to tell you once in Monte Carlo. Something must be done about it. You don't realize a great many things about me. I am terribly and unashamedly passionate, *how* passionate I don't suppose even you know. I wouldn't like you to know. All the force of that passion is centred on you. I want you, I desire you, in addition to everything else, as I have never desired anyone in my life. (I can't see anyone even ordinarily pretty without being emotionally stirred, so what do you suppose I feel about you?) In the tunnel I shut my eyes and I seemed to feel you bending over me, and kissing my lips. O Mitya, mon amour, ma vie, reviens. Il faut que tu reviennes.

Parfois, avant de m'endormir, à force de te désirer, je finis par sentir ton corps allongé à mes côtés, toute la tiédeur de ta chair frémissante, les baisers de ta bouche, et les caresses de tes doigts, et je défaillis, et je me sens sur le point de mourir....

N'éprouves-tu jamais de telles sensations, voyons, un peu de franchise?

C'est que je te *veux* que c'est de la frénésie! Il y a des jours entiers ou je ne pense qu' à cela. C'est de la démence, tout ce que tu voudras, mais aussi j'en meurs. Je suis sûr que tu n'as jamais rien éprouvé de tel.

Mon amour, ma joie, reviens, je t'en conjure![3]

---

[1] a dead love.   [2] with you.   [3] my life, my love, come back. You *must* come back.

Sometimes, before going to sleep, by dint of desiring you, I end by feeling your body stretched out by my side, all the warmth of quivering flesh, the kisses of your mouth, and the caresses of your fingers, and I feel faint, and I'm on the point of dying.

Have you never felt such sensations, come on, a bit of frankness?

It's that I *want* you. I want you to the point of frenzy. There are entire days when I think only of that. It's madness, what you will, but also I'm dying of it. I'm sure that you've never suffered so.

My love, my joy, come back, I implore you.

FERAI TOUT AU MONDE POUR TE GARDER TAIME TANT
SENDING YOU COPY OF LETTER TO PAT IMPLORE YOU TO
RING ME UP WILL DO ANYTHING YOU SUGGEST IF UNABLE
SPEAK TO YOU ON TELEPHONE GOING TOMORROW CROWN
HOTEL WILL YOU COME THERE 12-30   TIRI LUSHKA

16 May 1919

Mitya, darling, I *beseech* you to try to understand about this afternoon. O Mitya, I *do* love you so dreadfully, and you *know* I do. You know also that it would have been a very happy day for Pat if she succeeded in parting us for good.... Good God alive! Surely you can't fail to see that. What has she been looking at while you were away? What did I tell you this morning?

Mitya, I *swear*. I only lied to save us both, and in order that everything should remain [*scored over*]. It was horrible to lie, but I felt safety lay therein, and it never dawned on me I couldn't get you to understand. I am prepared to make *any* concession! I will go to Pat with you on Thursday, and tell her I lied from beginning to end, if by so doing everything remains unchanged between us....

I am so tired and wretched, Mitya. Why not keep your anger and resentment for when I had *really* done something dreadful? [*scored over*] If I had, then your anger would be fully justified, but God knows, I haven't. Please, please believe me, Mitya. I never for a moment dreamt that you would not see through my lies. I want so *desperately* to tell Loge everything from beginning to end....

I went to Charing X in the vain hope of seeing you and travelling down to Sevenoaks with you, but you must have motored. O God, I do want to see you so, my darling, my darling. I know if only I could talk to you you couldn't fail to understand. If you don't ring me up I shall come down to Sevenoaks (Crown Hotel) in order to see you in the morning....

---

[1] I will do everything in the world to keep you. I love you so much.

[May 1919]

I have heard nothing for so long. All my worst fears seem to be confirmed.

Have you forgotten me? I cannot bring myself to believe the worst of you.... Are you really only heartless and a coward? Was it never love, and only jealousy? It is horrible to have to think such thoughts, but how can I help it.... Perhaps the you I loved exists only in my imagination, alas!

It is dreadful the way in which you make me suffer.

[May 1919]

O men tiliche! I have told Loge everything. I said you meant more to me than anything on this earth, and that if you ceased to care for me I should die. He said he understood and that everything must be done to keep you for me. He said he would do everything he could to help me, and that he could have told me this as far back as Paris. Why not make him an ally, darling? ...

[May 1919]

... Another climax has arisen with Loge. Each one is worse than the last. I don't know what to do. He is furiously angry with me and talks now of telling men chinday about the unnatural compact[1] which will absolutely finish her. What am I to do? ...

31 May 1919

Darling, Much as I dislike it, I find it my duty to send you extracts from all the papers. You can draw your own conclusions. You might forward it to your mother.

'She worships the ground he treads on; they mean to have an old-fashioned family? ...' HOME CHAT
'They were observed during Tuesday night at the Ritz: neither spoke.' LONDON OPINION

[1] That Denys and Violet's marriage should remain unconsummated.

'It is very pleasant to note in these callous times that Major Trefusis and Miss Keppel have decided on a house that contains large well-ventilated nurseries.'
BANGKOK BOURGEOIS

'Is there any truth in the rumour that a certain society bride intends to elope on her wedding day with a dark-eyed stranger?' 'Things We Want to Know', LONDON MAIL

'I was much touched on my way through the park at seein' Miss Keppel (who is, of course, known as 'Birdie' to her friends) in blue gabardine over the dinkiest petties, sittin' hand in hand with her 'future' O they have exchanged hats – quite a touch of old Hampstead, what, Betty?' 'Letters of Eve', TATLER

'I'm told things don't half hum in London town. Of course, there's no doubt about it that Miss V....t K....l lived with the G....St chef for three years previous to her engagement to Major T...., and that she had much difficulty in housing her large and obtrusive family.' Auntie Tiare in 'Where Things are Hot', TAHITI TIMES ...

[1919]

O Mitya, your letter has simply shattered me – you *can't* mean what you say about never coming back. O darling, surely you know by now that I am most odious when most unhappy? ...

Your fortnight is up next Wednesday. Have you forgotten, or are you now so happy in Paris, you don't want to come back – Last night I succeeded in putting off the romandinado[1] till the beginning of July; it was not difficult: I said everybody would be away in June! ... I hate him again and he knows it. He is fed up with the whole business, and I think will break it off himself. He may do so at any minute. He is beastly to me – and made me cry yesterday.... I think he is beginning to hate me....

[1] marriage (gypsy).

137

[6 June 1919]

Men tiliche, so the worst has happened: you have gone and left me to go to somebody else. Just the one day when I would give *anything* not to be alone! – You must admit, it is the cruellest day to be alone;[1] to have no one to talk to – O Mitya!

You will have to make me *very* happy, darling, to atone for all the misery I have suffered on your behalf. I know it isn't your fault, but it is so frightful, just today, to have no one to speak to! ...

12 June 1919 (four days before marriage)

I make a resolution: I will write the most mad, obscene, relentless book that ever startled the world. It shall be more than a book. It shall be all passion, insanity, drunkenness, filth, sanity, purity, good and evil that ever fought and struggled in human anguish.... It shall be the eternal strife between Good and Evil. It shall be Truth.... The whole of humanity finds its echo in me, bought through pain. Thank God for my own suffering.

[1] It was Violet's birthday.

June to December 1919

After those terrible days in Paris from 17 to 19 June, there followed a three-week nightmare 'honeymoon' in St Jean de Luz in the Basque region of France, with Violet and Denys in separate rooms. Violet, more than ever in love with Vita, began to detest her husband. In late July they returned to England and went to live in Possingworth Manor, in Uckfield, Sussex, only twenty miles from Long Barn. Over the summer the liaison continued and the lovers again made plans to elope. Harold meanwhile was having an affair in Paris with the fashionable dress designer, Edward Molyneux.

On 19 October Violet and Vita left for Monte Carlo, via Paris, where they stayed for the next two months. On 18 December Violet was left in Cannes while Vita went to join Harold in Paris over Christmas.

23 June 1919

... O Mitya, when I am not actively unhappy, I am bored, bored – it is the only respite I get between hours of intense misery, when I think – but you know what I think. Do you know the poem by Sully Prudhomme which ends 'Des débris du palais ... j'ai bati ma chaumiere'[1] – well, that's what they're trying to make me do.

It's as though a voice were saying incessantly: Your ideas are too spacious, too wide your horizon, too lofty your ideals. They must be pruned and trimmed and made to fit everyday life! ... Try to think only of luncheon parties, clothes, luxury, social successes, flirtations. Be *small*. You who were so unlimited. It is much better: it *pays* to be small. ... Split your heart up into little fragments and give each one to a different person. Substitute Deauville for Tahiti,

[1]'From the ruins of the palace ... I built my thatched cottage'

amourettes for Amour, comfortable dilettantism for romance, the rue de la Paix for your Petroushkalike fair, Mozart for Wagner.

I can't. I can't. I never shall as long as I live. . . . I feel desperate.

Loge gets so much on my nerves I could scream! So does this empty-headed pointless existence, the banality of which is eating into my soul. I counted the number of cigarettes he has smoked today: up till now, he has smoked 19.

Hotel Ritz, Place Vendome, Paris
23 June 1919

My beloved, I am in a state of utter collapse. I have been crying all the morning – I simply can't bear to be parted from you, Mitya. I told D. why I was so unhappy. He would have stayed on here. Only unless I went tonight there would be no wagon-lits till the 6th of July. So I've got to go –

Mitya, you've no idea what I'm like. I sobbed all the morning in front of D. He is willing to do anything to make me less unhappy. O my love, I want you to come to St Jean de Luz; he will leave us alone – Mitya, you must come!

. . . I'm sure Harold would let you come if he knew. I know he would do most things short of giving you up for your happiness. Ask him to let you come to St Jean de Luz – I swear nothing will happen to give you the smallest cause for jealousy, and D. will leave us alone as much as we like. If D. is willing to make that sacrifice for me, I'm sure Harold will make it for you.

Golf Hotel, St Jean de Luz
24 June 1919

Men cheringue, you very nearly lost me for good last night. The part of the train I was in caught fire. A terrified wagon-lit man rushed in and said I must get out at once and that there was no time to lose. The compartment was full of smoke, and reeked of burning.

I got out onto the platform (a train had stopped at Poitiers); but nothing would induce D. to get out until he had collected every particle of luggage, every lozenge and every magazine! The whole station was raving but him. I expected to see him swallowed up in flames at any minute – our nickname would have seemed more appropriate than ever – Loge in flames!

O Mitya, you don't know what yesterday and today have been like. I can't attempt to tell you. ... If I've got to stay in this place for three weeks I shall die of it. ... J'ai perdu mes forces et ma vie et mes amis, et ma gaieté. J'ai perdu jusqu'à la fierté qui pensait encore à mon génie.[1]

Golf Hotel, St Jean de Luz
[June 1919]

... Outside the most frightful tempest is raging; huge angry waves are almost lashing my window; the wind is battling with my door, and shrieking down the chimney – outside nothing but great scudding clouds; and the sinister Spanish coast looking more sinister than ever. ... I've never known anything to equal the grimness and desolation of this place! ...

Alas, a quoi cela nous avance-t'il, Mitya?[2] all that you say in your letters? You are never going to try and put an end to this intolerable situation, that is quite clear. ...

You told me you were returning to England on Wednesday; in your telegram you say you are staying in Paris till Saturday; on Saturday you will say you have decided to stay another week.

Ah, Mitya, tu nous as bien ruinées – est ce que tu te rends bien compte de ce que tu es en train de faire?[3] ...

Golf Hotel, St Jean de Luz
[June 1919]

Men cheringue, you needn't worry about my getting on any better with D. We have nothing but money rows – the last phase of squalor – all day long.

He is *maddening*.

At the present moment I am waiting for the motor which is to take me to Spain. It is easier to motor. The trains are execrable. O Mitya, if I were going with you, even to San Sebastian! The day before yesterday I made friends with an old man, half smuggler, half poacher who lives near some caves on the frontier. You would

---

[1] I have lost my strength and my life and my friends and my gaiety. I have lost even the pride which still believed in my genius. [2] in what way does that help things. [3] you have truly ruined us – do you realize fully what you are doing?

have loved him! Half the cave – they are grottos, really, not caves – is in Spain, the other half in France. They go for miles, and look like the entrance to the infernal regions! They are supposed to have an entrance in Pamplona! – O Mitya, if only we were together. Loge counts no more than a fly on the wall.

Golf Hotel, St Jean de Luz
[June 1919]

My beautiful Calisto[1] – What wouldn't I have given to have had you here last night. You would have simply adored it – Darling, I am not saying this to make you cross, but I must tell you about it, and we must come here, for la Saint Jean in another existence, if you persist in mismanaging your present one.

La Saint Jean here is the signal of an orgy or of local festivities, a sort of Carnival, much more like the feria at Seville than anything else. If only you had been here! We would have gone mad with joy! Petrushka come to life, a Spanish not a Russian Petrushka –

Last night was the most perfect night; at about half past nine, when it was beginning to get really dark, the entire population, half Basque and half Spanish, wended their way to the little place in front of the Church. (The Church is XIII century and exclusively Basque architecturally, I think, quite lovely, with tiers of sculptured wooden galleries, and the most sumptuous altar made of twisted columns with vines curling up them.) The doors of the Church were shut. There was first a trickle of yellow light visible through the chink.

The place was *packed*! You couldn't have moved an inch. All the men wore their black boots, and some of the women had flowers in their hair. There were not more than about two or three foreigners, as the 'season' here only begins a month later.

We waited what seemed a very long time. La foule trepignait.[2] Then the Church doors opened very slowly, and two immaculate 'Suisses'[3] emerged, and stood on each side of the door. At the same

[1] In Greek mythology Calisto was the handmaiden of Artemis. Zeus took her as his lover, thus infuriating Hera, who, very jealous, transformed Calisto into a bear. Arcas, the son born to Calisto and Zeus, grew up and one day went hunting. As he was about to kill a bear, not knowing it was his mother, Zeus appeared as a whirlwind and transformed Calisto into the Great Bear galaxy.   [2] The crowd was stamping its feet.   [3] Swiss guards.

time the municipal band, the members of which all wore red berets, assembled round the Church, and began to play Basque music. Finally, the curé, in a gorgeous chasuble appeared, mumbled something in Latin and put a torch to an immense bonfire piled up in front of the Church. Apparently, this custom has been in existence some seven hundred years!

Huge flames leapt up instantly. I swear I have never seen anything so picturesque or mediaeval in the whole of my life! The background of those great cavernous doors, half open, full of yellow light, the gigantic Suisses with their halibards[1] (don't know how to spell them), the old shrunken curé, like some faded Ribera,[2] the swarthy flame-lit faces of the population, and the throbbing torches of the Garde municipale[3] like satellites of the huge bonfire in the middle. ... It was marvellous!

Ah Mitya, if you could have seen it. But this was only the beginning! The crowd then swarmed to the Place de la Mairie, decorated with magic lanterns and multicoloured booths. A bandstand was erected in front of the Maison de l'Infanta. I've never seen anything so delicious except the feria. Gypsies were standing in front of their little booths trying to entice the jeunesse dorée to have their fortunes told; a haze of confetti hung over the whole scene. An old fat man in evening dress, a cigar puffing out of his mouth (for all the world, like the Jew in Petrushka!) was lurching about with two pretty fishergirls on either arm —

And O! the wonderful Southern night with its velvety sky, and immense stars! But the best was yet to come! When the place was absolutely thronged with laughing, singing, gesticulating people, the band struck up a fandango! – Instantly the whole mob began to dance! I never saw such a thing in my life! Old women, young women, middle-aged women, fisherwomen, soldiers, sailors, peasants, gendarmes! Those who had castanets played them, those who hadn't snapped their fingers! The young women and the gypsies nearly went mad with delight – I never saw such dancing, and the great clumsy fishermen became as agile as cats! bending this way and that, shouting 'Olè!', clicking their heels, dancing as only Spaniards can dance!

My goodness! I thought to myself, and people live in England,

[1] halberds: an ancient military weapon, a combination of a spear and an axe, the traditional arm of the Swiss Guards.   [2] José de Ribera (c.1588–1652), one of the Spanish painters of the 'golden age'.   [3] city guard.

and read books, and try to improve their minds and consciences, when it is possible to live in a country like Spain, when it is possible to dance oneself drunk at a fair, when you can wander from country to country, when all that matters is sun and love, and singing and dancing!

Anyhow, that is the life I intend to lead si tu veux pas de moi.[1] I must lead it alone, but O God! how I longed for you to be with me last night – more than I ever have in my life – and in the midst of my longing a little phrase shot through my mind, 'Calisto était beaucoup trop savante....'[2]

Mitya, what is the good of your culture, your books, your learning, your so-called 'principles', your intellectuality? Believe me, my conception of life is the true one, and the rest is .... dust.

Golf Hotel, St Jean de Luz
[June 1919]

This reads like a Caucasian fairytale! I am alone. Loge is on the top of La Rhun (the highest peak in the neighbourhood) shooting vultures with a basque poacher! He left last night at midnight, having worked up till then on a translation from Pushkin. He motored about 10 miles, met his poacher (who they say may cut L.'s throat if he thinks he is carrying many valuables). They were then to dismiss the motor and ride for two hours on mules. The ascension of La Rhun is very difficult; it was pitch dark last night, and if the mules make a false slip, they were done!

I would have gone like a shot, only unfortunately I am not well – I shall try and go tomorrow night. It will be my best adventure but I hope not my last. Sunrise on the Pyrenees must be too marvellous, and today is the most delicious day into the bargain. O God! it must be exciting! A vulture can break your leg with one stroke of his wing.

Wed. afternoon. My sweet, I spent the morning shopping. I have bought you several little things. Perhaps L. has been eaten by a vulture: as he hasn't returned yet....

I discovered the patron of this establishment to be a Monégasque,[3] so I talked to him all through lunch. I talked to him

[1] if you don't want me.   [2] 'Calisto was much too knowledgeable....'
[3] A native of Monaco.

144

simply drunkenly of Monte Carlo, of the Mediterranean, of the Casino, of M. Gaillard,[1] of the sporting,[2] of everything you can think of. He said how divine Monte Carlo was – 'seulement il faut être amoureux –'[3] I thought to myself, Oui, mon gaillard, si tu savais à quel point je l'étais, et je suis encore![4]

O Mitya, will there be a Monte Carlo – or something equivalent for us again? . . .

Darling, I've just got a perfectly foul little post card from you – what do you mean by sending me a Post Card – Damn you. That means no more letters till Saturday morning – BLAST!

You'll be sorry if I AM eaten by a vulture tomorrow night! I forgot to say I was going to the Ritz – O Darling, how could you send me a Post Card??? I am almost crying with disappointment. . . .

Golf Hotel, St Jean de Luz
26 June 1919

I am writing to you so miserably, darling. Miserably because il y a tant de choses qui demandent à être éclairées.[5] *Why*, the last time you were in Paris, were you quite content to remain by yourself at the Hotel Roosevelt, and why, this time, did you seek out every opportunity of being with Harold? First you lived together at Versailles, then you go the Majestic; next you went together to Geneva, finally you come back to Paris and leave your Hotel Roosevelt in order to be with him again – In short, you have contrived to live all the time in the same house. All this seems very damning. Why this craving to be with H.?

I give you my solemn oath, Mitya, that if ever I find you out as having been deceitful and disloyal to me in the way I mind most, if ever you have played me false, if ever it came to my knowledge that you had broken your promise to me a year ago, you know very well what that promise was, *as long as I live*, I will never speak to you again. Not only that, but I swear I would behave exactly as you have behaved in every respect, in every detail. How can I trust you? How do I know *why* you left your hotel to be with H.? If you are

[1] Not identified.   [2] Sporting d'hiver, an elegant place to gamble in Monte Carlo.   [3] only one must be in love.   [4] Yes, my good fellow, if you only knew how much I was, and still am!   [5] there are so many things that must be explained.

in love with him again then why not tell me so? *Everything* points to that. My God, ce serait le comble![1]

But you can't have him and me too! . . .

O Mitya, all I ask for is an explanation, and an explanation I MUST have. If only I could trust you! . . .

Look here, Mitya, I can't bear this. You must wire on receipt of this: Post Restante San Sebastian. I advise you to do so without delay. . . . If only I knew the truth about you and H.! If only I knew for *certain* that you weren't playing a double game! . . . Oh God it is *degrading* to trust you so little. . . .

I put the hypothetical case to Loge of a person in exactly your circumstances, who had treated the person they loved in the same way as you had, and I asked him what conclusion would he draw? He said there is only one conclusion: She didn't care sufficiently to make the sacrifice of her husband and her children. In the bottom of her heart, she must have known they counted more for her than her lover. She didn't care for him enough. And all yesterday something kept repeating in my brain: 'She didn't care for him enough. She didn't care for him enough.' . . .

Golf Hotel, St Jean de Luz
28 June 1919

. . . What ages letters take from Paris and vice versa. I go for yours every morning. Yesterday morning there were 4, today, but one. Perhaps I shall get another tonight. This morning I went out and bought you a ring. There is a shop here where they sell all the stones they find in the Pyrenees: aquamarines, chrysolites, topaz, garnet, tourmaline, jacinth, etc. . . .

Darling, how happy we should be here! The Pyrenees would smile instead of frown – and you would love the Basques peasants. They wear berets like the chasseurs alpins[2] and they are so good looking à la manière espagnole:[3] lean, brown-skinned, blue-eyed, tight-lipped: ascetic-looking men, and women with equally brown skins, flashing white teeth, and delicious hair growing in a peak, low on their foreheads. Half the population speaks nothing but Basque – an entirely uncomprehensible and extremely guttural

---

[1] that would be the last straw!   [2] Alpine hunters.   [3] in the Spanish way.

language of which I only know one rather characteristic morbid little sentence, which you see written over every church door: 'bun guzek dute gizone kolkatzen askenekdak du Hobireat egoitzen,' – which means: 'Toutes heure blesse l'homme, la demain le tue.'[1]

I am chronically miserable. It never changes – the same yesterday, today, and tomorrow. I have just got two letters from Paris. . . . You said you mightn't be allowed at the Majestic; so in order that you shouldn't be found out, you inevitably shared Harold's room! How delightful for him! You moved to the Majestic *in order* to share his room. . . . What else might you have shared! You deliberately move from your hotel in order to be with Harold!

Gr. Hotel Eskualduna, Hendaye (Basses-Pyrénées)
1 July 1919

Men tiliche, I couldn't stand Spain without you: it was agony to think how you would have enjoyed things. So I told Loge I had suddenly taken Spain en grippe,[2] and I left San Sebastian accordingly, yesterday afternoon. I raised a motor with infinite difficulty, and left so hurriedly that there was no time to have the passports viséd.

God, what a journey! I motored straight from S.S. to Fuenterrabia, which I think one of the most attractive places in Europe. It is as Spanish as anything south of Madrid. . . .

Darling, I wonder what you were doing at 6 o'clock last night? Did you have people for the weekend, and were sitting on the terrace, talking about the newest novel, or the League of Nations?

If you had looked into your magic mirror, you would have seen Lushka cowering beside a punctured motor, outside a bull-ring near the Spanish frontier, in the middle of a Carlist demonstration, consisting of about thirty young men in red berets firing off guns at random (not in anger, but apparently to gain attention, and to punctuate what they were saying). I was terrified, and nearly got hit in the shoulder. It was an unfortunate place to break down in.

At Fuenterrabia I came in for the usual religious procession. . . .

All my incipient passion for Spain has burst into flames! I feel I

---

[1] 'Every hour wounds man, the last one kills.'   [2] a dislike.

would like to live and die there, sans bouger.[1] There is something so grandiose and changeless, something so remorseless about Spain; it makes you feel so impotent and infinitesimal!

Men tiliche, it is such a tribute to my love for you, that I left Spain. It was like being offered caskets of jewels innumerable, and saying 'No' only out of loyalty to you. . . .

Gr. Hotel Eskualduna, Hendaye (Basses-Pyrénées)
2 July 1919

This afternoon I went for a long walk amidst what appeared to be undiluted Scottish scenery, bracken, heather, etc. This coast of France (and Spain) is extraordinarily northern-looking. The illusion was further heightened by a 'conscientious drizzle' and penetrating cold. I was passing a hedge when my heart gave me a little stab of pain. The hedge was covered with convolvulus . . . Bacco. . . . This time last year. . . .

That which I don't know about your past, my imagination supplies admirably. I know how great was your intimacy, and it tortures me intermittently and intolerably. How terribly in love you must have been! It is too horrible for me to realize. . . .

I shall never forgive you the damned lie you told me at Monte Carlo, which I never believed then, but now, less than ever. . . .

Gr. Hotel Eskualduna, Hendaye (Basses-Pyrénées)
3 July 1919

. . . Ah Mitya, where shall we go this autumn? Ceylon, or Jamaica, or Tahiti? Don't forget that you have promised that. If it weren't for that constant hope, I should have committed suicide long ago, when I first came to St Jean and life was hanging by a thread. . . .

O God! Another whole week of this –

There is nothing to do in this damned place! (How *we* should love it!) I wish there were shops, and cinemas, and theatres, and luncheon parties.

I suppose I shall go for another long and dreary walk this afternoon. . . .

[1] without stirring.

148

Violet Keppel at about age three, 1897.

Violet costumed
as a Bacchante.

Alice Keppel
c. 1890,
aged about
twenty-one.

A drawing of Colonel Keppel,
Violet's father, by Philippe Jullian.

Violet (far right) and Violet de Trafford at the Albert Hall, March 1916.
Copyright BBC Hulton Picture Library.

Denys Trefusis in yachting attire *c.* 1922.

Vita Sackville-West, 1920.
Copyright BBC Hulton Picture Library.

Violet's sketch
of herself holding
on to Vita, dressed
in a man's suit.

A sketch by Violet
of herself with
Sir Basil Zaharoff
at Deauville entitled
'If V. accepts
Sir Basil's offer'.

Violet at L'Ombrellino
in Florence in the
early 1920s.

Alice Keppel (seated, far left)
next to Violet with
Sir Arthur Colefax,
George Keppel (right),
Mrs James, Lady Ridley
and Lady Lowther, *c.* 1922.

NORTH MYMMS PARK,
HATFIELD.

Saturday

I have been saying goodbye to Pat on the telephone O Mitza, I am so lonely, I am so lonely, I cant bear it, my heart is breaking, Mitza. I have nowe to go to, nowe to talk to, o Mitza, Mitza. What shall I do, what shall I do. Pat was

A letter from Violet.

Golf Hotel, St Jean de Luz
[July 1919]

... Mitya, you don't know to what a pitch I have brought my truthfulness with Loge. This is the sort of conversation that takes place constantly:

L: What are you thinking about?
Me: Vita
L: Do you wish Vita were here?
Me: Yes
L: (All this actually happened) You don't care much about being with men, do you?
Me: No, I infinitely prefer women.
L: You are strange, aren't you?
Me: Stranger than you have any idea of.

The above conversation took place word for word last night and it is a typical one. I will *not* lie to Loge, save in an absolute extremity. I know the truth hurts him frightfully, but I should feel absolutely beneath contempt if I lied to him. I almost think that if he asked me point blank to tell him the whole truth from beginning to end, without omitting a single detail, I should do so. It would kill him, you know what I mean, but he is essentially a person one cannot lie to.

I have never felt the smallest scruple about lying to anyone else. Almost everything I say makes him wince, poor thing, but it is better than the other alternative. I know it is. Darling, you hold different views, don't you? And I know if you could overhear some of our conversations, you would be desperately sorry for Loge.

I will never deceive you, but *you* must never deceive me. Tu me dois cela.[1] Don't think it amuses me to see L. writhe in agony sometimes. It does *not* − nothing has ever amused me less, but I know the answer to things he asks me, if it is the truthful one, will hurt terribly, and I know I would be disloyal to withhold it or to modify it in any way, so I never hesitate. ...

O Mitya, you must be straight with Harold about me! *You must.* It is *so* despicable to tell lies to someone who cares for one. All the time I have been here I have neither done nor said anything you could possibly have taken exception to. Are you as straight with Harold? ...

Mitya, why didn't you think of Venice a fortnight ago? How can

[1] You owe me that.

149

I go there now. . . . I have this beastly house from the 15th. A detail, and squalid at that: I am frightfully hard up: I have in three weeks contrived to spend about £400. Men chinday would be frantic if I didn't go to the house once I have got it. Then the biggest reason of all! I hate Italy. . . .

You want me to leave my threatening Pyrenees, my storms and my hurricanes . . . all that is proudest, most austere, most wild and intractable in nature and mankind, for jingling, simpering, gushing, soppy, giggling Italy?!!

Gr. Hotel Eskualduna, Hendaye (Basses-Pyrénées)
8 July 1919

Men tiliche, I hardly slept at all last night. I thought of you. . . .

I am alternately miserable, heartbroken, cynical, disillusioned, apathetic, resentful, then miserable again, jealous, despairing, listless – then, my inexorable temperament reasserts itself! All the rest is temporarily swept aside. . . .

O mercy, the things I want to write!

You remember the caresses. . . .

It seems I have never wanted you as I do now –

When I think of your mouth. . . .

When I think of . . . other things, all the blood rushes to my head, and I can almost imagine. . . .

Hotel Ritz, Paris
14 July 1919

URGENT

I am back in Paris, which I look upon now as a prison. . . . I shall never forget my joy on arriving in Paris last November: c'était le comble de tous mes voeux[1]. . . . It was the happiest day of my life. Then the deterioration, the gradual, inexorable deterioration of circumstances began. We were here, but not alone in March. . . . Loge was then a casual friend, an outsider. He lunched and dined with us – our guest. The other day, *outwardly*, the positions were reversed. *You* were the guest, the visitor – O my God, the irony of it! And now worst of all, I am in Paris alone with him. . . .

[1] it was the height of all my wishes.

20 July 1919

... From the first time we went to Polperro ... O Mitya, how happy we were! And the second time, still happier. Mitya, do you remember Plymouth, the second time? How triumphant we were – that little room of Hugh Walpole's,[1] with the sea almost dashing against its walls, the tireless and undated cry of the sea gulls, the friendly books – the friendlier atmosphere, the complete liberty of it all! And I was yours, yours to bend over and kiss if the fancy seized you! And sometimes we loved each other so much we became inarticulate, content only to probe each other's eyes for the secret that was secret no longer....

Mitya, the scene changes – now we are back at Long Barn – Outside a breathless summer night, full of scents and sounds, and suddenly I see someone incredibly young, incredibly wild and beautiful, clad in a leopard-skin, and laughing triumphantly....

Bacco....

Now it's Clovelly, I, separated from you, but nevertheless haunted by you day and night, the caressing blue sea so unlike the unbridled grey waves of Polperro – the masses of hydrangeas, the village cruelly parodying Polperro ... The nights of music and ineffable longing for you – I used to stand by the open window, between the music and the garden. And in the garden were irises which cast very black shadows, and sometimes I would catch my breath: *surely* that was a figure in a leopard-skin that darted out into the dappled moonlight....

If ever anyone was adored and longed for it was you, all my heart and soul cried out for you, Prince of Romance, and most beloved....

[July 1919]

My Mitya, I have just been about your ring. I wanted a signet, with an emerald but apparently such a thing is unobtainable. Green: symbolical of jealousy! So I shall have perforce to content myself with either a sapphire or an amethyst. Failing either of these my taste is disposed to become biblical: chrysoprase, chalcedony or beryl?

... Poor little Alushka, she is being more in love with Mitya than ever! The Grand Duke Serge Sergevitch, he will be having a very

[1] Hugh Walpole repeatedly loaned his cottage at Polperro in Cornwall to Violet and Vita.

dull companion tonight. . . . I long to see you in your Russian clothes, so tall, so proud, so magnificent. Magnificent of all adjectives is the one that suits you best, my Mitya. A Magnificent – yes – gypsy – paradoxical but indisputable!

Darling, I have been thinking things over and I *insist* on your burning my letters. You ought to know by now that jealous people stop at *nothing. It is so dangerous.* If ever they were read, then where would we be?

[July 1919]

Darling, if you knew how mad I felt! Is it necessary for Mitya to wear anything but the signet ring Alushka gave him *whilst he is away? Don't say anything about it* to me. You can silently comply or not comply, as you like, but please don't allude to it. My God, Mitya, what business have you at the present moment to wear anything but what matters to you and me? . . .

[July 1919]

Men tiliche – O! the emptiness of this house. . . . I felt absolutely crushed after you had gone: I couldn't do anything: I sat there dazed and stupid. All my worries crept back and snarled at me like wolves from the dark corners of the room. . . .

I felt so desperate, Mitya, I did something you may think naughty? I telephoned and asked Hwth[1] to lunch. I felt I simply couldn't sit through lunch alone. Darling, please don't be cross about this: she is going away tomorrow for good, or at any rate, three weeks, and after that she goes to America.

She arrived with her face streaming with rain, her herculean shoulders broader than ever in a dripping heathen mixture. I need hardly tell you, she had scorned both umbrella and mackintosh! She talked about Buddhism versus Christianity, the Romans versus the Greeks, her parents versus her! The house shuddered and rocked with her leviathan indignation! But, darling, the charm didn't work! All the time I was wishing she were you. I see now what it is. I see her attraction when I'm with you, not when I'm alone. She's too

[1] Unidentified.

152

overwhelming. I felt tiny and forlorn. Before I could say knife! she had grabbed hold of my poems which were lying about, and further annihilated me with the most ruthless and admirable criticism! My goodness, she *is* clever! She has much more your sort of brain than mine. . . .

She told me she went to a fancy dress ball the other day as a Valkyrie! (How right she was.)

Mitya, something beastly and altogether *damnable* has just happened: a wire from Loge saying he is coming tonight. I wanted to wire to tell him not to on my account, but it is too late. O men tiliche, I hate it, I hate *him* for coming like this just after you have gone – O God, I am miserable. . . .

[July 1919]

Luz de mi vida,[1] my pearls have been stolen now! So nearly all my jewels have gone. I am sending the rest to the S.F.T.M.O.O.B. (Society for the Maintenance of Overworked Burglars). It saves such a lot of trouble in the long run. . . .

I went to a horrible dance, and (though I say it and shouldn't) I was what I consider quite the best-looking and the best-dressed person there –

Diana arrived in lavender muslin, looking more subdued, dowdy, and changed than anything I have ever seen! However she was delicious to talk to.

O Mitya, Mitya, tiri Lushka really looked her best! May I tell you about her? Her hair was too marvellously done, quite 'lisse'[2] – and she wore a diamond bandeau string just over her eyebrows – She also had the most lovely dress she has ever had in her life, partly and ingeniously, and advantageously transparent; the whole effect was of the demure impropriety, and 'everybody stared!' . . .

The last time I danced was at the St Jean de Luz carnival and the contrast was a devastating one. . . .

I hardly spoke to anyone at that party – mai più![3] If you are farouche,[4] I will be twenty degrees more farouche. If you are friendless, I will be twenty degrees more friendless. Besides, you are no

---

[1] Light of my life.   [2] sleek.   [3] never again!   [4] wild.

longer farouche, and you were never friendless, except at the age of 14! ...

Quidenham,[1] Attleborough
5 August 1919

O God! It does seem strange to be back here! The last time I was here I was seventeen – que de chose se sont passé depuis lors....[2]

This place brings back all my childhood to me. The days of bird-nesting, red Indians, bed at 8.30, hide and seek, Saturday evenings, historical charades (in which Betty always contrived to play the part of Richelieu), endless dressing up, and 'consequences' played after tea....

Hence a slight soppiness for this grim, austere, un-gemütlich[3] house, and a more pronounced soppiness for the generations of stupid, pig-headed, truculent, talented Keppels who have lived here.

Here in my room they look down on me reproachfully: William Anne,[4] fat, and sallow, and Dutch; Elizabeth Caroline, powdered and 'pimpante' and Georgian, Augustus,[5] pointing to a beautifully symmetrical fleet on a marcel waved sea. Arnold Joost – the dandy![6] In his curled periwig, begartered robes and red-heeled shoes! And, oh Mitya! In all that stiff and dignified assembly, Louise[7] suddenly thrusts her roguish ringlets, extremely décolletée mustard-coloured satin dress, gleaming white shoulders and sensuous red mouth, with its rather prominent under lip (like Mitya's). Her tapering Lely-white[8] (O darling, for shame!) fingers play luxuriously with a string

---

[1] The Keppel family residence in Norfolk, owned by George Keppel's elder brother, 'Uncle Arnold', 8th Earl of Albemarle.   [2] what a lot has happened since....   [3] gemütlich suggests a cosy petit bourgeois style; Quidenham was quite the contrary.   [4] William Anne, the second Earl, named after Queen Anne, his godmother; he was a distinguished general and ambassador to France, who married the Duchess of Portsmouth, daughter of the Duke of Richmond, himself the illegitimate son of Charles II and Louise de Kerouaille.   [5] Rear Admiral Augustus Keppel, who joined the navy at the age of ten and at fifteen accompanied Baron Anson on a voyage around the world.   [6] Arnold Joost van Keppel, of a noble Dutch family, who accompanied William of Orange to England in 1688 as a page of honour. The King created him Earl of Albemarle and he later served as a Major General under the Duke of Marlborough.   [7] Louise de Kerouaille, Duchess of Portsmouth, mistress of Charles II.   [8] Sir Peter Lely, seventeenth-century portrait painter of the aristocracy.

of grossly inflated pearls and her grey green eyes look heavy with unexpressed avowals. . . .

> Louise was pretty,
> Louise was witty,
> Louise was a naughty girl!

She alone of all that satire looks friendly and encouraging.

Saturday Morning. I slept very badly, but awoke a few minutes ago with a strange sense of freshness: it seemed as though all the intervening years since I was last here had slipped away: for a minute or two I felt marvellously young and innocent. . . . I had never loved or been loved; had never bothered my head about such things. It is a lovely spring morning, and with any luck I shall get my lessons done by 12. Then I shall go bird nesting with Betty. . . . I dare say Uncle Arnold will give us a lump of clay and we can mess about with it all the afternoon. . . .

I like my Uncle A. I like his massiveness, stupidity, and sheer brute strength. I like his hooked nose, like an eagle's beak, his inability to see anyone's point of view but his own. I like his great hairy hands with a sculptor's finger, supersensitive for all their thickness. There is something monumental and splendid about him; something feudal and unshakable. O God! I know so well the sort of people who appeal to me. . . . And Heaven knows, they're different from the sort of people you like. You like wit, flexibility, humour (funnily enough), intelligence, and a certain amount of mental skittishness, accessibility, sparkle, fizz, and bubble! That sort of thing amuses me, but doesn't attract me, especially in men. It is too like myself – I know this is immodest, but more or less true.

9 August 1919

Men tiliche, I am writing this in the train, on my way to London where I am going to have my hair washed!

Please don't begin your letters to me 'My own darling Lushka' – it is a beginning I dislike, for a reason I would rather not tell you.

Darling, I'm so glad you're multiplying your rides. I may live to see you become the glory of the shires yet! . . . I can't tell you how much I applaud your equestrian prowess! It is one of the things that appeals to me most, anyway. . . .

O mercy to be so feminine! Evolution of Lush à travers les âges.[1]

---

[1] through the ages.

Roman: she insists on Julian becoming a gladiator.

Moyen Age: She forces Julian to enter 'les lices'[1] at least once a week on her behalf, one of her handkerchiefs (heavily scented) tied round his sleeve, as a gage d'amour.[2]

Renaissance: She wants Julian to cut out Bayard[3] at any price. . . .

Dixhuitième:[4] She contrives that he should fight innumerable duels to defend her honour.

1914: She says she will have nothing further to do with him unless he brings down a Zeppelin –

1915: She is determined he shall capture a U-boat –

1916: A [*indecipherable*] is the least tribute he can lay at her feet –

1917: After all, why shouldn't he bomb Berlin?

1918: or the Kaiser?

1919: *Surely* Julian will try to fly the Atlantic?

Etc. . . .

Bring your riding breeches – I've got a toppin' little hack for you – but afraid she isn't much of a weight carrier – pretty stiff goin' down in my part of the world, too! Stone walls and all that reminds you of the Duke's Country – So long, old bean. Yours till the moon turns pink. . . .

In the train
15 August 1919

My Mitya, you are being taken away from me already in the motor. The sense of our closeness begins to diminish. I simply can't begin to tell you what I suffer . . . I want to be able to put my head on your shoulder and sob my heart out. Even here in the train I can scarcely keep back my tears. My darling, my darling, how endlessly this horror seems to repeat itself.

. . . Oh! to think that instead of being with me tomorrow you will be with someone else. Not only him, but the *four* of you.[5] I could kill myself, Mitya. I don't know what prevents me. As you love me, Mitya, keep your promises – keep them to the letter – tell him about me. . . .

---

[1] 'the lists', the field enclosed for a medieval combat.   [2] love token.
[3] Pierre Terrail, Seigneur de Bayard (c.1473–1524), French soldier, famed for his heroic exploits.   [4] Eighteenth century.   [5] Harold and the children, Benedict and Nigel.

To think that you should have belonged physically to anyone but me – and to such an extent! That all the things you said to me, you should have said before to somebody else! I feel half crazed with misery and jealousy.

Oh Mitya, to be together constantly, without interruption! To know a little *real* happiness, not just a few days' bliss between two long stretches of wretchedness. *You* had it, darling, you had it for five years with somebody else! You could afford to be prodigal. You had your whole life to draw upon! You didn't spend those days with him only to be torn away by a relentless Fate the fourth day....

Claridge's Hotel, Brook Street, W.1.
16 August 1919

... You might have been a little kinder to me on the telephone? I had been waiting for hours for the call.

O Mitya, one word would have made such a difference. L. and D.[1] are scarcely on speaking terms. I told him last night I was quite wretched; he said he could see I was, and I told him why, and that I could never care or think of anybody but you.

I loathe being with him, Mitya. You sounded like a stranger on the telephone: all that you thought about was your trunk....

21 August 1919

Mer Dmitri, I have been reading Lord Redesdale's memoirs in a desultory fashion, and have come across some succulent anecdotes of your great grandfather, the Duque D'Osuna. He must have been too perfect – You told me that he objected to the representation of 'Lucrezia Borgia' but your narrative was incomplete.[2] Allow me to

[1] Lushka (Violet) and Denys.   [2] In *Pepita* (1937) Vita elaborated on the ancestry of her grandmother: 'Officially the daughter of Catalina Ortega and Pedro Duran the barber of Malaga, ex-dockhand and journeyman, Pepita could claim a far more romantic story current in Spain regarding her birth. Catalina, born a gypsy, was said to have leapt through paper hoops in a circus in her youth; and to have been the mistress of the Duke of O____a (Osuna), on whom the existence of Pepita was unofficially fathered. The obscure barber of Malaga completely disappears behind this cloud of wild romance. For the Duke of O____a is himself a vivid and well authenticated figure with a terrifying ancestry. ... A descendant of the Borgias on their Spanish side, all Paris had trembled when he was observed to enter a box at the first night of Victor Hugo's *Lucrèce Borgia*, for it was feared that he might rise up in magnificent wrath if any slight were offered to his illustrious if questionable forebears. ...' Nigel Nicolson (*Portrait of a Marriage*) dismisses the romance of ducal ancestry as wishful on the part of Vita and of Pepita.

quote Lord Redesdale: 'He is a great dandy, and looks like Philip II, but though the only living descendant of the Borgias, he has the reputation of being very amiable. When he was last in Paris, he attended a representation of Victor Hugo's "Lucrezia Borgia". She says in one of the scenes: "Great crimes are in our blood. All his friends looked at him with an expression of fear." "But the blood was degenerated!" he said, "for I have committed only weaknesses!"' And another, equally endearing: 'In the great hall and jardin d'hiver[1] were tables, each to hold ten guests, each dressed round an orange tree in full fruit. The illumination, with the usual fabulous number of candles, was an entrancing sight! "Mon Dieu: Que c'est joli!" "Mais c'est ravissant!" "Oui,"[2] said George de Lucit. "C'est positivement féerique! Ah," said the Duc d'Osuna, in his Spanish French, "n'est ce pas que c'est zoli! C'est l'uniforme du régiment que zé commande."[3] The good Duke had taken all the utterances as a well merited tribute to his own personal appearance!' Mitya, what *marvellous* ancestors are yours!!! You must live up to them.

I adored getting that telegram from you, Dmitri. You can telegraph as often as you like, provided you sign Dmitri, because nobody knows who Dmitri is, and I just say it is my sobriquet for – anyone. Do wire often. How wonderfully fluent you have become in Z.[4] . . .

I heard from D. this morning. I quote: 'Again I find myself, Oh Fialka,[5] in the slough of despond about leave. It looks like another month to wait though it *may* be less. I am weary unto death of this constant postponement.' So the next time you see me, it will be minus the fiery one, only Chinday mustn't know, else she would pack me off. . . .

Oh, and Mitya! I was characteristically forgetting the one portentous piece of news! I started to pave the way about going abroad, encountering *no opposition*, and only sympathy – 'Yes . . . I should certainly go! I wish I could come too, but I can't leave London – Holland if you like, or anywhere else –' With creditable adroitness, I then introduced you, saying how much you longed to get away too, how fed up you were with England, etc. . . . I left it at that for

---

[1] winter garden.   [2] Good God! How lovely it is! It's ravishing!   [3] It's positively a fairytale! Isn't it lovely! This is the uniform of the regiment that I command.   [4] Probably a linguistic variation on Zincali – i.e. Spanish gypsy (language).   [5] Denys Trefusis's nickname for Violet.

the moment, but, Mitya, why Holland? Wouldn't we prefer Italy? O God the country for us, par excellence, is Russia, but *not* under present day circumstances. Recently I have done nothing but pick people's brains about Russia – and the more I hear the more I realize how extraordinarily Slavonic are the joint dispositions of Alushka and Dmitri. How they would adore the mixture of barbarism and luxury....

5 September 1919

... O my most beautiful, I know incurably that I shall never care for anyone but you. You will probably become bored with 'the doglike devotion of a lifetime' and what then, my poor Julian?

Darling, I don't think I shall show my book to Hugh [Walpole]? I'm so terrified of his saying it is rotten – and I'm *sure* it could be licked into shape by you. I must confess I hope terribly that something may come of it. Otherwise I shall have to take in washing, my sweet! But I don't care what I do so long as I am sartuti – nothing is too squalid!

6 September 1919

... Mitya, for mercy's sake, write me long letters; we'll both regret it if you don't. It is not very easy for me to be good and patient and I mean to try so hard, but I can only do so if you write me reassuring letters, and long ones at that.

I can see from the tone of the few lines I had this morning that your unhappiness has begun to wear off, and in a few days you will be quite reconciled to your old life. ... Had you sent me a wire from Brighton to say you were staying there till yesterday, I could have written direct there. I suppose you didn't find time. ... Mitya, again, I *implore* you, don't do things to provoke odores[1] on my part; you will regret it as much as I shall.

I have been, and am still perfectly miserable, which the letters you found at L.B.[2] must have abundantly proved. I suppose you will be unable to get any written promise from a certain person –[3]

---

[1] meaning Denys.   [2] Long Barn.   [3] Harold Nicolson.

... How I'm going to stand possibly another ten days of this, God knows! I shouldn't make it longer if I were you – this isn't a threat, it's a supplication. ...

Possingworth Manor, Blackboys, Sussex
9 September 1919

Mitya, I don't know what's come over me suddenly: the most extraordinary craving for excitement and movement that won't any longer be gainsaid!

The old incorrigible craving for trains rushing south in the night, the bustle of frontier stations, the blue-chinned garlic-infested porters, the rocking, stifling wagon-restaurant, the parched southern landscape, the sawdust-strewn cafés, the mauve-powdered ladies. And not only that, Mitya!

I want adventure. ... Adventure veiled and elusive in great cathedrals, wanton and provocative in the [indecipherable] place, sly and surreptitious in a baignoire,[1] flippant and derisive in the streets, romantic and difficult in the Earth's open places! ... I want to dash my glove in the face of Convention. I want to fly and sing and dance. ...

If you don't feel as I do, leave me alone!

Claridge's Hotel
13 September 1919

Men tiliche, I have had a beastly little luncheon all by myself at Claridge's. I have exercised my proverbial glamour over the orchestra, and they are going to play 'Alma di Dios'. Do you remember the chef d'orchestra at Nice, who came a step closer with every tune?

O God! I am excited. They're playing 'Alma di Dios', your tune, par excellence. How it reminds me of that sunlit café: the glaring white terraces, the irresistible Casino, the décor de théâtre coast. ...

Amor di mia vida, how I *long* for it all! The sun and the passion of it! I am the world's most incorrigible vagrant, the world's worst nomad! Nous nous completon! (Mon gigolo!) Ce qu'à va rigoler à Paris, on s'amusera dans les grands prix??[2] ...

[1] theatre box.   [2] We complement each other! (my gigolo!) What a wild time we'll have in Paris, we'll have tremendous fun?

[September 1919]

O Mitya, you are wonderful – my lips are still burning from your kisses! I talk to you of misery and jealousy, and spite and malice, and you seem to take it all in, and you talk to me in turn on similar subjects with a face of stone, and a 'bang' of granite – then suddenly – Crash! What happens? God knows: You kiss me furiously, passionately, possessively, jubilantly! I see you for a second as you really are – eternally young, eternally uncontaminated by the sorrows and frailties of this wicked world! Incorrigibly healthy and inimitably sanguine!

Dionysius! of all your 'travesties' the most successful! You are beautiful, splendid: full of fire and youth, creative, invigorating, not *human*!!?? *NO*!

(*How* I adore you). . . .

Possingworth Manor, Blackboys, Uckfield, Sussex
23 September 1919

. . . Darling, sorry to be so tiresome, but I *do* think the drawing might be adapted for the cover,[1] if it were preferably done in a decor other than a Paris boulevard. I think the dignity and concentration of the tale loose indeed. Julian makes such a good contrast to the waywardness and caprice of the other figure who resents his being absorbed in a cigarette! Darling please don't misunderstand me: it isn't perfectly drawn, but it *might* be. However, I'll do it for you when you come. . . .

[September 1919]

. . . I didn't go to London to see Loge. I went to have my hair washed, idiot. . . . This weekend I probably shan't set eyes on L. I've had another row with him, anyway. O darling, I do so LONG for Monday. You don't know. Please don't be horrid and spoil everything. . . .

If you really want to know, both L. and his friend bore me stiff! I am sitting with them now. I almost wish they could see what I'm

[1] of *Challenge*.

writing. L. has got on an awful woolly sweater which he wears to spite me, and looks too untidy for words in. (That in itself is enough to provoke a quarrel.) They are both talking politics. L. looks too frightful with his hair standing straight on end! I should dearly love to box his ears! . . .

Darling, you are not entirely right in all your suppositions about me. But I agree about being a changeling – plus je vis, moins je ressemble au reste de l'humanité.[1] Who was my father? A faun undoubtedly! a faun who contracted a mésalliance with a witch. . . . Seriously, sometimes I think there's something rather eerily queer about me – I frighten myself. When I am alone, I would believe anything. You know, ever since I was a child, I have had the vague obscure terror of being 'taken away' – *claimed* by someone or by something. You will laugh, but that is partly why I hate being alone. . . .

Mitya, there is an Arab proverb which says: 'He who thinks the truth must leave his hand on the bridle; he who sees the truth must leave his foot in the stirrup; he who says the truth, must be in the saddle and off!'

My God, but the truth is blinding sometimes! . . . One day I shall be in the saddle and off!

27 September 1919

Men tiliche, I have been so good scribbling away at my old book ever since I left you! – It was *beastly*, not having you sitting next to me, darling, when I got into the other half of the train. The person you call Cow and I call Con is being quite charming to Diana?[2]

Mais je ne t'en dirai pas plus long.[3]

There is sitting opposite me, the exact portrayal of Mélusine aged 45 – quand les beaux jours sont finis[4] – French, fat, and flirtatious, smothered in rouge, pearls, and marabouts. Voluble. Voluptuous. Rings on every finger. A darling old cocotte. I love her. She has a lady friend, younger, less assured (or insured). We have had conversations. . . .

[1] the longer I live the less I resemble the rest of humanity.   [2] Characters in Violet's novel, now lost except for fragments.   [3] But I won't say any more.   [4] when her good days are over.

3 October 1919

Men cheringue, it is only a week since you left, and it seems like months! I have never missed you so much, or felt so distracted. I never heard from you yesterday, which made it worse. If you don't write to me I shall prevail upon D. to let me have the motor to take me to L.B. I know he would consent as we were able to get quite a lot of petrol yesterday. So, if I don't hear, I shall just motor over. You can't very well turn me out? I want to see you so *urgently*: I can't, I simply can't wait much longer. ... I know _____[1] will be there, but I don't care a damn! I shall simply have to come, if I don't get a letter from you – I am completely reckless, Mitya. I have suffered too much all this week to be anything else. I can neither sleep nor eat. Yesterday I was really ill, and I know it was directly attributable to unhappiness and anxiety....

That wretched Rosamund[2]! What she must have suffered! I mean when you fell in love with _____! I wonder she didn't kill you! Si tu avais compris quelque chose à l'amour, tu m'aurais tuée, plutôt que de me laisser passer 3 semaines seule à St Jean de Luz avec qui tu sais![3] But you don't, you don't, you don't! You like a thing so long as it is smiling, sunny, comfortable, and contented. The moment things become chaotic, tumultuous, difficult, and tortured, you want to get away! You hate having your peace of mind threatened, your serenity molested!...

Possingworth Manor, Blackboys, Uckfield, Sussex
6 October 1919

Your letter was like kicking a man when he is down. I telephoned to you in my misery and despair, imploring you to reassure me, and you choose the cruelest moment you could to write me that letter....

To cheer myself up, I have remembered all the things you have said recently about chepescar.[4] If I believed what you wrote in your letter, namely that surreptitiously and deliberately you were trying to make me release you from your promise, life wouldn't be worth continuing....

[1] Harold.   [2] Grosvenor.   [3] If you had understood something about love, you would have killed me, rather than have left me for 3 weeks alone at St Jean de Luz with you know who!   [4] escaping together (gypsy).

O my love, I am so sad. Another separation is upon us. I can't bear
to go back to my poor little house deprived of your presence. The
secret of my love for Possingworth is so pathetically easy to guess:
it is the nearest approach we have ever had to having a house
together. I always look upon it as 'our' house. And now you are
going to share another house with somebody else. Your house, your
life, your thoughts, and your laughter....

We have been so divinely happy at Possingworth! We take up all
our old habits again. That house is haunted by your presence, and
the sound of your voice calling me.

Oh Mitya, no more 'Lushi, where *are* you?' – no more rushing
after me upstairs, no more monopolizing the bath for hours....

You say you admire moral courage. It will take tremendous moral
courage to disregard the world, fight it eventually, and eventually
overcome it. We must fight to prove that Love, no matter where it
springs, is mightier than anything in the world.

[1919]

I'm so frightfully pleased you like what you are nice enough to term
my 'poetry'. By now you must know how terribly sensitive I am on
the subject of anything I have written – even worse than drawing
parce qu'on met plus de soi.[1]

But of course it's not poetry; it is words strung together anyhow
that just *had* to get written down. I never write anything unless I
feel I have to. And I have been too lazy to master even the rudiments
of technique. If you only knew how lazy I am! Sometimes I write
a lot, wrapped in impenetrable secrecy, as tho' I were committing
a crime – I nearly always tear up in the morning what I wrote at
night (the reverse of Penelope's embroidery). I never show anyone,
with the exception of your bête-grise![2] – anything I have written.

---

[1] because one puts more of oneself in it.   [2] Violet's twist of the phrase *bête
noir*, for someone a shade less than dislikable.

It is generally so rotten, and to my shame – be it said

> ONE OF THE BIGGEST
> CONFESSIONS OF A
> LIFETIME
> not to be missed at
> any cost!

I have tried to write with intervals of inactivity which have extended over as much as 3 years (can you place the three years?) ever since you first knew me – not poetry, just anything; needless to say, nothing has ever been finished. And I've got 'nothing to show for it' because with the exception of about 5 things, everything has been committed to the flames.

Mitya, you don't know what you said when you said that you preferred my poor miserable attempts at writing poetry to my drawings. I held my breath. Possibly I have always preferred what I wrote to what I drew, but have scarcely dared *think* it, let alone confide my opinion to anyone! One can only achieve originality in drawing if one has knowledge and accuracy, originality based on good draftsmanship *not* on colouring and fluke effects, the true originality is the only one that counts for anything and which I cannot aspire to because I haven't the knowledge or accuracy of life to back it up. As I told you in my letter of yesterday, there is nothing I loathe so much as *bad* drawings; well, there's a thing I loathe more: it's *mediocre* drawings. The nigger is a good instance of fluke originality which just *happened* to come off, not based on any sound or reliable knowledge. I won't say theories because naturally one has theories, but my work is not yet strong enough to be influenced by my theories, tho' thank God! my theories are strong enough not to be influenced by my work. I *could* draw well; I know I could draw well, but to that end I require unlimited time and worse still, unlimited patience!

Accordingly, I do mediocre drawings with the little accuracy I can command; my drawings lack verve, they lack enterprise. Why? because they're not allowed any, they *can't* have any – bah! I loathe drawing; it cramps me, binds me in, holds me down. No sooner has my imagination got the better of me than a governess's voice in my ear says: Look out! can't you see that line is incorrect? The proportions are all wrong. Your pencil's running away with you!

That's precisely what *does* happen: I think *beyond* my drawing, my work is unable to compete with my theories – It's as tho' I stood on a mountain and my hand drew down in the plain. It drives me wild. God knows how long it would take to raise my drawing to the level of my theories!

My Lord, what an egotistical letter! And how bored you must be – I don't care, I'm going on, this is the épanchement[1] of a lifetime. You see, the beloved, the perfect, the sublime medium was denied me. Needless to say, I mean music. I choose the nearest within my grasp, which happened to be drawing, and drawing has been found wanting. Darling, I must go through life a jack of all trades, and master of none! Am I to be cursed with dilettantism till I die? Ye Gods on high, answer me that? Am I, most inveterate and consistent worshipper of the shrine of Beauty in all my life never to accomplish something beautiful? Something flawlessly and completely beautiful?

What you know of me, what does it amount to? You know but one side of me, *even now*. This letter is the first glimpse I have ever given you of a side of me that is wholly isolated, indomitably proud, and quite inaccessible. My God, Mitya, you've a lot to learn about me yet – Nobody will probably ever find out that there's such a side to me again. What do they care? To them, yes, and to you, I am a vain, pleasure-loving, amusing, humorous, provocative, sensual woman. True, I am every one of these things – and that is how the world will remember me – if it remembers me at all. But, Mitya, it *shan't*; it shall have more than that to remember me by, I swear it shall, something more – what form it will take, I don't know, but O my God, am I a fool to tell you all this?

Don't you understand, Mitya, there is something fierce and terrible that is gnawing into me, as the eagle gnawed into Prometheus? Fool, fool! Why the side of me you know is that side that *doesn't count*. I've escaped you again, and I'm still free! And no one in the world has possessed me, or ever can!

10 October 1919

... I forgot to tell you, there is a Gypsy caravan not far from here ... and a blue spiral of smoke curls insidiously around the haggard pines. ... Also there was a tall girl, with glittering brass earrings, great tawny braids of hair, and a face as brown as a berry. She stood, her arms akimbo, scowling into space. ...

[1] outpouring.

166

I think I will go and see if I can find them again this afternoon, but like you and everything else, they will have fled.

'Rebellion'[1] will be acclaimed as a work of genius (you have no conception how good it is). Julian (in the flesh will be acclaimed as a junior Don Juan, hélas) and I shall by then have developed into a sort of secretary drudge (expected to dust and cook as well) with no higher mission in life than to typewrite your MS. and address your love letters.

Also, you will drink, you will gamble with *my* money. You will sell *my* jewels in order to keep the Mélusines of this world in silk stockings and black onyx wristwatches! Mais je t'adore, tout admettant que – suis bête!![2]

12 October 1919

Men tiliche, I have just got two delicious letters from you, but please tell Julian not to use amber gris scent! I'm afraid he must be becoming rasta?[3] ... I urgently want to be reassured; if you don't, it will go on getting worse and worse – I am not joking: I implore you, write and give me your word of honour that you are not lying to me, in that, or in any other minor infringement of the written promise[4] that lies in my writing table. *Please, Mitya.*

[October 1919]

Last night, I talked about you for hours to Loge, and was terribly indiscreet. He said that it was so awful knowing that as long as I lived I would never fall in love with him – and that on the other hand I would always care for you.

Mitya, I hate feeling myself alone so much that I could scream! It is making me feel quite hysterical. ...

Even the servants frighten me; they have ghoul-like faces: I'm sure they are thinking: How can we bleed her dry? If we murdered her, no one would find out. She is weak, and entirely stifled.

... I am all alone in this house: I know I shan't be able to stick it! I have never spent a day alone in my life before.

---

[1] The title of the novel Vita was writing, later changed to *Challenge*.   [2] But I adore you, still admitting that – I'm mad!!   [3] aroused.   [4] Most probably Vita's promise to have relations with no one else.

The sound of my own voice frightens me; I go into the kitchen to talk to the servants on the slenderest of pretexts! I am more jumpy and nervous than words can say; my own shadow causes me to gasp with terror! There's no doubt about it, a week of this, and I should be a raving lunatic? I could never, *never* live by myself. To show you how intensely I hate being alone, I have invited the Peareth girl[1] (the dullest woman on earth, and almost the plainest!) to come and stay with me till Friday, when I shall go to London. If she can't come, I don't know what I shall do —

17 October 1919

... I do hope you *really* paid attention to what I said yesterday; I never can tell if what I say to you doesn't go in at one ear and out at the other! Therefore I can't impress upon you sufficiently that this time it is more in the nature of a tragic undertaking than an adventure (like last year). And once again I must absolutely implore you not to go unless you are unmoveably sure. Think over it very seriously and weigh everything in your mind. ... This time you would absolutely do me in, and I swear I don't deserve it at your hands. You see, you are really such a child in some ways. I am like a nurse saying to you: 'If you steal that jam you will presently have an awful pain —'

But you don't care and your imagination doesn't stretch beyond eating jam. But what I want you to make quite sure in your own mind is that the jam is worth it.

Darling, this is not to be funny, but I feel rather like a distracted widow of forty (still moderately pretty and attractive), who has promised to elope with a twenty-year-old undergraduate. He looks grown-up, but the ghost of a bib collar still clings to his neck, and he still toboggans down the stairs ... and she doesn't know from one day to the other what he might turn into!

These are precisely my feelings! What hold can one have over such people? I say to you tremulously: 'Try to remember, dear, that when you're only thirty, I shall be fifty!' And at the time, you're thinking: 'What a lark! The fellers at Balliol will think me no end of a wag!' That exactly defines the whole situation! And the unfortunate widow dotes on the undergraduate, but is putting up

[1] not identified.

168

a stiff fight before taking the final decisive step – and instead of seeing the underlying pathos in this simile, you will go into screams of laughter, and say to yourself: Darling Lushi. She is funny. What a scrumptious time we shall have, or words to that effect! Is it any use asking you to reassure me? You *might*, all the same. ... Bless you, CHILD, and try to grow up! – Je t'aime!

Possingworth Manor, Blackboys, Sussex
[1919]

You won't get this letter but it must be written.

Yesterday I flew – for the first time.

Before I went up, I thought: I have offended the gods so much and so often that they won't be able to resist this grand, blatant and picturesque opportunity pour me renverser d'une chiquenaudo.[1] They'll say: 'There! puny atom, that'll learn you to go messing about among your superiors!' And a little mangled heap would inevitably be the result of so much impudence. So with a wildly beating heart and the absolute conviction that I should be smashed to smithereens, a few minutes later, but not caring much either way, I clambered into the seat behind the pilot. I heard a harsh voice rapping out instructions: 'Contact! Release! Contact!' The roar of the engine was such that I felt my head must split: then it was like being whisked up an interminable sky escape in jerks by the Selfridge lift (which is the fastest I know).

I shut my eyes, fearing to look down ... the engines began to throb rhythmically like a great heart.

Then I looked.

Rip Van Winkle after his hundred years' slumber didn't feel more changed than I! My old self was dead, I knew with complete assurance and indifference – whether it would remain dead was another matter.

Between the spread planes I saw, looking down, a little map dotted with little towns, and a little sea. We were flying back – 3 thousand feet, the pilot told me afterwards – I thought: what a wretched little place the world is! Humanity had been wiped out....

I suppose I was near the gods. Near enough for the 'chiquenaudo'.

---

[1] to overthrow me with a flick of the fingers.

Well, why didn't they? I was actually bearding them in their den. Only a few planks and an uncertain engine separated me from annihilation. Really it was cheek. It was doing a pied de nez[1] in their faces!

Then the absolute marvel of it swept over me and inundated me with ecstasy. It was so daringly like perfection! It was so surprisingly like the fruit of the forbidden tree. Should I die for having attempted to pluck it. I was between Death and Perfection—so near both. . . .

If a thing were more perfect, then one would be killed for having forced the gates of Paradise whilst yet living. . . . It seemed to me that I had become suddenly and miraculously purged of all meanness, all smallness of spirit, all deceit . . . the words had lost their meaning. Perhaps very good people feel like this when they die. I wonder?

Suddenly the pilot shut off his engine. We began to drop, silently.

Never have I felt so impotent. Dropping through limitless space . . . I saw the little map becoming larger, more definite every second. I hated it bitterly. I didn't want to see it. . . .

Then – thud, thud! We were back down, we were back! The aeroplane was jolting recklessly across the field and I could see two men through my bleared goggles, rushing to our assistance like grooms running to bring in a mettlesome horse!

Hill Hall, Theydon Mount, Epping
[October 1919]

. . . I have been playing some very strenuous tennis. It is rather pathetic, isn't it? that I would give almost anything to be really good at games. . . . I think my tastes are extraordinarily wholesome really. The sort of people I like proves that abundantly.

Poor calisto,[2] she little knows what is in store for her! . . . But she may play as much tennis as she likes, and she will be encouraged to ride, play golf
> pole
> baseball
> hockey
> pelota and shoot with a bow and arrow, because I like

[1] pulling a face.   [2] See note 1, p.142.

the line. . .! I'm so like the Frenchwoman who said: 'Moi j'adore la campagne . . . ça repose les cheveux.'[1]

---

[1] Me, I adore the country. . . it relaxes my hair.

January to April 1920

In January 1920 Violet and Vita were both back in England, planning what they hoped would be the definitive 'escape'. On 17 January Vita told Harold of the decision to elope; he had returned ill from Paris and she agreed to spend the next two weeks with him at Knole. Violet, meanwhile, was subjected to the strictures of her mother and threats of financial withdrawal. Violet afterwards confessed that it was on the evening of 2 February that she had yielded sexually to Denys, though it is unclear to what degree.

The two women stayed in Lincoln until 8 February and on the 9th travelled to Dover. To avoid attention, Violet crossed the Channel alone, while Vita stayed overnight in Dover, where Denys turned up. He and Vita, making unlikely travelling companions, joined Violet on the 10th in Calais and continued on to Amiens where he left them and returned to England to find the Keppels and Sackvilles in concerted alarm.

On 11 February George Keppel appeared in Amiens and on the 14th Harold and Denys arrived in a small plane. The ensuing scene was the climax of Violet and Vita's affair. After tears and recriminations, Vita left with Harold for Paris and on the 16th Violet, emotionally devastated, motored with Denys to Toulon, where her parents awaited them. Alice Keppel's chief concern was to avoid a scandal that would jeopardize Sonia's engagement to Roland Cubitt, son of Baron Ashcombe, the famous builder. The possibility of a divorce was dismissed and it was finally agreed that the Trefusises would travel to the South of France. Violet stayed in Pat Dansey's villa in Bordighera and Denys took a room in Monte Carlo in the same hotel as Nancy Cunard. On 20 March Violet met Vita in Avignon and from there went on to Venice via Bordighera, returning to England on 10 April.

6 January 1920

Men tiliche, Isn't it a bore? Men chinday has just this minute come in to announce she has bought the house! She promised this morning that she wouldn't until I had 'thought it over'. However, it can't be helped. Tonight, after dinner I am going to try and tell _____[1] again. I must, I *must* –

... How I wish she had not bought that house. I feel I ought to give her back the money. Mercifully she got it very cheap – Quelle triste farce![2]...

My nomadic soul s'y accroche déseperément[3] at best ... and yet ... and yet. ... How about having nothing, nothing, nothing but the sky, and the wind, and the stars? Granada!

29 January 1920

You can't seriously mean what you said about not publishing our Book.[4] It would be too *idiotic*. It is quite admirable – What rotten judges people are of their own books (i.e., you, Clemence Dane)[5]....

You've no idea how good 'Rebellion' is. I suppose I might say it is superlatively interesting as it is about us, but it is for all that. Wait and see this doesn't prove me right. I believe Clemence Dane is jealous of YOU – of 'Heritage',[6] I mean. (How lovely to think that my book will suscitate no jealousies – it is too *putrid*).

D.T. looks too ghastly tonight. I ought not to have been beastly in front of E. Bagnold.[7]

What do you think is wrong with 'Rebellion'? It is original in plot, brilliant in style, psychologically it couldn't be more accurate.

---

[1] Denys Trefusis; Violet was referring to the elopement to Amiens planned for February.   [2] What a sad farce!   [3] hangs on desperately.   [4] Vita's novel 'Rebellion', later published as *Challenge*.   [5] Pen-name of the novelist, dramatist and artist Winifred Ashton (1885–1965).   [6] Vita's first published novel.   [7] Enid Bagnold (1889–1981), prominent playwright and novelist, and a friend of Violet and Vita during the period of the love affair. In an obituary letter to *The Times,* following Violet Trefusis's death she wrote: 'I remember Violet (preTrefusis) young in years but an old spirit; luxurious, gay, elliptical, witty. ... She was a great loss to me.'

What more *can* you have? It has none of the awkwardness of
'Heritage', no rather difficultly drawn character like Malory. I'm
not crabbing 'Heritage'. It was *frightfully* good, but nothing will
induce me to think that Rebellion isn't ten times better. Why
'superficial'? I should have thought quite the opposite – You can't
say that either you or Julian are superficial. . . .

I don't know that I shall particularly enjoy steeping myself in
Trefusis this weekend. . . . Mitya, BE GOOD. I trust you. Don't
relax, don't relent, don't sigh and soften: it's absurd, disloyal (to
me), and useless. . . .

My address is Stonewall Cottage, Langton Green, Tunbridge
Wells. WRITE, WRITE, WRITE!

Hotel Ritz,
Place Vendome,
Paris
14 February 1920

My darling beloved, I am simply dazed and sodden with pain; it
seems incredible that I should go on living –

My God, and happiness was so near. . . . What is so perfectly
awful to me is the feeling that our separation is partially due to a
misunderstanding. There has NEVER never never in my life been
any attempt at what you thought from that person. *Never* – He said
his pride wouldn't allow him to say more, and he particularly doesn't
want anyone to know, but O Mitya, I do swear – may I die tonight – that there has never been anything of that nature and scarcely
anything of the other. I loathe having to write this, but what I told
you this evening is exactly true down to the minutest detail. O
God – if only I – or he – could have explained. I have told him I
hated him and that I would rather go to St Moritz[1] than stay alone
with him if neither Pat nor [Enid] Bagnold can come. At the present
moment, he is sobbing next door.

I told him I was going to write to you all the time, and you to
me. If you don't believe all this you can write and ask him. I will
force him to answer your letter. I feel absolutely merciless towards
him. He has completely and irrevocably done for himself, and he
knows it. I told H[arold] to tell you that it was against my will, but

[1] Colonel and Mrs Keppel were at St Moritz.

now you know more about it than he does, thank God. O Mitya, why didn't you give me time to explain? It was even less than you imagine now. You must know, you must know. It kills me to write it, but you *must* know all this. . . .

That man has ordered a motor at 11 to go to Toulon – it will take days – but I don't care what I do or where I go. It's Toulon, because I've asked Pat to meet me there. Mitya, and you are so near and so supremely unavailable you might be on another continent. . . .

Whatever I may have done or said to you, I have never loved anyone like I've loved you, and I shall never love anyone but you in this life. . . . O my beloved, I feel there has never been sorrow or pain or suffering for me till now.

I implore your forgiveness, Mitya, for all the lies and pre-varications I have told you. I implore it with the contrition of an absolutely broken heart. Try to forgive me though I have been unpardonable. . . .

Hotel du Rivage,
Gien (Loiret)
[February 1920]

My beloved, I am writing to you in a filthy little 'bouge'[1] in a village called Gien. I am dead tired, thank God! My only idea is to travel till I drop. The road was dreadful: one was nearly shaken to pieces. There is a great smooth oily river which I suppose to be the Loire just outside. Shall I throw myself into it? It would save much trouble and much pain. . . .

Denys is ill: he nearly fainted at Fontainebleau where I stopped to have something to drink. He is in great pain, he says, and looks like a ghost. I have hardly spoken to him. It will be too awful if he is laid up here which seems to me more than likely.

O Mitya, my being torn away from you has made me harder than any granite. In case you don't understand, the wire that Harold had from Denys referred to my unwillingness – but aren't I being punished sufficiently?

It would kill Denys if I stayed with him; he says this is far far worse than anything. I am hard ... hard. ... I can't feel, I hardly know what I'm saying. If you left me for ever, you would have killed us both. How can you say you were so sure of my love? . . .

[1] hovel.

Denys burst into tears in the middle of dinner. He has now gone upstairs to his room. I shan't see him till tomorrow morning. It was the worst thing that could happen to him, your leaving me now.

Tomorrow I suppose I shall go to Bourges –

My beloved, this is a nightmare: Denys is half delirious next door and the chauffeur has been tearing backwards and forwards from the chemist's getting him quinine and aspirin. Whenever I went in he had a sort of paroxysm, and kept on gibbering, 'Go away, go away, you say you hate me; it is in your face, I can see it, go away.'

What shall I do if he is no better tomorrow? This is a filthy hole, a sort of farmhouse; it is no more an hotel than I am. O my God, Mitya, why did you leave me? I told you the truth when I said I could only be decent to him as long as I was with you. I am inhuman now. Tonight I told him he must get his sister to come and look after him if he was going to be ill, as I couldn't. I know I shall kill him if I stay with him. O Mitya, come back to me, come back before it's too late –

Mitya, I *CAN'T* live without you. I am simply crazed with pain. If I had committed every crime under the sun, none were bad enough to merit this punishment.

My only crime has been *weakness* and *terror* – terror of him – terror lest he should prevent our going – O Mitya, if only you knew how true this was! I am guilty of nothing else. Perhaps one day he will write it to you, but I know he wouldn't do so now....

[Telegram]
16 February 1920

BOULE D'OR BOURGES JUSQUA DEMAIN ENVOIE MOI DEPECHE[1]

16 February 1920

I came here this morning, after having vainly tried to speak to you on the telephone. Denys is a wreck; he does nothing but cry and whimper: it fills me with repulsion, and I can't conceal it. My

[1] Boule d'Or Bourges until tomorrow, please cable me.

obsession is to get away from him côute que côute.[1] It is horrible and disgusting. As for me, Mitya, je ne vaux guère mieux.[2] My promise holds good, but *not* for two months – I couldn't, oh my darling, I couldn't![3]   Denys is a little better today, but he can scarcely walk, he is so weak. I *loathe* being with him, and he knows it. All the former pity I had for him has turned to disgust. . . . It is hideous, nightmarish. Tonight again I shall try to speak to you on the telephone – by tomorrow I may be too far away. I think I am going to Moulins (wherever that is). If *only* I could hear your voice tonight. Denys has ceased to be anything but my jailor, and I look at him and think: yes, if it wasn't for you. . . . Prisoners aren't afraid of their jailors, Mitya, and something terrible and inexorable is taking hold of my heart. . . .

Oh my darling, this afternoon I passed a little stall like the one at Amiens, full of mimosa; it went through me like a knife to see it. Mitya, how can you imagine that I could live through two months of this? You might as well have said two years!

My love, come back to me – *you must*! Whatever you had done or not done I could never bring myself to banish you for two months. . . .

Mitya, at least *shorten* your sentence. The supremely ironical thing is that my having wanted to go with you so unbearably is responsible for this.

. . . This time it may be indirectly my fault, but I don't deserve to be parted from you for two months. It is as though every time you saw a tree covered with buds ready to open, you plucked them all off one by one. Surely a day would come when the tree got tired of trying to flower, and just withered away.

I have never actually *belonged* (not in *any* sort of way) to him any more than I have to Andrea (I only use Andrea illustratively). If only you would realize that I am speaking the truth, and yet you are surprised that I loathe men incorrigibly and look upon them merely as animals. . . . If only I could have told you more fully in Paris, or better still, if he had. . . .

---

[1] at all costs.   [2] I am scarcely better.   [3] Vita had said that she could not bear to see Violet for two months on the evening of the Amiens crisis two days earlier.

[Telegram]
17 February 1920

SUIS A MOULINS POUR DEUX HEURES COUCHE A CHAR-
OLLES CE SOIR TELEGRAPHIE MOI DE NOUVEAU POSTE
RESTANTE MACON[1]

Grand Hotel du Dauphin,
Moulins (Allier)
17 February 1920

A line to tell you, my darling, that I'm not going to Mâcon after
all. They say the road is impossible. So I thought I shall go to Vichy
instead and shall probably get to Nîmes by tomorrow. I have just
sent you a wire telling you my change of plan. I have also sent a
telegram to Mâcon, telling them to forward any letters or telegrams
there may be for me to Nîmes.

O Mitya, I am tortured with longing for you. . . .

The motor has broken down so I shall have to spend two hours
here. O Mitya, the grimness of these motor drives! Me huddled in
one corner, he in the other, never speaking, looking endlessly out
of the window at the flying country. . . . I make the chauffeur drive
faster and faster: the car jolts hideously over ruts and holes like
shell-holes and sometimes we bounce a foot in the air, but I don't
care: I put my head out of the window and shout: 'Plus vite! Mais
vous ne pouvez donc pas aller plus vite que ça?'[2] I don't like
stopping anywhere. I get sort of stupefied with speed . . . We crash
over impossible roads, this morning we killed a dog – poor thing!
After that we went faster than ever.

I am going mad with longing for you, Mitya. Denys is ill again.
He has had to go and lie down. He has scarcely spoken all day. I
suppose if I go to him I shall find him in floods of tears.

If he goes on like this, he will certainly kill himself. I can't do
anything, I am frozen. Nothing touches me any more.

The Toulon hotel is the Grand Hotel, it appears, so write there.

---

[1] I am at Moulins for two hours. Will sleep at Charolles tonight. Telegraph
me again poste restante Mâcon.   [2] 'Faster! But can't you go faster than
this?'

Tonight Charolles, and tomorrow Mâcon and a letter from you, I hope.

Oh my God, why don't you come back to me? . . .

17 February 1920,
Monday night

My beloved, I can hardly bring myself to write to you tonight. You are really breaking my heart, Mitya. Do you think I deserve it? You know au fond I don't. God have mercy upon me, Mitya, I shall die if you won't come back to me for two months. I have hardly eaten and hardly slept since I left Amiens. . . . Two months, and what then? . . .

If it had been you, I would have been furious, but I would have come back to you the same day.

I am going to get rid of this motor and fly instead, if I can get a machine; perhaps I should think less then? I think it would be the only thing that might take my mind off you at all, so I shall fly anyway either now if possible or when Denys leaves me. I should have no difficulty in persuading either Pat or Enid Bagnold to come with me (flying, I mean).

O my sweet, and I have still got the money that was to have been for *our* house. I nearly threw it away when Denys gave it to me. How *could* you give it back to him? It kills me to see it in my purse. . . .

I found one of the lozenges you disliked . . . and your lip salve . . . It was silly, but I sobbed myself sick. How can you doubt for a minute that I should kill myself if I thought I was never going to see you again? . . . How I hate D. with his tears and humility, and utter dependence on me. Two days ago he destroyed his novel. All this shocks and disgusts me beyond words. . . .

Hotel de Beaujolais,
Vichy
18 February 1920

My beloved, I am writing to you from Vichy, not from Mâcon. I got here fairly late last night. O Mitya, it is so ghastly – this flight from the being one loves – each day a hundred kilometres or so further away.

Tonight or tomorrow it will be Nîmes – the alternative to Nîmes was Avignon, so you can imagine how I jumped at Nîmes – I hate having to stop. I should like to motor all day and all night; when I stop, such a flood of despair surges over me, that I feel I can't bear it, that I must break my promise. I loathe increasingly being with D. and I take care to let him know it. I would sooner be with men chinday or Papa – the fool! I suppose he thought I would stay with him if I didn't go with you – well, he is going to find his mistake out! If Pat fails me I shall telegraph instantly to Bagnold, and pressure must be brought on her to make her come.

As for D., I don't care what he does, or where he goes. My pity is dead . . . dead: only disgust remains. . . .

O Mitya, I shall die if you don't come to me soon. I look nearly as ill as D. and my hair is coming out in handfuls. . . .

16 February 1920

Men tiliche, I have just written to your mother to tell her we have left each other and that I am utterly heartbroken. I considered whether to tell her everything, then thought better not. So don't say anything about it when you write. I said *nothing* except how unhappy I was, and told her my plans, and asked her to write to me. I really care about your mother, Mitya, and her sympathy would be precious to me. O my darling, my darling, you *mustn't* call me faithless, you mustn't – *it's not that*. O my God, if only I could tell you the circumstances very fully of that horrible evening. . . . It was a sort of price to pay; I don't know, but I think he looked upon it as such too; he was *never* like that before, and O Mitya, it *wasn't* consummated – I know how awful it is for me to tell you all this, but the reality was so very far from you – what you shrink from – if only he could have brought himself to tell you more, namely that he desisted. . . . O my God, Mitya, you must have seen the horror on my face when you said you would leave me in South Street, the morning we went to Lincoln, and when I started telling you what a terrible time I had had with him going to the station. I would have told you then, Mitya.

If you lead me to think you are never coming back to me, there is but one way out for me, and that is . . . Death.

18 February 1920

SUIS AU PUY SERAI NIMES DEMAIN ECRIS MOI TOULON[1]

Le Puy
19 February 1920

O my love, I *hate* him so. I should kill him if I stayed with him another week. I loathe the very sight of him. He is abhorrent to me, with his tears and servility. I told him just now that he has absolutely killed any sort of pity or affection I may ever have had for him. I told him I merely looked upon him as my jailor, and that my ambition was to get away from him – I hate him, *I hate him.* O Mitya, I am SO unhappy. I cry and cry for you. . . .

What a *fool* that man has been! Anyhow, he has ruined his own happiness as well. At least, before he had my compassion, and that is dead – never to revive.

He is responsible for everything. If it hadn't been for him and his behaviour, you would not have left me, – we should be still together.

Apparently I have misjudged D. in one respect. He says he hates being with me as much as I hate being with him, and that once he has 'handed me over' to either Pat or Bagnold, he is going away for good, either Jamaica or elsewhere. He says he would only allow me to join him, if I were prepared to spend the rest of my life with him!!! Also if I had ceased to love you!! but he added that as this could be nothing short of a miracle, it seemed unlikely that I should ever see him again. . . .

Nîmes
[February 1920]

O Mitya, Mitya, why do you pretend not to understand my telegram? . . . I thought I should get an answer from you today. Mitya, if you have any love left for me, tell me the truth: have you changed towards him? I am sick with anxiety. What shall I do, what shall I

---

[1] I am at Puy. I will be at Nîmes tomorrow. Write to me Toulon.

do? I have been sobbing for hours. Mitya, how can you leave me in uncertainty?

I got three letters from you, one in which you say H. has written to D. I pray he makes no reference to my seeing you on your way to Florence, because if he does, D. will most certainly refuse to leave me. If he thought there was any chance of my seeing you he would stick to me like a leech.

I am going to send you a wire, and if H. has made that allusion he or you *must* telegraph to D. not to open the letter. I suppose it will be at Toulon.

... Denys is going away for good. He doesn't want to see me again so long as I care for you. ... Only, if you refused to see me again, you know what would happen. I have told you and Denys and everyone else countless lies; I have been utterly weak and utterly despicable. I shall never forgive myself as long as I live. As for D., I have *never* loved him, but I have been sorry for him at times, which led to further lies, but I never *never* gave him to understand that I loved him. If you remember all the letters you have seen from him to me, they have nearly all been reproaches of one kind or another; in not *one* has he ever said he thought I loved him....

[Telegram]
20 February 1920

MES PARENTS SONT ICI RIEN DE TOI[1]

[Telegram]
20 February 1920

WON'T FLY BUT SHALL GO MAD UNLESS YOU ANSWER MY QUESTION BY WIRE HOTEL LUXEMBOURG NIMES

[1] My parents are here. Nothing from you.

Nîmes
20 February 1920

... You have never answered my telegram in which I asked you if you were being 'good' – you know very well what I mean by 'good' – if I think you are being different, the same thing applies: I shall not keep my promise to you. ...

Write to me, my sweet, tell me that you are unchanged towards H. and that you will at least see me soon. I am so terribly unhappy, Mitya, and I love you more than I have ever loved you in my life. Why don't you sign 'Your Mitya' any more? Have you taken to wearing your wedding ring again? O Mitya, *please* not. I do hope I shall get a reassuring telegram from you today. Everything is cinders and ashes without you.

I thought for a moment that D. was going to strangle me last night. I told him I was going to sleep early because I had a headache, but started to write this in bed. He saw the light in my room, thrust his head in and said: 'You're deceiving me again. You said you were going to sleep – '

I lashed out at him, and said it was no business of his whether I went to sleep or not, and livid with rage, he yelled: 'I hate you. I hate you! I'm going to get even with you for all your deceit. I'm going to make you as unhappy as you've made me. I'm going to ruin your life as you've ruined mine!' Say what you want to say about plans in your letters in Italian which he doesn't understand, in case he ever snatched one of your letters from me.

[Telegram]
21 February 1920

T AI ECRIT AU MOINS DEUX FOIS PAR JOUR T AI ENVOYE DEPECHES INNOMBRABLES SI TU VAS EN CHINE PROMESSE NE TIENT PLUS MEN TILICHE NE ME TOURMENTE PAS[1]

[1] I have written to you at least twice a day. Sent countless telegrams. If you go to China the promise is no longer valid. Men tiliche don't torment me.

[Telegram]
21 February 1920

NOTHING FROM YOU NOT EVEN A LETTER GOING TOULON
TODAY PROMISE IN DANGER IMPLORE YOU TO WIRE GRAND
HOTEL TOULON

[Telegram]
22 February 1920

ECRIS MOI VILLA PRIMAVERA BORDIGHERA PARENTS
SONT PARTIS[1]

[Telegram]
23 February 1920

AH JULIAN JULIAN

Toulon
24 February 1920

Men tiliche, I am trapped, trapped, trapped on every side. When I arrived here my mother and father were waiting for me. They had come all the way from St Moritz. They say I must either go round the world with D. or they are going to have nothing more to do with me either financially or otherwise. (They propose giving me a little allowance – 600 per annum.) O God, what am I to do? They have a lawyer coming out from England. It's too awful. I could only obtain one thing from them, that is that I should go straight to Bordighera to stay with Pat for a fortnight before going to Algiers. Denys has promised to go to a hotel.

Listen, Mitya, this is desperate; either I must get him to divorce me by hook or by crook, or I must do a bolt from Bordighera to join you. It wouldn't be difficult, as he would be at Monte Carlo gambling all the time.

[1] Write to me Villa Primavera Bordighera. Parents have left.

Which is it to be? If I get him to divorce me, you must come here at once and see my parents, the lawyer, etc, (only it would be annulled, not divorce. Isn't it horrible? It entails a medical examination).

I have got 24 hours in which to think it over. I want him to divorce me. Whatever *you* want, nothing will induce me to stay with him. I shall do a bolt from Bordighera. ... Even if he does divorce me, men chinday will make me go with her. Listen: I have no longer an atom of compunction about leaving him either openly or surreptitiously. He has told me he would marry again. He says the only reason he hesitates about divorcing me is that he doesn't think it would be for 'my good'. And he has got someone in his mind, so there is no reason why we should feel guilty about him.

Only in the meantime, what *am* I to say to men chinday? It's so awful being taken by surprise like this. ...

My mother says she is going to write you a letter — what about I don't know, as she says she won't show it to me on any account; so for mercy's sake, don't think I have had anything to do with it. Mitya, if he consents to divorcing me, I will wire you, and you must come at once.

If only I could speak to you, and discuss all this verbally! I shall go straight to Pat as soon as possible, and shall escape to you from there. I am terrified of saying much in a letter. I have never felt so caged and watched in my life.

Sunday morning

Mitya, what am I to do? I spent hours imploring Denys to divorce me last night. He said he'd let me know this morning what he had decided. He has *completely* gone back on what he said, namely that he was going away for good, whatever attitude my parents adopted, and that I was only to come to him of my own free will. This morning he said he had decided to annul the marriage. My mother sent for him, and told him that if he did, she would have nothing more to do with me, and that she refused to give me anything to live on.

She retracted what she said about the £600 a year. I rushed down to Mama, and told her I would come with *her* if Denys would divorce me. She said I should never set foot inside her house, and that she would never speak to me again. I went on my knees to her,

I told her he filled me with repulsion, and always had done. I told her I would even go away with Duckrus[1] anywhere she liked, if only Mama would let me be divorced. He had said to her apparently that it would be on the grounds of 'undue influence', − I mean the annulment, and she told me about the medical examination. She is inhuman, Mitya, they all are, but I will *kill* myself rather than stay with Denys whom I loathe and abominate. I have just been into him, and he says he is going to annul it whatever she may tell me. I said I would rather starve than stay with him. I don't know *what* or whom to believe. Mama says he told her he would take me away if she refused to give me any financial support, and of course, she refused. Mitya, I *swear* I will kill myself sooner than go away with him. If he refuses or is coerced by Mama into refusing to divorce me, I shall go to Pat, and *make* her take me away with her somewhere. I know she would.

O God, it's so awful. They are three to one and utterly unscrupulous. I told Mama just now, I would give *anything* for him to divorce me, and that I would be quite content to live somewhere on a hundred a year. He still says to me he will annul the marriage; if he sticks to that, it means waiting here till the lawyers come out from England. ... If Mama gets round him, I shall go with him to Bordighera, and there induce Pat to take me somewhere where you must meet me. Wire and write instantly to Poste Restante Bordighera. It is safer than writing to the Villa. Even if I don't go there, the letters will be safe. Mitya, please believe me when I say I will kill myself rather than go away with him. *I MEAN IT.*

Not a line from you today. Why haven't you written since Wednesday, or answered my question. ... Oh my God, what is going to become of me. *Don't* telegraph here.

Later. My mother has just been in to tell me she has induced Denys to stay with me, to take me to Algiers for two months, then return to England. That settles it; I shall bolt from Bordighera at the first opportunity in a motor. You must meet me in a town in the South of France − Marseille for preference. If I fail to get away, I shall put an end to my miserable existence, but I *mustn't* fail. Write *not* Poste Restante Bordighera, but to the Villa Primavera. Denys will not be staying there. Mitya, I mustn't fail. She says (my mother) if I refuse to go with him now, she will never let me out of her sight for an instant. Have you any conception how much I loathe and detest that man!

[1] The nickname for Violet's Aunt Jessie (Mrs Winnington-Ingram).

Toulon
24 February 1920

... Papa and Mama have gone away and left me and they won't come back. When Denys came to tell me he had promised her he would take me away, whatever I said, I tried to jump out of the window but he caught me just in time. O Mitya, you don't know. I am absolutely at the end of everything. If I can't see you, I must kill myself. ... Even Mama relented a little at the end. She said I might see you later, when she saw how miserable I was; she even said I could have you to stay with me in England. I told her I loathed him, and she said it was all a hideous mistake; she said I must go with him now, but I would sooner die than stay with him. Pat must take me away, and you must come to me or I to you. ...

I cried so when I read your registered letter. I cried with pain and despair at having hurt you so, and having lied the way I did. O Mitya, if anyone was kind, they would put a bullet through my brain. I have never never cared for anyone but you, *never,* however much I lied to you.

Denys told Mama I had tried to kill myself but even that didn't make her say I needn't go with him. ...

She can't ever have been in love herself, or she wouldn't treat me like that. But Pat will be kind and sorry for me, and I think she will take me away.

Toulon
24 February 1920

Denys is climbing down rapidly. He says he will so contrive that I shall not set eyes on him the whole time I am at Bordighera, and that, at the end of that time, if I still refuse to go to Tangier with him, he will not use force, and that we must then separate completely. He says he will not annul the marriage just now on account of Sonia (which I have since found out was Mama's strongest argument,[1] and which induced him to say he would take me away now). He is very much ashamed of having deceived me the way he has, not only about having gone back on his promise to leave me at once and for

[1] Mrs Keppel believed that Sonia's pending marriage to the Hon. Ronald Cubitt would be in jeopardy if Violet's divorce were permitted. The scandal would greatly upset the very 'old-style' Ashcombe family.

ever as soon as I joined Pat, but also for having concealed from me that he had asked my mother to be here, which apparently he had done without telling me. I hate him irrevocably whatever he says or does, so that it doesn't make much difference. He said last night that he knew I always would, unless we (toi et moi) came together again, and for always.

Today, my darling love, I am going to Bordighera, but I shan't be able to do it in the day as it is nearly 400 kilometres (so the chauffeur says). It will be too awful if I have got to stop the night at Nice, which is about half way. . . .

The post hasn't come yet; if it brings no letter from you (you haven't written for days) I shall draw only one conclusion, namely, that what I feared most in regard with your relation to Harold has happened. I feel quite sick with apprehension. That would be the end. Are you going to stay for two months with Harold? What about your going to Italy by yourself? Not a word about that or what I asked you particularly to tell me? Are you so happy in Paris with Harold?

Denys has just written me this: the 'trust' refers to his having promised to leave me for good and having failed to keep that promise.

[*Note enclosed in Denys Trefusis' hand*]: I know that just lately I have not deserved your trust. I will not undeserve it again.

Don't take *that* away too. Even if you must hate me, try just now to be a little generous and give me back the last vestige that remained to me of anything I cared for.

I will not fail you again in that way. I will try and earn your trust again anyway – even if it comes with your hatred.

I know there is nothing *immediately* that I can do for you. But if you feel that in future you can at least *trust* me – it may help a tiny bit.

Nice
24 February 1920

This place has filled me with rebellion. To begin with, the beauty of the drive, over the Esterelles! Majestically they kept a wonderful secret: the Mediterranean! One comes upon it suddenly at a height of about three thousand feet. O Mitya, there it was, unbelievably blue, miraculously shining. ... The sky is of a deep throbbing blue, that it almost hurts to look into – O Julian, and you're *not* here.

We are invited to Happiness, and we don't answer the invitation. Our places will be filled up. ...

Denys no longer stands in our way. He said that from yesterday, I was free to do as I choose. He is only accompanying me to Bordighera to save me from my mother. But I shan't see him while I am there –

At the end of a fortnight, he is going to ask me if I am still unwilling to go to Tangier. If I say yes, I needn't go. I told him if you were going to pass through Italy, I should see you. He asked me not to tell him exactly when that was, and to leave no communication with him in the meantime. ... I could meet you *anywhere*, only it had better be in Italy, as I don't want to run across my mother, and D. is not going to tell her anything about this – Let me know quickly, quickly.

Your Eve[1]

Nice
24 February 1920

Denys has been filling my mind with the most loathsome doubts about you. He says my having deceived you was only *one* of the reasons you left me, the chief being that you went because Harold told you to go. I asked him if he thought you were as fond of Harold as of me? He only shrugged his shoulders, and said he didn't know and wouldn't commit himself. *Is this true?*

I told him I loathed the sight of him, and he said I was free to do as I liked, and that he 'cursed me with every breath in his body' – I tried to throw the lamp at him, but it was attached to the wall and wouldn't throw –

If it is true that you care for Harold as much as for me, you have but to say so. You will never see or hear of me again.

Please wire your answer to this.

[1] Julian's lover in *Challenge*.

[Telegram]
Bordighera
26 February 1920

VIENI[1]

[Telegram]
27 February 1920

SO GLAD IM WRONG DONT KNOW WHERE YOU ARE TELE-
GRAPHED YOU TO COME HERE DENYS AT MONTE CARLO
MAMA HAS ARRANGED FOR ME TO GO TO TANGIER ON
TENTH MUST SEE YOU BEFORE THEN

Denys has gone to Nancy [Cunard] at Monte Carlo.
Bordighera
2 March 1920

Men cheringue, how *could* you send me that telegram? Have you no
pity, no understanding? Have you never received any of my letters?
Pat is simply tearing her hair out with despair. You have never
answered any of her telegrams. She says she sent you three – surely
you might have answered them? She showed me the first, asking
you to come here. It was very nice of her, considering the rows you
have always had. O Mitya, I have been more than touched at her
efforts to bring us together. I do think you might have taken some
notice of them? As for me, I really don't know what to think; you
are so utterly unkind and unreasonable. You completely ignored
what I said about coming to you for always if you still wanted me?
How do you suppose I got Denys to consent to our being here
now, except by agreeing to go away with him for a time? Do you
suppose I want to go with him? *Fool, fool, fool*! Besides which, as I
said before, short of going away with you *for good,* which I would
rather do than anything, and which you very well know, my mother
absolutely *insists* on my being with Denys; if I were with anyone
else, say Bagnold (Pat and Joan are shortly going to Venice and
don't want me), they would start the same persecution all over

[1] Come.

again – to put it bluntly, whatever woman I were with! For mercy's sake, try to understand. If you want me ... say so and D. will clear out.

Mitya, I implore you, be a little kind and pitiful. ... Now listen carefully: Denys has to go to England on business as soon as the trains are running from the Riviera (or he may go via Switzerland). Shall I get him to take me with him, surreptitiously, which would mean my being in England about a week at the outside (I should have to conceal the fact from my mother) and then returning with him, or shall I contrive to stay in Italy for 3 weeks?

I can only be here till the 15th, and if you have not come by then, he is going to Venice – and I shall have to go too. I could come to you for a few days from Venice to Milan or Florence, or wherever you suggested. I know he would consent to this without my asking him (he is at Menton today).

Mitya, I *implore* you to be sensible and realize that my being with him till May is my mother's arrangement. It can only be avoided in one way, that is if I tell him on the 15th of March that I wish for complete independence, and that I am going to join you, in which case we must see our family, and have it out with them.

Otherwise, I will either come to England (against my mother's wish, but I don't care!) or you must meet me somewhere in Italy within the next three weeks – the strike will be over *long* before then, but see you somehow I *will,* so you must decide which it is to be.

If you bring me to England, darling, I shall look for something better than a few minutes snatched in Grosvenor Street or a hotel. I mean, I should either have to come to Long Barn, or we could go somewhere else in the country together. All I implore is, send me a telegram on receiving this letter telling me which you have decided upon....

Bordighera
2 March 1920

I am in absolute despair: you don't seem to have grasped anything. Either you have never got my letters, or you deliberately choose to ignore them – which is it? In the letters I wrote you from Toulon I told you that my mother had first said I must go around the world with D. She then relented and said I must go to Jamaica for 4 months. Finally, I got her to say (by tears and supplication) that if

I was abroad till *May,* it would suffice. All this I told you in my letters.

She then wrote (or wired) to the Laverys[1] and said she wished me to go to Tangier with D. She said that I couldn't stay there for very long, and D. told her he wanted to take me to Ragusa, which she jumped at. You suggest my coming to England. ... Even supposing I came, I could only stay at a hotel in London; if Mama found out I was at Grosvenor Street, she would certainly come after me – moreover, I could only stay a week. You would have to come up from Long Barn to see me for a few snatched hours. Instead of which, if you are willing, you can come to me now and stay at Genoa or anywhere you like, alone and unmolested till the 15th! D. is going to be in England all that time, and is very anxious to know what day you're coming. Your fruitless and endless discussions by telegram and letter are simply driving me mad with fury – God knows, the time is short enough, yet you still persist in wasting it. Why on earth did you go to England, when you were so much more easily 'got at' in Paris? You must be mad. ... If you knew how Pat and I have worked at this! She has been an absolute angel, only she says she is at her wits' end. As you were *always* going to Florence and as Harold has never raised any objection to your going, why can't you go a little sooner? ...

No, if you don't come, it will be simply because you don't want to. When I was in Paris, you told me you were going to Florence in a few days. I *know* there aren't strikes on all the railways in France; besides the strike is now over. If you don't come – and my heart is leaden with despair at the thought – *you won't see me till May – that is to say, nearly three months since I saw you in Paris,* which was on the 14th of February. It is tantamount to saying you never want to see me again. In one of your letters you say how delicious it would be to spend a few days in Italy together! ...

Mitya, you will have broken my heart if you don't come.

You know how straight and honest I've been about this! Denys says that it was owing to my honesty that he finally consented. It is *Mama* who is keeping me abroad more than him. ... He said that if I wanted to go to you at the end of that time, I could still go. And you never even alluded to it in your letters! But short of leaving him for good, I have got to go with him now. Mama won't hear of my being with anyone else – not even Duckrus.

[1] The artist Sir John Lavery (1856–1941), and his wife Hazel, who had a winter retreat in Tangier.

It makes me so tired, darling; you are forever accusing me of lying and deceiving you. I have been alone here ... he has been staying at Monte Carlo, and if you don't believe me, you can ask Pat. ... Think how divine it would be! Even for a week – I could meet you at Avignon or Nîmes if Italy is too far.

[Pat Dansey to Vita]
Villa Primavera,
Bordighera
2 March 1920

Dear Vita,

It is a queer world!! You and I mutually agreed we loathed each other, and here I am having to take as much trouble and worry over your and Violet's affairs as I might be expected to take if I entertained feelings of great affection for you! It *is* a mercy I can see how comic my position is, isn't it? However, the main point is you are two very unhappy people; therefore such a thing is not right, so I am only too pleased if I could do any-thing however small.

I am afraid this constant telegraphing is leading to bad muddles. Listen, I honestly believe Violet has been perfectly truthful, and all she has wired – as far as I know – has been *absolute* truth. If you could have come here all would have been well – curses on the railway strike. Violet *is* reasonable. *Can* you believe it? Also *very* unhappy. She is trying now to go to England to meet your wishes and really I think for her to go to England is the best plan.

Don't blame *her* about Tangier. It is not her plan or wish, and when she sees you she will explain it completely. What on earth you both will arrange in the future beats me –

Yrs Pat

Pat and Joan have
gone to Monte Carlo.
Bordighera
3 March 1920

It is almost unbelievably hot. I have climbed up here by myself, and feel exhausted. I am sitting in the shade of the olive groves on the top of a hill. I can't begin to describe how lovely it is: there is a mosaic of wildflowers winding amongst the olive trees and peach blossom everywhere. On the high peaks the snows are melting, leaving only white coronets. The Mediterranean is wrapped in a blue haze and without a ripple. O Mitya, to have you here! ... If you can't come, I shall get back to England by hook or by crook....

How little I want to see England. How intensely I hate the North!

Damn it all. My great grandmother was a Greek! We don't belong to the North, I still less than you.

[Telegram]
Bordighera
3 March 1920

AM FORBIDDEN TO GO TO ENGLAND TILL MAY BY MY MOTHER EVERY THING SATISFACTORILY ARRANGED WITH DENYS TANGIER PUT OFF TILL FIFTEENTH SO I CAN BE WITH YOU HAVE MOVED HEAVEN AND EARTH IT IS OUR LAST CHANCE OF SEEING EACH OTHER TILL MAY YOUR FAULT IF PLAN FALLS THROUGH IN DESPAIR CANT DO MORE

Bordighera
3 March 1920

Sometimes it seems so impossible that you shouldn't be coming, that I should be doomed to yet another failure.

... I want you so, Mitya. I lie awake for hours at night, longing for you hungrily, hopelessly. ... If you ceased to care for me, I should cease to live. ... Never say I don't love you, if I have to travel across Europe sitting bolt upright, to England which I detest, braving the fury of my mother, merely to catch a glimpse of you! Je t'adore....

[Telegram]
Bordighera
3 March 1920

IF YOU WONT COME TO ME I MUST COME TO YOU FOR FEW
DAYS IF CAN GET PLACE IN TRAIN TANT PIS[1] IF MOTHER
FINDS ME OUT STRIKES OVER

Bordighera
5 March 1920

... Surely I am sufficiently unhappy already without your taunting
me with vulgar 'reprisals' at the Casino de Paris! – And reprisals for
what?

I wrote to you always twice a day, if not three times before I
came here. I have not written to you here, because you were so
remarkably obtuse about my question. You say, Mitya, that you are
'not in a fit state to consider anything now' as if you were barely
convalescent from a very serious illness, I daresay, but it's rubbish,
all the same. If you don't choose to consider anything now, you
will not see me for two months from the 10th of March. That is to
say, nearly ten weeks from now. I shall have to go to Tangier with
Denys, and after that, wherever he likes – probably Jamaica.

... One dreary day limps after another dreary day – if you don't
come back to me, there will be no love for me, Mitya – ever. I must
content myself with watching other people's happiness, it appears.
If you want me, you can have me, if you don't want me, say so. Je
ne t'ennuierai plus.[2]...

My darling beloved, I shall post this letter in Monte Carlo, but
you mustn't mind my going there with Pat. I so hate being alone,
and if I didn't go with her and Joan, I should be alone all day. I
shan't see D.T. Pat let him know we were going. (He doesn't wish
to hold any communication with me.) So he will keep out of the
way. He does not want to see me any more than I want to see him.
He has already met my mother there ... so I expect there is a nice
old row going on, if she has found out he is staying at Monte Carlo.
Of course he may have told her so quite openly, but he promised
he wouldn't. But then, I can't trust him....

[1] so much the worse   [2] I will not bore you any more.

195

Anyhow, what does it matter?

Nothing matters except you, and my seeing you again. . . . O darling, please *please* write to me; I shall die if you don't. A tiny misfortune is that I have had a great deal of money stolen from me, but you know how little I worry about that sort of thing. It isn't worth mentioning, and you may scold me for being squalid! I miss you more and more each day. Poor Pat, who is kindness itself, is miserable about us. . . .

Bordighera
5 March 1920

Men tiliche, how could you think that, whatever Mama said, I would give you up? You can dismiss that theory for ever. . . .

It infuriates me not to know where you are. I got about 4 contradictory telegrams from you yesterday, some saying you were going to England, others saying you were not.

Why the devil are you going to England? I hope Harold has to go and is dragging you with him. And why Long Barn? It can't be business then? 'Pour revivre le passé?'[1] O God, I am in such a Hell of jealousy and uncertainty about you.

I have sent you a telegram – in fact two – asking you to come here. Pat has also sent you one. She has been angel – she says she would let you share my bedroom if she thought it wouldn't be a scandal! You must be very nice to her, my sweet. She is the most forgiving and generous person I know. She and Joan seem flawlessly happy to-gether. . . . I simply can't tell you how I envy them – alone, independent, unmolested. O Mitya, why can't *we* have a house together?

I am so relieved to have got away from Denys. I believe he is at Monte Carlo; he may go to Rome. He told me this on his way here, also that he was going to spend most of his time with Nancy [Cunard] (who is at Monte Carlo) and if possible, take a room at the same hotel. I don't care what he does or where he goes, so long as he leaves me alone. Nancy would be a satisfactory solution. He knows I propose to see you one of these days. Mama is under the impression that he only spends his days in Monte Carlo, and comes back here every evening. I suppose there would be a row if she

[1] To re-live the past (with Harold).

knew. I don't care. I am hardened and completely indifferent. Pat has placed herself unreservedly on our side; she dislikes Denys intensely: so does Joan.

On the 10th, I shall either have to go to Tangier with Denys, or I shall regain my complete liberty. It depends entirely on what you propose to do.

O to have you here, my beautiful beloved! . . .

Bordighera
6 March 1920

. . . Darling, how can you be so unkind as neither to write nor answer my telegrams? What is there for you to be angry about? I am quite alone here; I suppose Denys will reach England tomorrow. I am not going to Tangier with him, or anywhere else. I am merely waiting for your 'orders'. Moreover I am completely free and independent. . . .

I am so unhappy because I never hear from you, darling. Perhaps you will get this on your birthday (the 8th)[1] which I had planned you should spend in the South with me.

I have got you rather a nice present, but nothing is ever nice enough. . . .

If your decision holds good, I shall try and get a place in the train at the end of the week –

Forgive squalor, but I must wait till I'm all right again. *I have got a pain this morning.*

Poor Pat gave a cry of genuine disappointment when I said you wouldn't come here. 'Oh, why won't she come to Italy?' she said. 'You two poor children could be so happy.' She and Joan are going to Venice. They want us to go too? I should so love to see Venice. I have never been there. Contrast Venice with Grosvenor Street! . . .

Sonia and Mama have either gone or are just going to Spain for an indefinite period. She won't have anything to do with me, and barely shook my hand when I saw her. I'm told Sonia is in love with a Spaniard.

[1] Vita's birthday was in fact 9 March.

[Telegram]
Bordighera
8 March 1920

NOT GOING TO TANGIER NOT THE END A NEW BEGINNING
AM ALONE AND FREE CAN MEET MEN TILICHE ANYWHERE
UNDER THE SUN YOUR LETTER WORLDS WORST RUBBISH

Bordighera
8 March 1920

... I lost ten thousand francs at Monte Carlo, because I felt
absolutely desperate, and gambling is the only thing which makes
one forget for the moment.

O my sweet, what frightfully silly notions you have got into your
head! I could afford to laugh at them! For instance, the one that I
was demented with jealousy about Nancy Cunard whom I *implored*
D.T. to go and console himself with!

Darling, it's too absurd! I wish you could ask him about it? I
wrote in relief, not in anger, and merely state the fact, because I
thought it sounded so dramatic!

T'es bête, mon pauvre chou.[1] ...

What can have happened to all the letters I have written to you
from here? I know the post office is hopeless; it is a private concern
owned by the family, and you can buy the whole place for three
thousand lire! The people say that letters sent from here seldom
arrive, and no more do telegrams, or else they arrive so distorted
that no one can make head or tail of them. If I were to stay here
much longer, I should certainly buy the post office.

And now to business: I can't live any longer without seeing you:
that's flat. If you won't come to Italy – and God knows you won't –
I shall return to England the moment you let me know definitely.
If it wasn't for you, I would not go back for ages – perhaps never –
I worship the South, and my freedom. I revel in the thought of
having no house, no possessions, no ties, no plans, and very little
money. ...

I live only for the sight of you again. As I said tonight in my
telegram, it is not the end, it is a new beginning. It is the end if you

[1] You are stupid, my poor dear.

insist on its being the end, and if you insist, you will kill me. . . . If you told me to meet you in Biskra, I would meet you there! Shall we both go to Ragusa, Mitya? Ragusa is as wild and uncivilized as you like – or Corfu or Cyprus – or merely Florence?

O Mitya, I can no longer write my book – our book – I can't, you know, when I am unhappy, and if it never gets finished, you will have killed it.

Don't pay too much attention to what your mother says – since when has she become a competent judge of literature? As to its maligning me in any way – I could not be more maligned and shunned than I am at present, partly, thanks to your mother, who wrote to someone I know who was staying at Monte Carlo, saying 'that arch-fiend, Violet, has been trying to upset the Nicolson's marriage, etc. etc.' *I* don't care, as you know, but she has made things pretty hot for me in London, which is rather a bore if I have to return there, especially as I don't want to be perpetually en tête à tête with D.T. and, if no one will come near me, that is bound to happen. People have told my mother that she has gone about telling everyone she met (people I have seen at Monte Carlo have cut me dead) and making the most frightful mischief – Moi je m'en fiche,[1] but an uninterrupted solitude with D.T. will be the result, if I do go back. . . . I would commit suicide (seriously) if I had to stay in Grosvenor Street alone. . . . If I deliberately step into my hated cage again, you must at least feed me through the bars! . . .

Darling, this is England:	Grosvenor Street
	ugliness
	shackles
	detestable people
	conventions
	restrictions
	watery sun
and the South is:	liberty
	la branche,[2] as a substitute for G.St.
	no conventions
	no restrictions
	no detestable people
	sun
	heat

[1] I don't care a straw.   [2] literally, the branch or bough (of a tree).

<table>
<tr><td rowspan="9">7</td><td rowspan="9">Alas, England for you is:</td><td>strange, unknown accessible</td></tr>
<tr><td>countries</td></tr>
<tr><td>adventure</td></tr>
<tr><td>Long Barn</td></tr>
<tr><td>your books</td></tr>
<tr><td>your garden</td></tr>
<tr><td>Knole</td></tr>
<tr><td>your father</td></tr>
<tr><td>people you like</td></tr>
</table>

But after all you know why I loathe it so – I submit three new titles for my book, which will never be finished unless my happiness is restored – 'The Comfortable Cage', or 'The Rut', or 'Sisyphus?' . . .

[Telegram: from Denys Trefusis to Vita]
Bordighera
8 March 1920

FORGOT SEND YOU WIRE YESTERDAY FROM VIOLET AT
BORDIGHERA SAYING NOT GOING TO BE OVER

8 March
(Your birthday)

Darling, why *won't* you come to Italy? Can't you tear yourself away from Long Barn? Aren't you a little inconsistent? You have told me all along how you hated my being with D.T. and now you are deliberately suggesting I should return to him! As long as I am abroad, I am *free*; there is *no date fixed for my return*; I can remain abroad *indefinitely*. There is a sort of vague idea that I may go back at the beginning of the summer, but there would be no fuss made if I didn't. I really don't understand, Mitya, darling. Why did you say you were going to Florence if you didn't intend to. . . . I suppose Harold has persuaded you not to go? What about your professed craving for solitude? If you are still adamant about England, *I will come,* but apart from seeing you, *it is completely against my will.* I know you will understand how I loathe giving up my beloved freedom, and returning to that loathsome Grosvenor Street. I don't do you the injustice of thinking you would drag me back for the pleasure of occasionally spending a day with me in London. *No, Mitya, it must be clearly understood: if I come back, you go with me to somewhere like Polperro for at least a week, AND AT ONCE.*

Besides, it is really a legitimate request – you will have been with Harold for a month by the time I come back. You can spare me a week. . . .

I made a mistake. Your
birthday is today.
Bordighera
9 March 1920

. . . I searched hungrily for letters when I got back but found none. Darling, how I sympathized with the woman I was reading about this morning:

'But if I don't see Lionel for long stretches . . .! Oh, I telegraphed him yesterday!' She said it vindictively.

' "Long stretches!" why you saw him before you came up here.'

'Nearly *three weeks*!' Alice stood an instant staring over the carved railing into the hall, as though looking back at Purgatory. 'Three mortal weeks! After all, Lionel's only flesh and blood. Three weeks is too long –'

And we have been parted for nearly four! O Mitya, don't you mind any more? What is it? . . .

I am really just as cut off from my family now as I would have been, had I run away with you! I think they have washed their hands of me! Save for that time I met my mother by accident in the Casino at Monte Carlo, she has neither written, nor taken the smallest notice of me, and though she is only 23 miles away, she has never asked me to go and see her, or suggested coming to see me. The time I saw her in the Casino, she said she didn't care a damn what I did, provided that D. was in London to look after her money!

At first I was a little hurt, but now *I* don't care a damn! (I think my sister's behaviour hurt me most.) But after all, those are unessential things, things that I have learnt to brush aside like crumbs off a dinner table – There are only two essential ones: You, and Freedom.

Life has become strangely simplified. . . .

[Telegram]
Bordighera
10 March 1920

DO YOU REALIZE SHALL HAVE TO BE GROSVENOR STREET
WITH DENYS NOTHING WOULD INDUCE ME TO RETURN
EXCEPT TO SEE YOU BY RETURNING SHALL LOSE MY
LIBERTY WHY DONT YOU GO FLORENCE AS ORIGINALLY
INTENDED CONSIDER WELL AND WIRE FINALLY

Bordighera
10 March 1920

My darling precious love, I have just got two letters from you, but
no telegram? Why? You can't *possibly* be angry with me for not wanting
to go back to captivity? It is so tiresome, not hearing, as I want to
get my wagon-lit, if I am going back to England –

... I was so wretched all today; I went and lost another 5000
francs at Monte Carlo, in order to drown the miserable conviction
that you no longer cared whether you saw me or not.

Mitya, at lunch, they played the Serenade from *Les Millions
D'Arlequin* – I nearly burst into tears. The last time I heard it was
at the Hotel de Paris, and you went out and left me, do you
remember? Monte Carlo is *us*; it is ours, that lovely coastline, that
limpid sea. I am keeping it for you, Mitya. ... You remember that
dowdy little dressmaker whom I used to talk to? ... I talk to her
by the hour, but she already *guessed*! She thinks you're lovely. I asked
her to lunch on the strength of that, and the next time I go in we
are going to lunch together – I bless the poor kind squalid people
in that Casino. I love them – I have no use for 'ladies and gentlemen',
Mitya. They are the only people, Mitya, the poor, the struggling,
the unsuccessful, the infinitely kind-hearted. *I hate success.*

Do you remember the 'Rideau' or 'L'école les Cocottes' – 'Mais
chère amie, rappelez-vous donc que le bonheur n'est que pour ceux
qui n'ont pas réussi!'[1]

And how I agree with Robert Browning! You know –

[1] 'My dear friend, just remember that happiness is only for those who have not
succeeded!'

'Thoughts hardly to be packed
Into a narrow act
Fancies that broke through and escaped;
All I could never be
All, men ignored in me,
This, I was worth to God, whose wheel the
   pitcher shaped.'[1]

Bordighera
12 March 1920

Mitya, you would try the patience of a saint!

I am positively tired out with explaining things to you! You are up to your old game of answering neither yes nor no. ... It's no use your pretending you don't get my telegrams, because you *do*! especially the ones I send you from Monte Carlo. I sent you one on Monday from M.C.; it *couldn't* have been more explicit – 'Shall have to be Grosvenor Street with Denys; shall lose my liberty by returning, nothing would induce me to return except to see you! Why not go Florence as originally intended? Consider well and wire finally.'

You have chosen to ignore this one completely. Very well, to please you, I shall drag myself back to that poisonous Grosvenor Street, that hated and 'watched' and restricted existence. I will put on my cast-off shackles – for you, in order to see you. I will make this sacrifice, but, if ever you dare say one word of jealousy, or attempt one single row with me, because, *owing to your own silly fault,* I am with Denys, I will clear out of that pestilential country and you shan't set eyes on me again. ...

Except for the week I took motoring here, I have never slept under the same roof as Denys. When he was on the Riviera, he wasn't, as you always seem to think, *here,* but at Monte Carlo. He occasionally spent the night at a hotel at Bordighera, but he *never* came here, except at my request, and I only sent for him twice in order to discuss plans, and to tell him I was going to see you. He promised me he would not come and he didn't.

All this time I have never bothered you about being with Harold, when you told me in Paris you wanted to be alone. You have been

[1] From 'Rabbi Ben Ezra'.

with him *consistently* since February 14th, except, perhaps, for two days when he preceded you to England. . . .

No, Mitya, You have played me a dirty trick.

[Pat Dansey to Violet]
Hotel Prince de Galles, Monte Carlo
15 March 1920

Darling, I saw your mother in the Casino yesterday – she does look so ill – worried and sad. And she is quite miserable over the whole beastly business. Cannot anything be done to arrange things without this horrible disgrace? Won't Denys change his mind?

Darling, I was so sorry for your mother. She does mind quite dreadfully.

Oh, Violet, what a hash you have made of things *and all for one person*. You fling all your real friends to the winds – not to speak of your wretched family. How often, darling, have I told you no good would come if you persisted in your downward path. I know, child, you are miserable. So are your friends. I loathe to think you are the one to suffer.

Your mother is a brave woman and I admire the courage she displays amongst this fire of hateful gossip. She is a proud woman, and it is hateful for her.

Make Vita promise that her mother shall never tell tales to your mother.

Bless you

19 March 1920

I am simply mad at odoros [Denys]. I have burnt his book, and in so doing, nearly set the house on fire.

Why don't you even mind when I tell you I'm ill? My head is burning with fever! What happened to you? Why are you so changed? . . .

A phrase of Harold's sticks in my mind: 'And she says to herself, "When I get back, I'll be so nice to little Hadji".' Are you being so nice then? . . .

That on top of all my unhappiness is too much. The pains in my head – O God, have pity on me – what have I done to deserve all this. . . .

All today I've thought of you playing with the children, especially with the one who is so like you [Benedict]. But not only like you, like him too. My godchild.

I wonder if the other [Nigel] is getting like you too?

He must be about four now, I suppose. I don't remember much about him except that he had ears like his father. When we were at Nîmes one evening, and the little boy played about and got entangled in the toiles peintes,[1] you thought longingly of your eldest boy. I knew it at the time.

It is astonishing how much and how often I think of your children – you would be surprised if you knew. How extraordinary it must feel to have children. . . .

I think of you as a mother sometimes for hours on end. I have today. Not only as a mother, but as a potential grandmother, great-grandmother. How my head burns. . . .

If you could have seen me last night when we were telephoning. If you could have seen my tear-stained eyes, and felt my burning head and hands, and known how ill and wretched I felt, and known that if you spoke to me as you did, I wouldn't sleep last night, you wouldn't have been sceptical and dry and impatient as you were. It was too unkind. . . . Even shop people in a shop I always go to were rude to me.

People say they couldn't be seen with me in public. I give you my word of honour this is true. Two people have said it who are by way of being my friends. Try to understand how deeply this hurts me. I come to you all bleeding and hurt, knowing that you have been spared the ghastly day I have just been through, knowing that you are surrounded with sympathy and affection – How can you expect me not to find it unjust? It's as though two people had been caught stealing, but one is put in prison, and the other is not. The one who is in prison can't help feeling the injustice. . . .

[1] painted canvas.

13 April 1920

My Mitya, bless you for being sweet to me this morning on the telephone – O please love me dreadfully to make up for all the beastliness I have to endure. . . .

The house[1] is a marvellous combination of all the things I hate: it amounts almost to genius. It is as if I had made a list of them, and the house is a faithful representation. To begin with, it is small, tiny, a doll's house! The rooms are tiny, and you bump your head on the ceilings. It is in a village street. I suppose the village is pretty, but I loathe 'picturesque' English villages; one can't breathe in them.

It is a tiny Georgian house, and some of it is much older. It has a tiny garden, and it has a gemütlich,[2] snug little atmosphere. Perhaps if Joan Campbell had it, it would look right; anyhow, she is 'to scale' – but me! What shall I do there? It is absolutely in the opposite direction of Sevenoaks – on the Great Western [railroad]. My heart sank when I saw it. . . .

This morning a nice thing happened; I bought the largest piece of bluejohn I have ever seen: a perfectly colossal goblet, like the Holy Grail. Also a lovely tanagra. O my darling love, how much I long to see you; you must tell me *where* we can meet. . . .

O for Space! O for a huge house, an immense park, great towering trees! . . . I think with longing of Possingworth – the broad horizon, the empty woods – the house was small, but it was strangely gracious, and there was nothing cramped about it; also it was quite a long way away from either a shop, or a village.

This miserable little country!

In the train
15 April 1920

O Mitya, I can't write. I just sit staring dully out of the window. Your place is empty. I can no longer turn my face to you to be kissed. You can no longer tell me you love me. . . . O my sweet, where are our rapturous journeys? Our joyful flittings from place to place? You, absorbed in some book, and me interrupting you every three minutes or so, just for a kiss, just to draw your attention to the scenery?

[1] The Dower House at Sonning-on-Thames.   [2] cosy.

And now you've gone....

O this grey and sunless country. How I hate it. The train seems to 'scandire'[1] Pri-Son, Pri-Son. It's taking me back to prison – Freedom lies behind me like some shed, radiant cloak. Freedom and happiness....

The whole country is a horrible illustration of the art of compromise – It was told: you cannot be Magnificent, so you can only be Pretty. The sky was told: you cannot be really Blue or utterly Black, so be grey. ... It is neither hideous nor beautiful, squalid nor affluent. It is *mediocre,* moderate, second best. ... It is the country of gentle Hypocrisy, smooth-haired Decorum....

[April 1920]

Darling, yesterday there was something 'soft and clinging' about you. You were well dressed, and tiny – Yes, feminine and most flagrant, of all inconsistencies. I like you to be rough and uncouth and fierce and untidy!

But I've noticed it before. You get like that when you are with ____ [Harold]. All that is feminine in you mounts to the surface – All that isn't remains in abeyance. Most scandalously, I prefer *all that isn't*! To put it brutally, a masculine interior beneath a feminine exterior. ... Your eyes were like a primeval forest, dark with some crouching, nameless menace....

I love all the ambushed atavism. ... I love the latent fierceness in you, the guarded sensuality. ... It makes me feel terribly insecure. ... You build walls and walls around you, and the sentry passes up and down, day and night. But if it were ever to break loose – ! I would go by the board, and so would everything else! You wouldn't have a scruple in the world! Everybody who attracted you would become your prey. The earth would be strewn with the bloody corpses of the people you had loved – for one night!

I don't think you realize it yourself fully, do you, Mitya? ...

[1] syllabize.

The Dower House,
Sonning-on-Thames
17 April 1920

I may be alone today again, for all I know. What awful waste! I think 'Sussex Gorse' too wonderful for words! What a giant book! It is rather Russian too; it has all the qualities which appeal to me. I think it is tremendous, and I love her concise, vivid style (Better style than Clemence Dane je le constate à regret).[1] I love the huge grotesqueness of it all. I must get to know Sheila Kaye Smith![2] It is rather amusing comparing her with Clemence Dane.

Kaye-Smith has a far more virile way of writing; she is much blunter, more direct, less circuitous, less wayward. She has a healthy and earthy directness which rather reminds me of you! She also believed in 'youth' and 'strength' – 'perfect health', my sweet!! (I smiled). . . .

[1] I regret to say.   [2] Sheila Kaye-Smith (1887–1956), a prolific novelist, devoted to the Sussex countryside.

May 1920 to February 1921

On Violet's return to England, Alice Keppel installed her daughter and Denys in the Dower House, Sonning-on-Thames. Violet's passion for Vita was unabated and her misery heightened by her isolation from society and family. She bitterly contrasted her plight to Vita's secure social life and Harold's unceasing devotion. In mid-May Vita went on a yachting holiday with her father and over the summer had tense meetings with Violet in London and Long Barn. Violet clung for comfort to Pat Dansey, who now began to play a prominent role as their go-between.

In August Violet and Vita spent five days together. The annual Keppel visit to Duntreath Castle in late August seemed a respite for Violet, but her misery returned during the next two months in Clingendaal where her mother persisted in publicly humiliating her. In November she was back in England for Sonia's marriage and once again her hopes centred on escaping with Vita. That Christmas she spent alone but in January 1921 Violet and Vita again went off together for two months to Hyères and Carcassone in the South of France.

1 May 1920

I have been so miserable all the evening. I sent you a wire to tell you so. I am so bruised and hurt. . . . Why do you see the secondary non-essential things, and not the vital ones? You are like a person trying to avoid getting bitten by a dog, when a tiger is preparing to devour him. You are constantly going off into side issues – I suppose it was foolish of me to be so angry about your sneaking off to be with poor Clemence Dane, but somehow it struck me as so extraordinarily perverse of you to go every year only to cultivate her, on top of all I had told you that morning. I thought perhaps you had realized how fundamentally unhappy I was. But no, all that time you were keeping something from me, a mean, sly, petty little secret – it doesn't matter, only as I said this evening to Denys, I get no credit for being truthful to either you or him.

Mitya, don't you see where we are going? I feel so terrified and alone in my dreadful clearsightedness. ... O can't I shake you out of your apathy, out of the apathy that is growing on you like some sort of insidious fungus? What has our love become? A debased, crippled, crafty thing of furtive pleasures and false generosities, of mean impulses and starved understanding. But to my mind the worst thing of all is its flagrant, its crushing hypocrisy. Under our skilful perversion – *not only ours but other people round us* – cowardice becomes prudence, selfishness is called love, misleading evasions are supposed to be 'kindness', meanness, blindness, and jealousy are all different manifestations of 'love'. Mind you, I blame myself every bit as much as I blame you – and I blame our circumstances more than anything. It is impossible for any love to expand healthily under such circumstances – it must always become a shrivelled abortion.... How can one make the best of anything that revolves on lies and deception?

The Dower House,
Sonning-on-Thames
4 May 1920

... We have done nothing but talk, and we are no nearer any sort of resolution. I try in vain to drive this tyrannous, all-absorbing love from my heart, but it returns undaunted, imperishable, to rage and storm through me like the wind through a roofless house.

The Dower House,
Sonning-on-Thames
7 May 1920

... One thing I revel in is my quite remarkably weak grasp on Reality – a little tug, and I should be free for ever, free from what most people term Reality –

My realities are quite different, only they're so 'insaisissable'.[1]

---

[1] unseizable, not to be caught.

They hide in the trees, they lurk in the tiny sibilant wind that steals in through the window and whispers to me as I write. They make music for me when I go for walks by myself, and above all, they are indissolubly mixed up with all 'free' things, with the flight of birds, clouds, the wandering of Gypsies. (Mitya, think of the divine people who have been wanderers: Jason, Odysseus, Lavengro, Coeur de Lion, François Villon. . . .)

Do you know, Mitya, that my only really solid and unseverable 'lien' with this world is *you*, my love for you? I believe if there weren't you I should live more and more in my own world, until finally I withdrew myself inwardly altogether. . . .

Sometimes I feel so queer, you don't know. Everything people say to me, even everything you say to me, slips off me like water off a duck's back.

And whatever you say and whatever they say, it makes no difference, I mean, about going away, for instance. You trot out your perfectly sane, legitimate and balanced arguments against going and something in myself, as it were, sits on the top of a tree and watches them curiously, amusedly, like a procession of ants. . . .

It's the very core of me that sits at the top of the tree and smiles, though the rest, the intolerably human part of me may be racked by misery at your obtuseness.

Don't you see, Mitya, that if you tried for a hundred years to make, say a Fijian, see things from your point of view, you would never succeed. And your trying to make me see is just as futile. I shall go on playing my own solitary games until you will listen to my point of view, which, in reality, is neither selfish nor immoral, but just DIFFERENT. In the Middle Ages, when people did things that the community didn't understand they were instantly burned at the stake for being sorcerers and witches.

Because you don't see things as I see them, because you don't really understand, you think I am wicked and immoral and selfish – so I am, according to *your* standards, but not according to my own. According to my own, I am singularly pure, uncontaminated, and high principled. You will laugh, *but it is true*. And you can laugh all your life, but it will still be true.

[Pat Dansey to Vita]
1a, Lower Grosvenor Place, S.W.1
8 May 1920

My dear Vita,

Your letter sent to Bordighera came back this morning. I am going to see Violet for the day Thursday next. I wish in many ways I could have seen you first, because I fear if Violet is not satisfied with the proposal made by your husband she will keep it from me! She *is* such a little monkey. She telephoned to me this morning and said she was worried but about what I don't know. Now, I am going to be very frank and you mustn't give me away otherwise I may have no influence in a future crisis. All through those scenes and storms at Bordighera and Venice I was working entirely on your side!

I tried all I could to persuade Violet to go back to England because I realized how cruelly hard it was for you to be nagged at to break your word to everyone who had been good and understanding for you. My dear, I worry for you as much as for Violet, more perhaps for you than for her. I wanted so much to talk to you when we were in Venice but did not like to – it is so difficult and I was so dreadfully afraid my intentions might be misinterpreted.

I think you *so* wonderful to Violet – but, oh, Vita, think sometimes of your own happiness – not only of Violet's. She, as I have told her over and over again, will always come out 'top'. I don't suppose for one moment she has ever told you what I have really said to her about the 'bolting' plan. She must prove herself stable, faithful and loyal before she can demand you to throw all away. We can never change the child's character, and we must accept the fact that to gain her point of the moment, she will say and do anything, but, dear me, she rarely takes me in. I am in future going to take as much trouble that you shan't suffer and be made unhappy as I would for Violet, and if the day comes when I give you warning you are going to suffer, you will know my motive is genuine. I have spoken very openly to Violet at Bordighera, and what is more she knows I speak absolute truth about her character. I do so want happiness for you both and will so gladly do anything for either of you.

Jealousy is impossible between us three, thank God! So we can all work together without any misgivings. Please, Vita, trust me. Nothing you choose to say to me will ever be repeated. I would be gratified to feel you knew you could speak about anything which worried you in tangles with Violet without having any idea I should be tactless and repeat it. When I see Violet I am going to tell her I want you to consider me your friend as well as hers and all I shall ever want is to see you both happy. I was so unhappy abroad about you both.

I brought home a few, very few, Macedonia cigarettes for your benefit!

Yours ever,
Pat

The Dower House,
Sonning-on-Thames
10 May 1920

... Last night another terror est venue s'ajouter aux autres.[1] I told Clemence Dane for fun that this house was haunted – now I feel certain it is. I woke up en sursaut[2] at 2, because someone had knocked at my door quite distinctly. I lit all the candles, and after waiting for about 1/2 an hour, I heard the most awful shuffling up and down the passage outside my door and little funny taps in my room – I nearly died of terror.

I didn't dare blow out the candles, and didn't go to sleep till it was daylight. I am simply praying it won't happen again tonight. I know I shall scream if it does. . . .

11 May 1920

Mitya, the bitterness of it – and though you haven't been with me, you'll be with *him*. He'll come back today and you'll be together. Always together till you die – O my God, I dare not think of it. He won't let you go. What a dreadful thing is marriage. I think it is the wickedest thing in the universe. Think of the straight, clean lives it has ruined by forcing them to skulk and hide and intrigue and scheme, making of love a thing to be hidden and lied about – as in our case. It is a wicked institution and I would almost go to the stake to prove it.

[1] has come to add to the others.   [2] with a start.

It has ruined my life, it has ruined Denys's – he would give his soul never to have married. It is ruined – not *your* life, but our happiness. It is all worry and dreadful and hideous.

... I have been ardently wishing we were ten years older; then people wouldn't care what we did or where we went – or even twenty years older. I don't care how old I am provided I may be with you....

Ever since I was a child I have loved you. Lesser loves have had greater rewards – You don't know what you have been – what you are to me: just the force of life, just the raison d'être....

Somewhere, tucked away in the recesses of your nature, there is something which understands – something which responds to my touch like a harp string – something alien, and wild, and uncouth – something savage and untender, something fiercely willing, and fiercely hostile to the rest of you – something which is not you but *me*! And to that something I make my appeal....

22 May 1920

... I had a detestable day yesterday; men chinday was beastlier than I think she has ever been, not only to me but to Denys who says that if she comes here, he will go away. He, by the way, has got one of his Julian (Grenfell)-esque[1] fits of morbidness and is again talking about killing himself. He was in an awful state when I arrived here last night. He said that if I hadn't come, he would have, and he is so miserable at the present moment that it really wouldn't surprise me....

Poor thing, he is so miserable that I think even you would be sorry for him. He has offered to go away for the nights of the 31st (Monday) and Tuesday, in order that you should come here, and he is going to help me get rid of my aunt. So please contrive to come *Monday, no matter how late*. Please, come late Monday if you can, as men chinday wants me to go up on Wednesday and I have to see Z.[2] It is so awful, knowing I can't even ring you up on the telephone; I miss you so unutterably.

[1] Julian Grenfell (1888–1915), poet and brilliant intellectual, and a former suitor of Violet. He died of battle wounds in France several weeks after his famous war poem 'Into Battle' was written.   [2] Sir Basil Zaharoff, the millionaire Greek financier who dominated the British munitions firm of Vickers and after World War I became the owner of the Casino of Monte Carlo, rivalling the princely family for control of Monaco.

Yesterday I went to a party and was introduced to Raquel Meller,[1] who is far lovelier at close quarters than on the stage.

She knows no English at all, so I had to talk to her in my Spanish which is nothing but accent and gesticulation.

Men chinday came up to her with some conventional compliment (I don't think more than about four people appreciated her) and Raquel Meller cut her short, by saying sweetly: 'Good-night!' which is apparently the only English word she knows. . . .

I can't bear to think of you in a boat in the sea with Harold.[2] It makes me quite frantic – the enforced intimacy. If you don't come back on Monday 31st I shall have Raquel Meller to stay with me. O Mitya, I do implore you not to waste your time. I do implore you to be firm. I am so tired of being unhappy.

The fragment you did for my book was exactly what I wanted, only my book is so difficult I think I shall give it up in despair – I am not clever enough or technically experienced enough to cope with it – alas!

The Dower House,
Sonning-on-Thames
25 May 1920

Z. has asked me to become his mistress with a house in Paris, a house in the country, and unlimited credit in every bank in Europe – 'Ginevra, quoi!'

I think it will be terribly inartistic to refuse.

The demand was made with every formality. This was the 'business' I had to go to London for yesterday, though I didn't know it was going to take that form, as in his telegram he merely said he wanted to see me 'on business' without specifying.

Well, darling, you always foresaw this, so at any rate it will not be a surprise to you. It is 'lift' with a vengeance, isn't it? to belong to the Richest Man in the World? On a son petit chic.[3]

I hope we shan't lose touch with each other altogether: my house will be in the Avenue du Bois, and I shall be at home from 5 to 7 every evening, only you had better telephone first. You will find the telephone number under the name of Mlle Thais de Champagne.

[1] Spanish screen beauty who later played the Empress Eugénie in *Violettes Impériales*.   [2] Vita was going on a cruise with Harold on Lord Sackville's yacht.   [3] One has one's little 'chic'.

I feel rather like a storm-tossed ship getting into a quiet haven at last, a sunny satiny haven, with gold-flecked waves!!!

After all, we have both always known I was predestined to become Z's mistress – it is merely a question of time. It is very soothing to have hit upon one's real métier at last. I shall – or rather we shall – be going to Deauville in August: I hope so much to see you there, my poor Julian – mais à ton âge on se console vite et tu dénicheras súrement quelque bonne petite amie à laquelle tu me présenteras.[1]

Z. always spends the winter at Monte Carlo, at the Hôtel de Paris, so we are certain to meet in the Casino! I shall be so weighted down with pearls that I shall be méconnaissable mais que veux tu? Faut se couvrir....[2]

Write to me sometimes: I shall often think with regret of the happy times we have spent together. On s'aimait bien, quoiqu'on n'avait pas trop de pognon?[3]

I shall always have a soft corner in my heart for you. Tiens, c'est plus fort que moi: je suis tout en larmes.[4]

Ta Vielle Louchette

P.S. Tu. Tu ne m'en voudras pas. Après tout se ranger. Tant qu'on est jeune, passe encore puis quand vient la vieillesse, si on n'a pas placé des petites économies, il n'y a plus qu'à crever en pleine rue. Mais tout de même, ça me fait de la peine de te quitter. ... Tu as toujours été un chic type ... comme je sais que tu es dans la misère, je t'envoie ci-joint un billet de mille. ...[5]

---

[1] But at your age one consoles oneself quickly and surely you'll pick up some pretty little friend whom you'll present to me.   [2] Unrecognizable but what to do? It's necessary to cover oneself....   [3] We loved each other a lot, although we were hard up.   [4] Well, I'm terribly moved; I'm all in tears.   [5] I don't want much, you know. After all, one must arrange one's affairs. When one is young it doesn't matter so much, but when old age arrives, if one hasn't made some small economies, one is left to starve in the street. But nonetheless it does hurt to leave you. ... You've always been a 'great sport' ... as I know you're rather hard up, I enclose attached a banknote for one thousand (pounds)....

The Dower House,
Sonning-on-Thames
26 May 1920

Men tiliche, I sent you a wire this morning to tell you not to take my letter of yesterday too seriously. I have not said definitely that I would accept the offer, and there has been the most awful row about it: anyway, I know it is terribly inartistic to refuse.

I lunched yesterday with Bagnold and for once we didn't get on at all. I said nothing but the wrong things out of sheer nervousness. She says she is very much in love with Sir Roderic,[1] which I am quite ready to believe; she can persuade herself of anything. ... Darling, she made me feel very murky and decadent and tropical, and I don't like to be made to feel these things. ... O DO COME BACK. ...

North Mymms Park,
Hatfield
5 June 1920

Men cheringue, I am writing to you in bed. It is awful to think that tomorrow I shall be 26! I am dreading it. It is dreadful to be as old as that. I *hate* getting old. ...

This is a lovely place, rather like Hurstmonceaux and rather like Montacute. The thing is it really makes my mouth water (for once) – the most gorgeous tapestries, Limoges enamels, and carpets.

In quanto alla gente, ils m'emmerdent[2] and they would you too. You can guess pretty well who they are. Moreover I feel too ill for words.

I am 26, passée, futile, pointless, and – letterless!

I have had no letters – there may be a post later and I am putting all my faith in that. Nobody has even wished me happy returns of the day, and you needn't have worried about Denys giving me a present, because he hasn't, nor did he remember it was my birthday, nor is he going to give me a present. You must think I *want* people to give me presents, but I honestly don't, only, I'm afraid rather childishly and perhaps soppily, I like to be wished many happy returns of the day. But I shan't ever again, because after today I want my birthday forgotten, because I am getting too old.

[1] Enid Bagnold's husband, Sir Roderic Jones, chairman of Reuters. [2] As for the people, they make me sick.

Last night at dinner I talked passionately about ostrich farming, manure, hunting big game, shooting, polo, golf. (I love being thought versatile.) There is only one other person here besides myself who isn't roped in for bridge, and we talk for hours in melancholy undertones for fear of disturbing the bridgites.

Quelle vie, mon Dieu, quelle vie![1] And all the time a little hammer goes on in my brain saying: 'mai più, mai più.'[2]...

Even the lovely things in this house bring it home to me how life wants simplifying: I have really forbidden myself ever to covet anything of that sort. It's all nonsense: one doesn't really need tapestries and carpets and pictures.

This is what one needs: the person one loves, the sun, freedom. Everything else is entirely superfluous....

You see, darling, wanting beautiful things really means wanting money, and one should never never start wanting that: it would be *really* lowering oneself. I have so very few qualities that I couldn't bear to diminish those I have. ... I want passionately to be hard-working and free, and you know what I want even more than that. There must never be any greed (in the material sense) or insincerity, or shirking, or slovenliness, or snobbishness, in my life....

The post has come, bringing only a letter from Clemence Dane, who *did* trouble to write. I *am* so hurt. You took jolly good care to both write and telegraph Harold for his.

The Dower House,
Sonning-on-Thames
[June 1920]

... I have done nothing but write since I have been back; my book is so difficult that it makes my brain reel.

Darling, I am *building* on your conversation with Harold. I feel beautifully confident (touch wood!) that you will achieve what you are out for. Also – this is a dead secret – Denys may be going away – abroad, I mean – only not a word.

[1] What a life, my God, what a life! [2] 'never again, never again.' [3] A letter and a gift from Vita arrived a few days later.

The Dower House,
Sonning-on-Thames
18 June 1920

... It is incredible how this place gets on my nerves: I am more restless and nervous here than I have ever been in my life. It is a small place, full of small noises: shrieks of children, babble of sparrows, 'honks' of motor bicycle horns on the road. It drives me wild with irritations, so that I can do nothing. Alas, I am feeling very unwell again. (How I loathe the sound of children's voices. There can be nothing shriller, or sillier, or more distracting.) This place is the apotheosis of fussiness.

To think of Berkeley[1] here is like paddling in an inch or two of shallow brook, full of bits of glass and ginger beer bottles, and then suddenly to step into a cool pool of luscious, limpid depths, and water lilies. ... Berkeley jealously guarded by great trees and a jungle of grasses, Berkeley with a voice singing in its heart, thunder growling round it like an angry watchdog. Was there ever such romance, such colour, such mystery?

I told Pat we had been there. She was miserable and really hurt as I feared she would: I said we had only seen the place from the road. (Though I loved you to love it, I feel guilty of an indelicacy.)

Lovely, lovely Berkeley, I shall be faithful to it till I die. . . .

And we go on, you and I, associating with the banal, the trivial, the unbeautiful, the vulgar, the clamorous, the prosaic.

2 July 1920

I want to write you the most serious letter I have ever written to you in my life.

I know you have cared for me and care for me still, but it is my unshakable conviction that you care not only for me. Heaven forbid that I should blame you for this! I neither blame nor condemn. All I want, all I *beseech* is that you should, *at any cost,* tell me the plain unvarnished truth. I implore you not to treat this part of my letter with your customary evasiveness. If I am to be hurt, hurt me once and for all. Don't toy with me like a cat with a mouse. It is so infinitely crueller than any coup de grâce could possibly be.

[1] Berkeley Castle, Gloucestershire, scene of the murder of Edward II, celebrated by Shakespeare, and where Pat Dansey kept house for her octogenarian uncle, Lord Fitzhardinge.

In the name of our love I appeal to all that is best in you to tell me the *truth* – to be brave and tell me the truth. It is the uncertainty of everything that is torturing me till I am half mad and don't know what I am doing. Make up your mind which it is you want – you can't have both.

This sharing business is revolting for both of us. If you give me up, I shall nearly die, but I can't stand the uncertainty of our future any longer.

Darling, I want to impress something else on you. There would be no question of 'reprisals' on my part. I am telling you this because this is not written in a mean or petty spirit. . . .

If you decide you want to give me up, I shall go away by myself or with some disinterested third person as soon as possible, and – I repeat – I shall be utterly heartbroken, but I can't stand this any longer. . . .

I want your happiness as well as my own, though I suppose you will not believe it, but O, I do! In cold blood I have been thinking everything over for hours. I know you care for me and if you give me up, I know it won't be because you have ceased to care for me but because you realize the futility of your efforts to free yourself, because you think it wrong to leave Harold and the children, and because I make you unhappy. Not a vestige of blame would attach to you.

You think I don't realize your difficulties, *but I do*. That is why I want you to make up your mind to lead a perfectly honest and open life either with your family or with me. You can't do 'la navette'[1] any longer. We must have a 'situation nette'.[2]

There is one thing I will never forgive you: that is if you put any misconstruction on the motives which prompt this letter. I never thought I could be so brave as to write it, because each word I write is torture to me.

I am tired of being a rotten character – tired of being selfish and spiteful and malicious – above all, I am tired of being jealous. It is killing me and making utter beasts of both of us. You will say it is selfish of me to want you to give up everybody for me. It is selfish, but it is honest, and would abolish deceit and jealousy for ever. But on the other hand I see it is wrong to ask you to do this. Therefore I won't ask it of you anymore. If you want to come, you must come of your own accord. I relinquish my rights and pretensions. I abdicate my claims.

[1] A boat that does a shuttle service.   [2] A clear situation.

You must do whatever you please, go wherever you please, see whomever you please. I shall not interfere.

I shall mind *hideously,* but I must not see you, for you must not know.

You said I gave you no liberty. You have complete liberty. I will neither reproach nor criticize.

You say I am ungenerous. You will no longer be able to say it. I will not do things by halves. O darling, *I want to get back* – I hate wickedness and lies and deceit. I am bitterly sorry for all I have done. I am bitterly repentant. I want to reconquer all I have lost. I want to be good like I was at sixteen. I want most of all to be good to you. If you are unhappy it would be good for you to give me up, even though it would break my heart. It is killing me to write these words but you owe yourself to your family – if you think it is right, you should give me up.

I know I have always shown in myself all that is vile, but I swear to you, all the good in me there used to be isn't dead. I am flinging it at your feet as a not unworthy tribute to our love.

I love you so utterly, you don't know – with such complete surrender.

I have wrestled all last night and all today with my selfishness and I think I have conquered it at last.

I shall love you till I die, whatever you do.

God bless you and make you happy, and Harold too. . . .

7 July 1920

. . . I have just seen the doctor. He says my 'irritable' heart is strained and that I must have complete rest – whatever that means? He recommends Evian – the great heart place – He thinks the baths there would do me good. He says the heart business is entirely the outcome of 'worry' and that I mustn't smoke, etc. Are you going to take me to Evian?

My mother has chucked me out of the house, on account of a letter she got from Denys this morning.

My precious darling, I had an utter collapse at Clemence Dane's (I nearly fainted in the Ritz) – where I dined. My head went all wobbly and my heart began beating almost to suffocation. I thought I should have died, and laid for ages without moving on the sofa.

After I had left you I thought of nothing but how awful it would be without you, and it worked and worked on my mind till I felt sick with horror and dismay, and hardly knew what I was doing.

... You said today that our love had become a debased and corrupt thing, that you couldn't trust me – O Mitya, you can trust me – you must have seen this afternoon what is at the bottom of everything – an incorrigible, insatiable longing to be with you – no matter where, no matter when. Can you blame me for this?

8 July 1920

... I feel so terribly tired and run down, and like what I felt in Venice, when I really wasn't responsible for what I said or did. You must forgive me. I was in such awful pain last night, real agony, my face pouring with perspiration. It has about finished me.

Mustn't it be awful for people who are always ill?

I was so pleased with my present,[1] darling. I'm sorry I sounded cross, but it was only because the letter didn't come in time, and because it didn't begin 'many happy returns of the day' when it did come! ...

[July 1920]

... The only time of day I look forward to is going to bed nowadays. I am so infinitely tired. ... My brain refuses to grapple with any new problems. I think until my head is ready to split. ... I feel quite stunned and stupid. ... If I go away by myself I shall try to make my mind a blank.

I wish I belonged to a lower organism of life altogether, halfway between a worm and a sea anemone. Denys has come in here, having 'changed his mind' about going for a drive, to inform me that he has written an insulting letter to Alfonso.[2] I have written to A. to say that as I was unaware that D. indulged in such housemaid-like practices as reading other people's letters surreptitiously during their absence, he had better cease writing in future, and that it makes no difference to our friendship. I am absolutely frantic with D. In

[1] For Violet's birthday on 6 June.   [2] Not identified.

spite of Alfonso's letters, I have always had a perfectly innocuous friendship with him, and he has never taken the smallest liberty with me. . . .

I am sick to death of D.'s insults and interferences, and if it wasn't for you, I would give him something to complain of with A. tomorrow –

In all my life I have never been treated like this – watched and pryed upon, and bullied. Heaven alone knows I have never bothered myself about his Jeannes and Yvonnes and Anne K's[1] – I don't care a damn what he does. If only he would take himself off to the other end of nowhere – If he comes in again, I shall throw something at him. You haven't been such a fool as to interfere with friendships that you knew were intrinsically harmless –

. . . I am sick to death of the man. If only he would elope with A.K., what a lot of trouble he would save everyone. I am so angry that my cheeks are burning and my pen shakes so that I can hardly write.

Please let me know as soon as you've had your talk with Harold. Because if you don't, I shan't know what to say to my mother. . . . If you fail it will be the end of everything.

10 July 1920

I am writing to you in great anguish of mind: please try to understand.

I write to you in the most homeless, friendless condition it is possible for anyone to be in. All the morning I have been making lists of my things. You know I don't crave a permanent 'home', but it is rather sad to have nowhere to put them – (you charitably said you would keep them for me, but since I have heard that they may go to Grosvenor Street) I mean nowhere where they can remain.

My picture seems to be solitude in hotels – hotels I don't object to, but I loathe solitude. You, of course, would be miserable with no house of your own, and faced with my future – mercifully, I mind that part less.

But what I *do* mind, acutely, devastatingly, is having no friends, no one who really cares what becomes of me. . . . You will say that you care: I am sure you do, but life is so different for you. You are

[1] Denys had *many* women friends.

223

surrounded by people who care for your comfort and care for your happiness, people who will never fail you....

There is nothing permanent in my life, not one person whom I feel will always sympathize and will always understand. As for you, darling, you are miles away physically and spiritually. You have been 'reclaimed'. Harold says you were weak. You *are* weak, darling. I don't mean in the sense of being soft-hearted; that is surely a most enduring weakness, and one with which I would never reproach you. *No,* I mean that whoever you are with, tu te laisses dominer[1] by that person – sometimes quite subconsciously.

Six months ago it was me, now it is him, and whichever it is, you are temporarily *blind* to the other person. When it was me, you were blind to Harold; now it is him, you are blind to me. *Don't misunderstand me:* I don't mean that you are hard and unkind to me; I mean that you are temporarily incapable of entering into my spirit and understanding my sensations. ... The mere fact of your getting angry when I tell you things like this is sufficient proof that you don't understand....

Think to yourself: well, it is thanks to me that she has no friends. I must be *all* her friends; it is thanks to me she feels lonely and desolate. I will see to it that she feels neither.

O darling, I am so abysmally sad. Year succeeds year, and there is no good done, no happiness accomplished. It is the old story of 'La Cigale' – 'La cigale ayant chanté tout l'été se trouva fort dépourvûe quand la bise fût venue.'[2]

I am la cigale. Don't – O don't say to me: 'Vous avez chanté tout l'été. Eh bien, dansez maintenant!'[3]

The Dower House,
Sonning-on-Thames
14 July 1920

Yesterday after Pat had gone, I burst into tears because I felt lonelier than ever; as she drove away, the other motor with Denys in it arrived. I felt I couldn't possibly talk to him just then, and rushed past [sic] him upstairs to Clemence Dane's room, where I knew

---

[1] you let yourself be influenced.   [2] 'The cicada having sung all summer, finds herself destitute when the winter comes.' (from La Fontaine's *Fables*.)   [3] 'You have sung all summer. Well, dance now!'

he couldn't follow me, with tears streaming down my face. She found me there a few minutes later, sobbing my heart out. She was very kind and comforting (she already knows a lot about me).

He apparently went out for I didn't see him again till dinner. He said nothing to me the whole evening, and I had no opportunity of speaking to him alone. I thought I would tell him why I had cried because I knew he must wonder. So when we all came upstairs to go to bed, I called to him to come to my room for a minute (knowing I was perfectly safe: Tu sais que je suis malade).[1] I said: 'The reason why you saw me crying was that I felt so sad and lonely after Pat went away.' Then he burst out, blazing with fury: 'Soppiness! You're soppy about her, you're soppy about everyone.' I said 'I'm devoted to Pat, and to lots of other people.' It annoyed me so, that he should resent even Pat, whereupon he cried out: 'Yes, you're devoted to everyone except me!' and struck me on the side of the head. He then yelled 'Go to Hell!' and rushed out of the room.

I am only telling you this, because it is the first time he has actually *struck* me – because the day before yesterday he twisted my wrist so that I cried out in pain, to make me say 'Goodnight, darling'. . . .

He likes hurting me, Mitya. It made me feel suddenly cold and sick when he twisted my wrist, half in pain, and half in terror at his face. He smiled all the time – his eyes were two glittering slits, and his mouth a thin, hard straight line. I thought of the war and shuddered. . . .

The Dower House,
Sonning-on-Thames
21 July 1920

. . . Denys has said *nothing* to me since yesterday; he told me last night that he didn't want to discuss it till I was better. Seeing me in the condition I was in yesterday has suddenly made him realize that I cannot stand the strain of another scene.

Pat told me yesterday she would only take me away on the condition she told us. Naturally, I would rather go with her – but I could not deceive her and let her think I was really trying to forget you. . . . I think the best would be for me to go with one of his [Denys's] sisters, who surely wouldn't exact such promises from me.

[1] You know that I am sick.

You must see, darling, that I *cannot* remain in England. It would be too intolerable. ... I *know* you realize how intensely and devastatingly I mind about my mother. I could not live in the same country as she was, to say nothing of Sonia, knowing that by living either with you (which would end in disaster) or near you, I will be insulting her more and more irrevocably, and making her hate me more and more each day. There is nothing to be gained and everything to lose by remaining in England.

In a sort of exasperation of loneliness, I might go to my mother and implore her to take me back on any terms – It is in order to escape from such dangers as this that I must go abroad ed aspettare fin che tu mi posse raggiungere.[1]

I am rather glad his sister is coming, as I like being with both of them. They are so spacious that the ordinary standards don't apply. ... Their coming to stay with me alone is sufficient proof of that. If they were any different, they would cut me dead! They always make one feel rather 'bedint' and limited. ...

Despair gnaws at my heart. I don't think you will ever get Harold to see. ...

I want, if possible, to defer my conversation till you can speak to H. in order that they may both coincide. Need you show the very abusive parts of that letter? I enclose you another letter of his, which I think helps to show the trend of thought. ...

All your letters have disappeared from the drawer of my writing table, so I suppose he has taken them. I have only just found this out. I always tore up the indiscreet ones, thank goodness! I'm sure he has put them in a box in his bedroom. I am going to take it to Reading and have the lock picked – tomorrow, if I can slip away from the vigilance of his sister. O my darling, all our struggles are yet to come, but we must be brave, and *stick at nothing* – if we do, we're done – and they will separate us for ever.

The Dower House,
Sonning-on-Thames
22 July 1920

... Most unfortunately, Denys is ill today; he was to have spent the night in London, but is too ill to move out of bed. He has a

[1] and wait until you are able to join me.

feverish cold and can hardly speak, his throat is so bad. The doctor is coming again this evening. Of course, I can't say anything today. Betty [Trefusis] came down with him last night. She is refreshing. It is like walking on top of a mountain with the wind blowing through one's hair. She is a theosophist, and, from what she has told me of theosophy, I think it must be a most comforting thing. She is writing a novel. You would like her, Mitya. She is very like her sister, but fiercely, courageously human. I shouldn't think she has ever told a lie, or done a mean thing. Those disdainfully immaculate, unattainable sisters! They are like beings of another sphere. ... Nothing small, material, social, comfortable has the smallest significance for them. They inhabit a high, free icy-clean world of their own, in spite of their humanity, where none but the unstained can penetrate.

They are emotional aristocrats – snobs, if you will. They will entertain nothing but the highest, purest, noblest emotions.

This one, with her fierce gold hair, and sensitive, arrogant profile, is like the daughter of a Scandinavian god of the ice and snows – the Aurora Borealis. I would not mind going abroad with her.

I am longing to have everything 'fixed up' – You will talk to Harold as soon as you can, won't you, darling? ...

I still look and feel terribly unwell. This morning I had hardly strength enough to totter round the garden. Darling, do be clever with Harold! Don't let him say that the best thing would be to give me up. ... I shall shortly need a lot of help with my book.

It is so urgent from every point of view that I should go away. I had better see H. as soon as possible. I am in a fever to have things settled. ...

Please let me know *what* peculiarities those sailing ships we used to see at Monte Carlo had, which so reminded one of Elizabethan ships – It's for my book, and *please* let me have the description of M.C. under rain. It is urgently needed.

The Dower House,
Sonning-on-Thames
23 July 1920

Denys is very bad: his throat is agony, and last night his temperature went up to nearly 103. The doctor comes three times a day. D. has had to be moved to the blue room overlooking the garden for quiet.

The only thing I have heard him say is that he wished he was in London!

I suppose it is influenza. I have asked Pat to come down for the weekend. She says she met men chinday yesterday, and that she was quite hopeless – adamant.

How desperate everything is.

Isn't Gaigneron[1] the man with whom you 'behaved less circumspectly than I should have wished' in Paris – Yes I know it is. *Please* don't start that again. We have got quite enough complication without that. *Do* let me feel that I can trust you implicitly to do nothing contrary to our interests. If I *can't* feel that, I shall really go mad. . . .

The Dower House,
Sonning-on-Thames
25 July 1920

Darling, you are an old humbug! You say 'I have got to go to a dinner party on Monday' and another on Tuesday. You know you haven't 'got' to any more than I have! I am not going to London because I have 'got' to – merely because I *want* to – and it's the same with your dinners.

On Monday you said you were dining with the Curzons'.[2] 'Corps diplomatique' dinner party, I suppose? I can't say anything, my tongue is tied, only I would rather you didn't try and humbug me over them. . . .

Oh, I am sad. Not because I think it 'chic' to be sad, but because I can't help it. I am also not at all well, and shall go and see my doctor as soon as I come up. Last night there was another scene – It would be worthwhile going to London, only to escape them.

I am so ill with jealousy and despair I feel I can't go on. I would sooner go right away. I loathe your being with that man to such an extent, that nothing short of one thing would ever improve matters.

I don't misunderstand you. . . . I know you are happy and well-cared for. Why shouldn't you be happy? You have got everything

---

[1] Comte Jean de Gaigneron, who became Harold's friend at the time of the Peace Conference and is not very kindly portrayed as the Marquis de Chaumont in Harold's biographical sketch of him in *Some People*. For half a century he was a friend of Violet.   [2] Lord Curzon (1859–1925), at this time Foreign Secretary in Lloyd George's government.

in the world you want – the one jarring note is me. *Let me go* – you have said you hated me. I make you hate me. You have no use for me. Just wipe me out of your life. Believe me, it is the only thing, short of being with me altogether. Nothing prevents my going any longer, either with or without you. . . .

28 July 1920

. . . I had a very painful time with Pat. She says if she wasn't so fond of me, she wouldn't go on seeing me on account of the current scandal about us. She says it has reached such a pitch that no decent person will shortly have me inside their house, and that she thinks I am going mad with the strain of it. She also said that if I lived alone, withdrawn from the protection of my family, no one would come near me. O God! How awful it all is. . . .

29 July 1920

I told Denys last night that I was looking for a flat for myself. He was perfectly furious. I then said that it would be for the intermediate time from returning from Holland to going away. I added that if it wasn't with you it would be with somebody else, as I couldn't stand being with him anymore – I said I had had a letter from men chinday asking me to go with her. And he roared with derision and said: 'Oh don't you see through that! I have told her that if you live with me as *my wife* in the fullest sense of the term from now till December, *then* you may go away for half the winter – three months. Otherwise even if you went with your mother I should dissolve (annul) the marriage after Sonia's wedding with the fullest publicity. The travelling with her is merely a bribe. She thinks that if you think you may go abroad, you may belong to me in the meantime! Short of that, I shall cast you off. You will become Miss Keppel again, and nobody will have anything to do with you.'

So you see, I was right even to mistrust men chinday's letter. They are determined to do me in. *What* I think of D.!!!

So it all comes to exactly as it was before. (You can tell Harold so.) If I refuse to live with him, they are going to have nothing more to do with me. . . .

2 August 1920

... Yesterday morning I'm afraid I said some dreadful things to D. in connection with what the doctor told me about him.[1] I think I was unnecessarily cruel. ... I also send an extract from men chinday's[2] which you can show Harold. I didn't send the whole letter, as it is sufficient for him to see that. I have put the rest in my bag to show to you.

I absolutely *beseech* you to do your utmost. If you fail, not only does it mean the end of our love but it also means the end of me....

[Early August 1920]

I told Denys last night that I was going away on Monday, for three weeks, that is to say, till Holland. If you would care to spend three weeks with me, you can.

As I told you yesterday, I am perilously near to agreeing to *anything* which gives you to me merely temporarily. Oh, yes! I've reached that stage.

I know there will be an awful row with men chinday about the three weeks, but that can't be helped. I think I told you that my father won't speak to me at all....

Men chinday is determined to take him[3] somewhere for the regulation cure; if the doctor approves it may be Holland. I wrote to him last night at her instigation to ask what would be best. I expect he will say Switzerland. It means sleeping out and lying up all night....

Men chinday told me last night that the allowance she would make me would be barely adequate – just enough to prevent me from starving. It *is* an inducement to give you up, isn't it? (Mlle.[4] is another.)

Listen, darling, *very carefully*. I am so terrified that Denys should *not* annul the thing, that I have not told him that the alternative is going sartute loude gayeres.[5] If he thought *that* – you never know with him, it is just possible that he might not do it. I don't know

---

[1] Possibly Denys was impotent.   [2] In Mrs Keppel's hand: 'I fear the scandal would be very great, and you would be the laughing stock of the country becoming Miss Keppel again.'   [3] Denys, who was showing symptoms of tuberculosis.   [4] Violet's governess, Hélène Claissac, also referred to as Melle.   [5] to elope with you (gypsy).

if I made this clear yesterday – indeed, I can't remember exactly what I *did* tell you, neither did I tell men chinday that it would be loude gayeres.

She forestalled that saying, 'Even if you went for 6 months with Mrs Nicolson, I could have nothing more to do with you.' You see, oh darling, do try to understand, my predominant fear is that she may use her influence – and she has an unmistakable influence over D. – and force him to compromise, to have merely a separation or something. You see, it is like this – if I say, 'All right, then I'll go with Vita for *good,* and make an open scandal', she may use *all* her influence over D. to prevent his getting rid of me.

You must see that at the present moment the supreme thing *is to be got rid of,* because you have *always* said that if he divorced me or whatever it is, you would stick to me whatever happened, and I believe that.

O darling, I am fighting with my back to the wall. *Please* help me all you can. Though he doesn't consider it at present, I am convinced that he is chronically jealous of you, and that the prospect of my living happily with you while he was languishing with his complaint would drive him to any measures. O darling, I advance these theories in all humility, as I know even less sometimes, how he is going to take things than you do. Only when I keep you scrupulously au courant with what happens from day to day, you are so disposed to doubt me, it really makes me doubly wretched. What object would I have now in concealing anything either from you or Harold? Please tell him the following, in order that he should know exactly où il en est:[1]

1. That the annulment will not take place until after Sonia's marriage.

2. That if I do *not* go abroad with you, men chinday will not cut me off entirely; she said last night that I must live abroad for 5 or 6 years at least to 'live it down', that she would take me to Jamaica, give me a small allowance, and provide Mlle. Though she *had not mentioned it,* I suppose she would have no objection to you coming to see me, 'if you happened to be in the same locality'.

3. That for the reasons I had mentioned (Had you better say this or not?), I have *not* said I was going with you for good. I'm afraid, darling, there is yet another reason why I don't – It is because I don't want my 3 weeks interfered with: they would probably think we were going to do a bolt. In some ways I think it would be an

[1] where matters stand.

excellent thing if Harold saw men chinday on her return from Scotland. You might tell him that from me. Also tell H. that D. is really ill. I don't want him to see D. when he is in one of his most excitable moods – but he is nearly always excitable so it can't be helped. They had better see each other *after* Monday, as I shall simply cut my throat if I don't get away with you, beloved.

Please understand and realize too, darling, how much I have to put up with on your behalf. If you only knew. Tu es toute ma vie.[1]

17 August 1920

... I played Tchaikovsky's 'Symphonie Pathetique' – the one you loved so much – on Pat's pianola. It is surely the most heartbreaking thing that was ever written! Do you remember how we loved it at Monte Carlo? Afterwards we walked by the sea. ... I hadn't heard it since then.

Before we left Monte Carlo you were mine, darling. I was absolutely convinced that you were going to tell H., and that, whatever he might say, you would return to me.... Do you remember the day you left me at Cannes? How completely we trusted each other! We were all in all to each other – ah, Mitya, what agony it is to remember!

There was little room in your heart for anyone but me. The other claims and affections had faded until they had become mere inopportune ghosts. C'était moi que tu aimais, moi que tu tenais![2] It *was* true, *then*, Mitya, that you cared exclusively for me – you know as well as I do that you can always tell – 'Le coeur a ses raisons que la raison ne connait pas'.[3]

Duntreath Castle,
Blanefield, N.B.
23 August 1920

The clock has been put back twelve years: I am fourteen, romantic, pedantic, mystery-loving. I haven't got over my stay in Florence: I

---

[1] You are my whole life.   [2] It was I that you loved, I that you cared about.   [3] 'The heart has reasons that Reason doesn't know.'

allude to Verrocchio, Donatello, Cimabue. I am deep in Marjorie Bowen – but I am not too old to surreptitiously enjoy L.T. Meade.

Nana is still one of the most important figures on my horizon: Moiselle is omnipotent. Mama is a remote, sometimes gracious, always stately and beautiful figure in my life. The boys aren't much fun, only Charlie teases me and pulls my hair. Mrs Strachen[1] is my only real conquest. (She has delicious lemonade in bottles, and she makes drop scones on Sundays.) And Vita – of course, it would be too wonderful if Vita came here. She is so beautiful and clever. (She knows Italian better than me – but I was in Florence longer than she was.) I simply adore Vita, but I don't know if she is really fond of me. . . . If only I could find out. But how? If Vita came, we would dress up and perhaps we could do *Le Masque de Fer*[2] again, only I'm such a bad actress. . . . Of course, Vita's so clever: there's nothing she can't do.

Look at the way she stumps all the others at Miss Wolff's![3]

Though it was a near thing between her and Sibyl Mettersdorf for the prize essay. . . .

I wonder if Vita's mother would let her come? How lovely it would be. . . . I would scatter rose petals on the carpet. . . . (Perhaps there are some tuberoses in the hothouse. I will get my mother to write to hers.)

Men tiliche, you have no idea how strange it is being here – finding everything unchanged. You must remember I haven't been here for seven years. It's like coming back to my lost childhood. The illusion is unexpectedly assisted by men chinday, who, so far hasn't made a single reference to anything – for which I am infinitely grateful. Mio Zio Archie[4] and Mia Zia Duckrus[5] (not Iscariot) are most kind and gentle. The other 'Zia' is away.

Men camelo tuti[6] so superlatively – it seems like an unbroken sequence – I did as a child – I do still. It seems the one thing that must last as long as I last. . . .

My darling, I have such a horrid sore throat – apparently – though it's not necessary to connect the two – there is an awful outbreak of smallpox in Glasgow, and my uncle thinks perhaps I ought to be vaccinated as I lingered there this morning.

---

[1] The wife of the lodge-keeper at Duntreath.   [2] *The Iron Mask*.   [3] The school attended by Violet and Vita.   [4] My uncle, Sir Archibald Edmonstone, Mrs Keppel's brother.   [5] My aunt, Jessie   [6] I adore you.

Monday morning

I haven't slept – and my throat is much worse – I have no remedies for it with me....

Yesterday men chinday, instead of being hard and inquisitorial and menacing, was kind and humorous and gay. She is quite brown and sunburnt. She says she has been so happy here away from everybody. She is so attractive, like she was yesterday, no one could help loving her – not even you!

She has moments – hours of complete simplicity. She laughs and jokes like a girl – in the intervals of locking up the retrievers and doctoring a poor wounded dove that the rats had practically devoured.

Then her manners and her courtesy are so charming. She took me for tea with an old lady who lives near here and several particularly tiresome and offensive neighbours arrived. Men chinday talked to them as if they were the most brilliant and attractive people in the world, teased and chafed the old lady, admired all her belongings, until her head was completely turned. Non, il n'y a pas à dire.[1] I couldn't bear Mama a grudge for anything in the world. Whatever she did, she could always be forgiven. There are some people like that.

There was a nice little man here called Sir Courtauld Thomson, who was quite ludicrously and blatantly in love with her. Oh! The charmers of this world, what an unfair advantage is given them!

[Scotland]
[August 1920]

I write quite near the place where I cried so, because I thought you weren't coming.[2] O, darling, I ought never to come here. You haunt this place. ... How young and happy we were – as free as the sparrow hawks that nest on the hill, as shy as the roe deer that feed on its slopes. How I loved you then! I was always afraid of your guessing how much I loved you....

The place is inviolably yours, the lanky, awkward, adorable you that wrote historical novels and had no sense of humour. You have changed more than I have, for I haven't changed at all. ... I know

---

[1] No, there's nothing to be said.   [2] to Duntreath Castle

how terribly alike we are in some ways – the most deplorable ways – but I have nothing but contempt for my shortcomings, and nothing but pity for yours. We are both weak, untruthful, and cowardly by nature. Don't wince, darling, it doesn't make me love you any the less – if anything it makes me love you more tenderly, more compassionately.

All I ask of you is this: don't do anything that could intrinsically mar or profane our love. It is too rare, too precious for that. It must always remain the one deathless thing in our lives. ... Years ago, you said we should always come together again. I pin my faith on that.

Darling, about your friend, what would you have thought, if after we were parted, I had gone out of my way to see as much as possible the one person with whom you had asked me, not unemotionally, to abolish all intimacy? It doesn't really matter; it is merely an error in taste. ... It is the brawny peasant strain in you. You are like a Titian, so rich and coloured and carnal, but you have not an ounce of spirituality. ...

Duntreath Castle,
Blanefield, N.B.
24 August 1920

... I am playing a game with myself: I am still (more or less) fourteen and you are still sixteen in spirit. Darling, how dreadfully happy we were before we grew up, you and I! I am terribly against being grown up. It does nobody any good. Hugh[1] always belongs intimately to this place. I can recall him so vividly: a gawky tongue-tied boy of nineteen. (I think the term 'boy' is legitimate in this case.) And you – why, you never left it – the whole place rings with your name.

Darling, it's true, I'm afraid, what you say. You have made a sad muddle of your life. You are neither fish, fowl, nor good red herring. But, while you admit the 'martyring' alternative, you don't admit the other – the burning of boats – and – flight! (Surely the more palatable of the two?)

It is more difficult for you to play my game, for you are not

[1] Hugh Walpole, whom Violet had first met at Duntreath where he was employed as tutor to her cousins during his summer holidays from Cambridge.

alone, whereas I am. It's funny, how, the moment I get away, how gloriously emancipated I feel. I shed certain aspects of my life as easily as a garment ... I feel so free. ...

There is something invulnerable, something inviolate in me, something that will ultimately triumph over everything, and carry me away on its wings of rapture! (Darling, you see how incorrigible is this belief, if I can write about it in this idiotic way at 11 o'clock in the morning!)

Perhaps no one will ever know, perhaps it will never see light, but it is there, it is there, it leaps and throbs and sings, and you are the only person in the world who suspects its existence. ...

Duntreath Castle,
Blanefield, N.B.
25 August 1920

... Here I can live completely withdrawn from all reality; here I could re-capture the serenity of my childhood. Here I can breathe freely and live freely – Sympathetic hills surround me on all sides.

I *hate* having to go to Holland and try not to think about it. Anyhow I shan't be able to, if my arm takes. ...

I am reading a delightful book about the late Dowager Empress of China – She lived in a place called 'The Palace of Winding Cloud' – O God, the imaginations of people – Why shouldn't we go and live in China and become naturalized Chinese? What *IS* there to prevent us? I am so sick of obstructions – for me they have merely ceased to exist. Anyhow they have no real significance – If you were here with me, I would get you to see that too.

Poor caged Mitya – O darling, I am so anxious about you really – *Don't* fall back into the frame of mind you were in when you first came to Hindhead and which you gradually grow out of when you are with *me*. O God, what will you be like after six uninterrupted weeks with *him*?

You say I am strong in some ways. Shall I tell you the secret of my strength, the secret of my unwavering desire. ... I never let myself be influenced by anyone under the sun – Infinitely harassed and distressed, no doubt, but never actually *influenced*.

O Mitya, don't let yourself go again. I hope he doesn't get sent to somewhere in the Balkans. It is bad luck: you are always wanted at places *we* would love. I would give anything for you to be with me here. I'd soon knock all the nonsense out of you. ...

I open my letter again to answer a question of yours. You say would he [Denys] have gone to Holland if he had been well. He would *perhaps* have come for a few days if he could have got away, but I should have been there practically the whole time by myself. There was absolutely *no* question of his coming for 6 weeks or a month or even a week. You can also remind H. that I asked him, when I saw him, if he couldn't go and see D. I wouldn't have asked him to do so if there had been any hankey-pankey. There is *no* reason why you shouldn't give H. a very brief letter D. wrote me saying he thought it would be better if we didn't meet till Sonia's wedding. I gave it you.

Darling ... you are the *least* resourceful person I know.

Duntreath Castle
27 August 1920

Mia hermosa, My cousin Eddie (the one who faintly resembles me!) has just arrived from Constantinople. From a rather stocky snub-nosed child, he has turned into a perfect Adonis! He is about six-foot-two, perfectly proportioned, has a deep bass voice (yes, deeper than mine!), almost classical features (the erstwhile snub nose having turned into a Geeek one), and a shock of impenetrable auburn hair! You never saw such a dream! I shall get him to sit for me.

The romance of sailors! I feel he is like a juvenile Lingard.[1] He has had every sort of adventure and skirmish and he is not quite twenty! *Really* young, darling, not fake young like you and me!

I foresee he is just my sort of person. If I were staying here longer I should certainly 'get busy buzzing around' – so it's just as well I'm leaving tomorrow, as little can be accomplished in 24 hours.

Isn't this a bare-faced confession? (Shall I ask him to Holland?)[2] I can see your face getting darker and darker but you deserve to be teased (besides all I have said is quite true) for not having said a single word about Sunday. I don't know where I'm going or anything. You are really maddening, darling.

... I shall think of you tomorrow having arty conversations with your flabby host, pompous diplomatic reminiscences at meals, gossip

[1] Captain Lingard, the hero of Joseph Conrad's *The Rescue, An Outcast of the Islands* and *Almayer's Folly.* [2] Violet was going to Clingendaal (near The Hague), where each autumn Mrs Keppel rented the home of her friend, the Baroness (Daisy) de Brienen.

about the latest lion, the latest book, cheap witticisms at the expense of Sibyl Colefax – and you can think of me with my deliciously young, debonair cousin, being shown tame tortoises and a parrot that uses unrepeatable language, a revolver that has been used as a means of defending life, not as an objet d'art in an 'old world interior'.

Oh darling, don't think I include *you* in that soulful, soulless, little set, that miserable intellectual clique – I don't. Mentally, spiritually, and yes, physically! you tower above them. They are certainly your friends, but there is nothing big about them, nothing that will live, not a spark of divine fire. As for *living,* they don't know how. . . .

They live their little padded lives in their little padded houses surrounded by valuable old furniture, the latest thing in poetry, the latest thing in prose. And they go out to expensive luncheons, and they come in to expensive dinners, and they *dare* to criticize, these miserable flabby, half-alive people, the people who *really* live!

Oh! They take jolly good care to protect their little lives, to keep away from any danger zone – Pah, I hate them. I could spit in their faces. . . .

When I think that I escaped in the person of G.W.[1] (for goodness sake, don't leave this letter lying about). Thank God for the people like Julian [Grenfell], and Aubrey, and Maurice – and the bright flower of youth and courage and keenness who perished in the war. *Those* were the people worth knowing – the people to admire and live up to. I *know* I am right, and in the bottom of your heart, you know I am too. You've only got to look at your own father. He's not exactly thrilling, but there's far more to admire in him than in all the tinselly people you are misled by. Darling, please forgive this outburst. You will, because of the truth of what I always tell you. . . .

28 August 1920

Darling, I was so spoilt yesterday: I had 4 letters from you, and in that lot only one nasty one which I dutifully answered. The last one you wrote after having received mine, I adored. Bless you for having written it.

As to the one about your book,[2] I think you ought to make it

[1] Presumably Lord Gerald Wellesley, who became the 7th Duke of Wellington and remained Violet's friend.   [2] *The Dragon in Shallow Waters,* published in 1921.

'end well'; as you say yourself, then Silas will have failed in everything, and personally I think that is more artistic than the other solution. It is an awful temptation to make one's books end badly. I experienced it over my miserable effort.

I have been writing a little – it is now 'starker' than ever – the barest possible statement of fact – no embroideries, no flights of fancy. It is merely an undraped chronicle of things that actually happened. It has no merit – it is abominably written – the only merit it could possibly have is one of the most undeviating concentration that looks neither to the right, nor to the left, but sees only straight in front of it!

I can never help laughing at my own austerity.

As to *your* novel, I was tremendously impressed with what I read of it. I think it quite excellent ... eschew prettiness at all cost, prettiness and its effete train bearers, Rhapsody and Sentiment....

Clingendaal, Holland
1 September 1920

Men tiliche, I got here in an absolutely exhausted condition after six hours of the most hellish crossing. I was to have had a cabin to myself – one was reserved for me, which my mother appropriated on the grounds that she must on no account be disturbed. I therefore had to share one with Sonia who alternately coughed, sneezed and snored all through the night....

I'm afraid I *hate* the sea – the cabin creaked like a fat woman in tight stays, and undulated like a Spanish dancer. ... I have never been so miserable.

Men chinday misses no opportunity of saying unkind and spiteful things to me; neither does my father. La châtelaine,[1] I need hardly say, models her behaviour on that of men chinday....

I do not see _____ [Denys] till lunch time. He exhibited no enthusiasm at seeing me, and appears completely absorbed in his régime. He lunches in the house, but has all his other meals in the hut.[2] He is looking slightly better.

You asked me to tell you exactly who was here: the Alington family, the Harry Lehrs and Lady de Trafford. ... Darling, you need

[1] Baroness de Brienen.   [2] A cottage on the property.

not worry about me here. There are no temptations of any sort or kind....

Clingendaal, Holland
2 September 1920

... To my joy and surprise I found a letter waiting for me when I returned from the Hague this afternoon. I went with an enormous party to the picture galleries, then on to the curiosity shops, where I saw several things we should have liked. ... I missed you so acutely the whole time, that I had to pretend I had been sneezing....

I simply can't tell you what _____ [Denys] is like! He is more odious and disagreeable than I have ever known him; never speaks except in grunts either to me or anyone else, and was so damnably rude to everyone at lunch that I went for him afterwards and scene No. 1 resulted. (I sometimes think he must be terribly conceited, otherwise he wouldn't dare be so dull. Also, I loathe his indolence: he is the most indolent man on earth, and is never so pleased with himself as when he is doing absolutely nothing.)

I couldn't help smiling at the picture your imagination had conjured up, of him waiting impatiently on the doorstep! What really happened is that he went for a walk shortly before we were expected, and only returned in time for luncheon.

Thursday morning – men tiliche, men chinday was so outrageously rude to me last night in front of everyone that Lady de Trafford went for her, and was perfectly charming to me herself. Everybody here says that men chinday is quite insufferably unkind to me. They complain that it makes them feel so uncomfortable.

Sonia is very nice to me, and even my uncle is amazed at men chinday's behaviour in public – It is so sad for me, darling, because I mind so dreadfully, and I think she knows instinctively that whatever she did, I would always forgive her. I can bear her no malice. She has only got to smile, and everything is forgotten. I do try so hard to be nice to her, but I can't bear her to make a laughing stock of me in front of a roomful of people – I shall have to go away....

6 September 1920

... This place is doing Denys no good. He is more emaciated than ever and can hardly drag one foot in front of the other. He has said nothing, but I know he will have eventually to go somewhere else.

O Mitya I long to hear what you think of the Prague idea? ...

With any luck I think I shall be able to get away from him at the beginning of October – but I want to go to Prague then.

Clingendaal, Holland
8 September 1920

I was angry this morning when I got your telegram. Now I am not angry, only infinitely sad and discouraged. Was it so magnanimous letting you out on a chain for five days, when you had spent the whole summer with him, except perhaps for a fortnight all told which you had spent with me? I see the theory: a day with me for every week you spend with him: five days, five weeks.

If I could have managed Prague in spite of Denys's being ill, why couldn't you? ... But taking into consideration your objection (on the grounds of the beggarly five days) you could come at the *end of the five weeks,* that is to say, the 7th of October? That would be quite fair from every point of view – H. will have had his uninterrupted five weeks with you, and it will be *my* turn. ... I take it you will be at Ostend for three days with H.

I suppose you realize that the mere fact of your being about three or so hours from here with him will drive me absolutely mad? It is about the most tantalizing thing you could have devised. ...

I expect the life at Ostend is very similar to the life at Monte Carlo. He will enjoy parading you there. I am sorry: try as I may, that and your reason for not going to Prague is making me see red. I can't help it. ...

You apply the adjective 'ghastly' to my life here: I have not your luck. I am not surrounded by people who amuse me. I have neither your brains, nor your beauty, nor your sanguine and impervious temperament. Our ways lie apart, and au fond I am chronically miserable and despairing, for I know that there is no hope for us, though this last year was Paradise compared to now. If you were still physically chained this time last year, you were mentally emancipated: *you wanted to go. This year you don't want to go.* In a letter you wrote me after we had been together, you said you despised yourself for shilly-shallying, that your life was neither one thing nor the other. Why don't you take your courage in both hands and settle *now* which it is to be? . . .

There is only one thing to be done: It is for you to ask the parties concerned *in front of me,* and if I see *for myself* that they are really adamant, I will renounce all hope of that forever. *But would they be,* if you were forever telling them – especially *him,* how much you wanted to go, how unhappy you were . . . instead of seldom mentioning it, and leading an, at all events, outwardly perfectly contented life, when I am away?

How hopeless and terrible it all is. . . .

Clingendaal, Holland
17 September 1920

. . . When I am here je reste les bas ballants à guetter les courriers.[1] My book is at a complete standstill and has been ever since I arrived – it is useless trying to get on with it; I can't. I go to seed quand sono lontana da te.[2] . . . Yesterday I trailed wearily over the picture gallery at Amsterdam, vainly trying to persuade myself that I liked pictures, when they really bore me to tears – except some modern ones. Today I trailed round a place called Gouda, where I tried – more successfully – to persuade myself that I liked stained glass. I really don't like sightseeing. . . . I find the only thing that keeps my mind off you is danger. . . .

This time last year, what a lot there was to look forward to. And now. . . .

Across my life only one word will be written: 'Waste' – Waste of love, waste of talent, waste of enterprise – what could be worse or more despairing. . . .

---

[1] I stand with dangling arms awaiting the post.   [2] when I am away from you.

242

Hotel Astoria,
Rue Royal,
Bruxelles
18 September 1920

Men colochin, I was so grateful to get a telegram from you this evening – I hate arriving at a place when there isn't a trace of you. . . .

Brussels brings back Paris too intolerably. At night it looks just the same. . . . The réverbères,[1] the dark narrow streets, the jostling, good-humoured crowd, the kiosks with their multicoloured 'affiches'.[2]

And my heart cried Julian! But there was no Julian, only a lank, chaffing girl looking like Alice in Wonderland. And my heart wept at the waste of it all, the wicked, stupid, waste. . . . We may be going to Bruges or we may be staying here until tomorrow. It is entirely a question of finances, because – another pang – I am in the usual penniless condition we both are in when I travel with you. In any case I expect to be at Antwerp on Tuesday. . . . I am so tired of these miserable little sophisticated countries. . . .

Hotel de Flandre,
Bruges, Belgium
19 September 1920

. . . Did you go to Bruges from Ostend? It doesn't interest me any more than any other Belgian or Dutch town; I dislike its diminutive houses, aggressive brass ware and complicated carillons.[3] The Memlings and Van Eycks are monotonously stilted (I hate primitives) and the Rubens and Brueghels make me sick. . . .

All today I have been regretting most bitterly that we didn't go to Greece. I must have been *mad* to put you off. I suppose my reluctance arose from some perverse and ridiculous distaste for an expedition I didn't plan *myself* – you know what an idiot I am when I have been *told* that I shall like something. . . . Why didn't you beat me into a reasonable frame of mind?

Tomorrow I shall probably go to Ostend for the day to where

---

[1] street lights.   [2] 'posters'.   [3] chimes.

you were only about ten days ago. I have only a few hundred francs to get me back to Holland, so I shan't be able to gamble – properly....

Ypres, Belgium
21 September 1920

... It seems to me, I am forever pursuing your ghost – yesterday, the Casino, today, Ypres. It is dreadful. This place, which is no more than a wooden hut of the most primitive description, rejoices in the name of 'The Splendid' – Anything so heartrending as the fictitious frivolity of Ypres with its matchwood 'Splendids', I have never seen.

It is so infinitely worse than I thought it would be: those acres and acres of barren land stuck with lamentable protests of blackened trees like broken antlers....

At Paschendaele I saw the most desolate sight I have ever seen in my life: a wizened and twisted little hunchback sitting on a pile of wire netting, alone in that vast and agony-haunted plain. It was such a terrible illustration of the God forsakenly grotesque, that I shuddered, and couldn't look.

'How are the mighty fallen' and how good was Osbert's poem:[1] the first thing that leapt to my mind was the last line: 'Too late came carelessly Serenity.' It couldn't be better said.

How forcibly it makes me realize the sufferings and privations of the wretched men who fought all through the war. Darling, I wish we had come here together.

I don't know what I shall do if I find no letter from you when I return to Bruges....

Grand Hotel,
Antwerp, Belgium
22 September 1920

Mon amour chéri, I began this very despondent letter last night meaning to post it on arriving here; then I thought I might perhaps

[1] Osbert Sitwell's poem 'There Fore Is the Name of It called Babel', in *Argonaut and Juggernaut* (1919).

get a nicer letter from you, and postponed sending it. There was another page which I wrote at 3 a.m. but it was so terrible ... that I destroyed it.

You say one horribly disquieting thing, namely how quickly people fade, how quickly you forget – and you add that you haven't forgotten me, but aren't you liable to any day, if you are so shallow? Are you so shallow, Mitya? It is my nightmare, your shallowness. And though you won't admit it, you haven't got the capacity for love that I have. ... When I woke up at 3 this morning, I was in a cold sweat because I had dreamt something dreadful about you – and I determined I would never come back to England, never, never. I was absolutely miserable and beside myself.

When I got up, my hands and limbs shook as though I had a fever. Mitya, you don't begin to know what it is! I know I live about four times as intensely as you do; when I am unhappy I am four times as unhappy, when I am jealous I am four times as jealous – you are in pastel what I am in oils.

You may have a Spanish grandmother, but you have 'le flegme brittanique'[1] for all that. O God, will you ever *live?* I remember and long for your beautiful stagnant face....

Antwerp is exactly like Paris, as far as I can see. This hotel is on a boulevard; it is incidentally extremely disreputable, and outside, under the awning sit rows and rows of little Alushkas, waiting to be 'treated'. There are masses of music halls and cinemas and theatres, and lovely clothes – It has Eve and Julian written all over it even larger than at Brussels. ... I am sick to death of this life of enforced chastity....

Grand Hotel,
Antwerp, Belgium
24 September 1920

... Ses baisers ensorceleurs, son étreinte rageuse, ses gestes impatients et cruels. Je revois ses yeux, assombris tout-à-coup, à la fois humbles et inquiétants; plus tard encore, sa bouche qui implore, ses yeux qui commandent. ... Et je lui dis: prends moi: je suis tienne.[2]

[1] British equanimity.　[2] Her bewitching kisses, her passionate embrace, her impatient and cruel movements. I see again her eyes, suddenly darkened, at once humble and restless; later again, her mouth which beseeches, her eyes which command. ... And I say to her: take me: I am yours.

I like Antwerp: it is neither Dutch nor Flemish; it is cosmopolitan. I like its bariolé,[1] strenuous crowd, dotted with an occasional Eastern face – generally Chinese. I went to the docks this morning and watched a great ship unloading; she had just arrived from the Congo –

It was swarming with negroes and there were great Cretes [sic] at work on board. With difficulty I restrained myself from booking a passage –

How infinitely I prefer the turmoil and unrest of Antwerp to the smugness and stagnation of Bruges! You don't know how the little prim houses annoyed me – the pleasant apathy of its population!

This morning I was thrilled, watching that Greek ship unload. She was alive, throbbing, exultant, safely returned from the perils of the high seas – but chafing to be off again! I felt her affinity. . . . I loved the jolly negroes who sweated and grinned, the competent business-like orders from the officers, the anxious-eyed, sweltering passengers – They were alive, those people.

And I went from there to the respected and invincible boredom of the cathedral, its dusty aisles, and pampered pictures.

My respect for antiquity is at its lowest ebb. I am emancipated from that snobbishness – slavery would be a truer word. If I can't be a peer of the future, I won't be a vassal of the past!

Clingendaal, Holland
25 September 1920

. . . Denys is looking very ill again, and has put on no weight. There is talk of his going somewhere more bracing – He and Ruby[2] (who has been here for the last week) are inseparable, and he hasn't spoken two words to me since I returned.

It's not settled about his going, but if he went, I should have to go too; it would be for a few days only. He hardly ever speaks to me, so Ruby will have lovely tales to relate on her return. . . . C'est comme si je n'y étais pas.[3]

R. asked men chinday if I was going to be divorced. Tu n'as pas besoin de t'en faire[4] about my going away, because it probably won't come off. . . .

---

[1] colourful.   [2] Not identified.   [3] It's as if I weren't there.   [4] You need not trouble.

Hotel de Flandre,
Bruges, Belgium
[September 1920]

I found two letters from you on my return from Ypres. . . . Both
rather upset me. . . .

Would you mind if I didn't come back? Tell me honestly, because
I want to know the truth. Also I beg of you not to write to me as
if I were a foolish and frivolous girl when I am really an unhappy
and tragic woman. . . .

s' Gravenhage, Holland
27 September 1920

. . . Darling, I want you to tell me more about your book. Have
you made it end 'well' or 'badly' – I like the title.[1] Please tell me
more about it.

Goaded to fury by your having finished yours, I have been trying
to write mine again, but it will be ages before it is finished, as I
write very slowly and anyway it is rotten.

I can't tell you how I miss my hotel life, and the bustle of catching
trains, and the joy of sitting outside a café sipping Malaga!

Elizabeth is a dear child; she was the only person I had to talk to
here. Now she's gone there is no one.

Denys – le diable au corps,[2] I think. He has flung his régime to
the winds, rides all the morning, plays tennis all the afternoon, and
bridge all the evening – Result: he is looking iller than when he
came. Everybody has remonstrated with him, to no purpose; ce
serait beaucoup mieux qu'il guérisse . . . s'il mène ce train de vie. . . .[3]

Do you realize that there are only ten more days after today –
and do you also realize that the 8th is a Friday? Vorrei naturalmente
andare – Sabato –[4] à toi d'y veiller[5] that we do – Il n'y pas de
prétexte qui tienne[6] – after nearly 5 weeks, Harold can just go
elsewhere for the weekend; d'autant plus,[7] I am going to stay

---

[1] *The Dragon in Shallow Waters.*   [2] the devil in the flesh.   [3] it would be
much better if he tries to get well . . . if he leads this kind of life. . . .   [4] I
will naturally go – Saturday.   [5] up to you to arrange.   [6] There's no valid
pretext.   [7] moreover.

with the Zanes (you know him: we met him at Monte Carlo) on Tuesday....

Otherwise men chinday would have insisted on my returning with her about 10 days later, and the Zanes provided me with an excellent excuse, which I naturally jumped at, so sois raisonnable, mon chéri,[1] und beschäftige dich sofort um samstag.[2]

This morning I had a hideous row with 'Not one' [Denys] because he had the impertinence to say *I* was a screw!! and ended up by calling me a b ... y fool, and telling me he hated me. This being the case, I took the opportunity of writing to remind him of a certain arrangement dopo il romandinado.[3] No doubt it will all be poured into the sympathetic ear of R. (Such a good person to confide in.) ...

s' Gravenhage, Holland
28 September 1920

... I have been writing all the morning, but have again got hideously hung up. I fear literature is not my vocation.

I was talking to men chinday about you all the morning. She was nice on the whole. She also says she thinks it would be best if Denys and I abided by the original arrangement despite romandinado, but I know she won't when it comes to the point....

Clingendaal, Holland
29 September 1920

Do I like your making political speeches? *No!*

I hate it. I think it is to be deplored. You, Mitya, my erstwhile gitana,[4] going and mixing yourself up with the 'landed classes' and education reform and such stuff! Pfui! It makes me both angry and sick. For Heaven's sake, leave that to other people. ... Besides, I know who to trace it to!

O God, it is time I came back and took you away from all such

---

[1] be reasonable, my darling. [2] and take care that you come on Saturday. [3] after the marriage (gypsy). [4] gypsy.

248

stuff. You know how I hate your sense of possession and all that is a part of it. My poor sweet, I know I am stupid and narrow-minded and rude, but oh! I *do* so hate social problems, and education, and feudalism, and possessions and laws and arguments! I realize that such things must be – but they mean less than nothing to me. . . . You whom I sometimes think should be wandering the high roads of the world with no roof over your head and nothing but a bundle to call your own, to go fraternizing with that galère,[1] the governing, legislative, disciplinarian galère – that is to me sheer anathema. It is treachery. . . .

Gypsy, come away!

Clingendaal, Holland
30 September 1920

Men tiliche, I am so thrilled about your book,[2] and longing to read it. I wonder if it will arrive in this afternoon's post. I know d'avance[3] that it is excellent, and you are a genius. I am trying hard to write my own, and spend hours of agony over it each day with little or no result. . . .

Clingendaal, Holland
2 October 1920

. . . This morning I went to see some pictures of the Barbizon School which I quite liked. There were one or two Mauves, and several Daubignys that really appealed to me. How infinitely I prefer the modern school of painting to the 'old masters'!

Now I come to think of it, I like almost everything modern best. . . .

A perfectly charming Russian dined here tonight. He is the only person I have liked since I've been away. He is a singer now, and before the war he was very rich – now he has barely enough to live on – He told me he sometimes went hungry to bed. . . . He told me stories about Chaliapin[4] that you would have delighted in – how

[1] literally gang (or crowd) of prisoners, here 'the establishment'.   [2] Probably a typewritten draft of *The Dragon in Shallow Waters*.   [3] in advance.
[4] The Russian opera singer, a sensation at Covent Garden in the role of Boris Godunov.

terribly attractive they are, those people, how gigantically simple. Darling, you mustn't ever allow me to get very intimate with a Russian – il y a trop de chances pour que nous nous entendions.[1] ... Not just this Russian in particular, but all Russians. They are so *un-smug*. This man was nearly killed in a duel. He then flung himself headlong into the War, and was very badly wounded again – He was then sent military attaché to the Hague, but hated being out of the Revolution and returned to Russia and his regiment. When he got back, he found that all his possessions had been confiscated and his house burnt; ultimately he escaped by the skin of his teeth in an absolutely destitute condition and is now condescending to make 200 a year in Amsterdam.

I have been struggling again with that miserable book this morning. My limitations are becoming more and more apparent. I can only feel things. I can't express them. I don't know English well enough, I can't analyse, I can't reason, and I am altogether too stupid. But my chief handicap is that I *cannot* argue! I can only see my side of the question; I am blind to the other person's. It is seriously much worse than I thought it would be. Parts of it are childish. It has only one quality: sincerity, and no high fallutin flights of fancy. I know that all I have just written is absolutely just and true. The question is, what is to be done with it? It isn't nearly finished, but even when it is, it won't be nearly good enough to be published. So my literary ambition has gone phut! with a vengeance –

I haven't the brain to make any sustained effort. If hard work and concentration can save it, it will be saved yet, but it's an intellect that's wanted to back it up, not a temperament. If you could only lend me yours for a month, I could do it. . . .

Darling, I hate to have to disillusion you, but I am NOT CLEVER. And if it wasn't for my book, I shouldn't care a hang – and with one exception, I hate 'clever' people. . . .

[October 1920]

Tonight the Russian came and played all evening. You know how fond I am of Massenet's 'Manon' – I've only heard it once in my life, and that was in Munich. I didn't have enough money for a

[1] There's too much risk that we'll get on very well.

stall so we went in the gallery. I love it also I'm afraid for rather soppy family reasons, because it is the one time that has always been very closely bound up with men chinday. C'est un peu sa vie, et un peu la mienne,[1] the story I mean, somehow. It brings back my little room so vividly, with snow on the window ledge. . . . In the street outside the droshkys (they always called them droshkys there) made no noise, the snow was so thick. . . .

[October 1920]

This household is solely concerned with Denys's health; men chinday fusses far more about him than she has ever about anyone in her life. There are plans afoot to send him to Davos, etc. etc. She means to go with him. My father won't speak to me at all; he leaves the room as soon as I enter it. In some extraordinary way he seems to think that I am responsible for D's complaint. . . .

I think perhaps you had better tell Harold that he is ill, (don't say what is the matter with him) otherwise it will all ricochet on to me for having exposed him to an unexpected interview. He had far better arrange it all beforehand, exactly when and where he is to see him, etc. and not suddenly assail him in the Marlborough Club. It will only mean further trouble for me if that happens.

Tonight by way of making himself worse he played bridge till 8 – from 4 till 8. I get all the blame. 'Oh, if you weren't so odious to him, he would come home; you were killing him.' I shall go mad. I am so *sick* of the whole business. . . .

Everything is tragic, grotesque, and horrible beyond any words. . . .

For pity's sake, let's have everything settled either one way or the other.

[1] It's a bit her life, and a bit mine. (This is a curious remark for Violet to make in reference to her mother. One music critic describes Manon as 'an eternal type: the embodiment of charm and beauty without moral sense. . . . She sees no earthly or heavenly reason why she should not leave her bewildered lover when she wants the luxuries he cannot buy, and then return to him and expect their love to begin again exactly where it left off . . .' – Stephen Williams, *Come to the Opera*.)

Clingendaal, Holland
[October 1920]

My life here is quite unbearable. Quite seriously, I think men chinday
is going mad. In the last three days, she has scarcely spoken to
anyone – save to insult them, and her behaviour to me has been
indescribable. They are unanimous in saying they have never seen
such an unprovoked exhibition of unkindness in their lives. She
walks – long solitary walks from early in the morning till late at
night, only coming in for meals. Her undisguised hatred of me is a
terrible thing. . . . I mind so . . . and she loves showing all the others
how much she hates me. She is diabolical in her intuitions. . . . She
knows exactly what to say to hurt me. . . . She watches my pain and
smiles cruelly . . . it must be fun for her. The other people here –
especially Lady de Trafford are horrified and nauseated.

But I have no one to turn to in my loneliness. Sonia despises me,
despises me for minding so much amongst other things. My uncle
is indifferent. As for Denys, our brief truce is at an end. I hardly
ever see him. Today I only saw him at luncheon, and I haven't been
near the hut since I arrived, save twice, to get a book, when he
wasn't in it. I haven't had ten minutes' conversation with him.

Today he looked iller than I have ever seen him look, and he
certainly looks thinner than when he was in England; there is
nothing of him.

You can imagine how miserable this house is –

Clingendaal, Holland
[October 1920]

. . . How vile of me to have written you a letter which made you
cry.

It is such a heavenly night – if only you were here; there is a
really lovely little Japanese garden in the middle of the wood. I
have just been out to look at it. It has a little paper house in the
middle, where it would be divine to sleep.

Darling, I am writing to you in a room by myself, after dinner.
All the others are playing bridge. I have never been so much alone
as I have been here. . . .

Clingendaal, Holland
14 October 1920

I love nothing in the world but you. Test after test is applied to my love, and test after test is vanquished triumphantly. For you I would commit any crime; for you I would sacrifice any other love. My love for you terrifies me.

I am writing this for myself, not for you. I am so hypersensitive where you're concerned that not the slightest inflexion of your voice, not the subtlest nuance of your letters, escapes me. I got one yesterday that was cold, almost impersonal. I worried myself sick over it.

My life is in your hands. If you deceived me in any vital issue, you could kill me. . . .

20 October 1920

. . . O darling, please keep on about chepescar.[1] I simply *implore* you − don't let him think you are not in earnest, or that it is temporarily in abeyance. If you do, all is lost. My tears no doubt seemed to you very pointless yesterday, but I was miserable at your going away and full of apprehension and forebodings. I never *pretend* to be unhappy. I have never done such a thing in my life. Yesterday I suddenly remembered something I had completely forgotten and which you can taunt Harold with until all is blue. What about the *6 MONTHS*??? What about the six months that were so 'grievously' granted in Paris??? You were to spend 6 with him and six with me. If he goes back on what he says about coming after you, you can remind him of what he said in Paris. . . .

How can I fortify you against the thaw which generally sets in when you have returned to the fold? How can I make you secure and invulnerable? Si tu t'attendris,[2] don't forget that you are not ruining us merely temporarily mais pour de la vie.[3] Darling, rassure moi, je t'en conjure. . . .[4]

[1] running off together (gypsy).   [2] if you soften.   [3] but for life.   [4] reassure me, I beseech you.

28 October 1920

... I have been writing like mad all the morning. I consulted Clemence Dane about the 'drunk scene' yesterday, and she thoroughly approves. She is wonderful in making one see that everything must have a *function* and that it is not permissible to introduce any episode, however picturesque, that has no influence, direct or indirect, on the main theme. She made me look for the 'function' of the drunk scene – I racked my brains and eventually struck it. But this will keep. It is fearfully difficult. I don't know how drunk people behave. I have never been in a room with anyone drunk. *Have you?* So considerable imagination has to be exercised. If only I could get the thing finished in a month. ...

If it were your book you could polish it off in an afternoon.

Yesterday I went to say goodbye to S. She was surrounded by becomingly saturnine Orientals, with limpid brown eyes and caressing voices. They looked at her with the devotion of dogs. ... They talked about places I had never heard of, with resonant guttural names, about camel escorts, and water supplies, and caravans. They talked sometimes in Arabic, sometimes in English.

She sat very white and upright in a circle of dark faces; she looked absurdly young, and absurdly feminine. London and civilization began to retreat. I crouched forgotten in a little corner. What a marvellous woman. Of course she is the most picturesque person I have ever known. How you would like her. Chin up! darling, she leaves on Monday, and I shan't see her again. ...

Royal Crescent Hotel,
Brighton
31 October 1920

Men tiliche, I have been writing hard all the morning. I'm afraid I cried a little over the only really 'sympathique' person in the book. My heart goes out to him. ... It depresses me to think of its probable reception at your hands.

You know I said yours was sensual. Mine isn't; it is suggestive, which is worse. Yours is like a person with no clothes on, and mine is like a person with ... one garment completely adequate as to length and breadth, but completely transparent. So all that is going to be done away with – ruthlessly scrapped. I *loathe* suggestive books.

I know there is going to be a row sometime today. Denys's idleness gets on my nerves and I could scream. In a book by Colette, I find the most wonderful description of what I feel. . . . It has never been so well expressed. How well she writes, that woman. Have you read 'Chéri' by her? It is one of the cleverest books that ever came my way.[1]

O Mitya, my book! If *only* I could be tolerably good? I should be so thankful. I write in a fever, almost blindly. . . . If it turns out to be rotten, it will really break my heart. I have so little confidence in myself. I am so stupid: how should my book be good? I write in the most abject humility. And you know what a fool I think myself.

One day you will wake up and realize how stupid I am. *Then* what will Calisto[2] do? It will be a terrible awakening. . . .

Royal Crescent Hotel,
Brighton
1 November 1920

Men colochin, I had nothing to do this morning, and it was pouring with rain, so I rang up your mother and asked her if I might go and see her. So I went – alone, of course – and she was very sweet. . . .

I am longing to see you – I haven't a notion when you are coming up tomorrow.

Darling, tiri chinday said one or two things which fairly astonished me. I'm afraid you haven't been quite truthful, mais je ne te gronderai pas.[3]

[1] Several years later Violet met and became a friend of Colette, a precious friendship which lasted for the rest of Colette's life. After Violet's death, Colette's husband, Maurice Goudeket, wrote: 'I have seen her and Colette together and one can hardly imagine two more different women – one of them earthy, always in direct contact with everything; the other ethereal, seeing everything as if through a prism. Yet they understood each other in certain deep-seated essentials of which they alone were conscious. . . .'
[2] See note 1, p. 142.   [3] but I won't scold you.

[November 1920]

... In consequence of your silence, my book waxes more vitriolic –
I have been writing all the morning. I wonder what on earth you
will think of it! It is everything a good book shouldn't be!
1. The style is jerky, careless, débauché, crude.
2. It is personal, biassed, prejudiced, passionate, intolerant,
   rhetorical, ranting, incoherent.
3. It is absolutely truthful, and indecently sincere.
   There! You couldn't have worse faults than that to cope with. . . .
Loge returns to London tomorrow. Perhaps Frank[1] will stay on
alone with me till Friday, but I haven't asked him yet. He is quite
nice and very brave – *not* clever – you wouldn't like him, but for
his really velvet voice.

Isn't is awful, the way I can't stand being alone? I am so ashamed
of it. If I were alone for a week, I'm sure I should end by cutting
my throat. . . .

53, Cumberland Mansions,[2]
Bryanston Square, W.1
3 November 1920

Mitya, I am waiting for you – I don't know if you are coming or
not. I have a faint wild hope that as you haven't let Pat know, you
may be coming all the same. . . .

I am hardly myself today; I have wanted you too much. My heart
is beating pitifully. I hardly dare breathe lest my breathing should
drown the sound I long for; the ringing of a bell.

I am sick with hope and anguish. If you come – ah, if you come!
All will be well. I say to myself: Mitya must have read between the
lines of my telegram – you must have read the plea that was behind
my words. You must have known – realized how I longed for
you. . . .

It is getting late, though; my knees and hands are shaking. . . . I
am going to telephone because I can't bear the suspense.

I won't go on writing till I have had an answer –
My God! You're not coming.

---

[1] Not identified.   [2] Pat Dansey's flat.

12 November 1920

Darling, you must not start being casual with me – like yesterday afternoon. One is not casual with one's julañi. One's julañi should be coaxed and bribed, and occasionally browbeaten, but *never* treated casually. . . . This is *not* a joke. . . . (Don't let me be better at my job than you are at yours?)

I never thanked you properly for my darling little cigarette holder. I'm afraid I like asking you for things, which is dreadful. . . .

No, darling I shall never take to drink; it is far too revolting – and has quite put me off my ci-devant[1] friend. . . .

I have behaved like a perfect swine to Denys this morning. Why am I so cruel? It always disgusts me in retrospect.

Men chinday says that tiri chinday has been talking again. I do wish she wouldn't, because I am the one to suffer, and I'm sure she and Ozzie [Dickinson] wouldn't if they knew – Can't you stop him, darling? You know how I hate having scenes with men chinday; besides it doesn't do anyone – including ourselves – any good. . . .

13 November 1920

. . . I met your friend, Reggie Cooper,[2] whom I took the most appalling dislike to – it has been maturing for some time, and now it is quite definite.

I will state my reasons. First, because he said: 'Have you heard the Nicolsons are buying the statue by Rosendick for £300. Harold wanted to get it as a surprise for Vita, but as he hasn't enough money, no doubt they will buy it together.' (It's silly to mention all this; you can regard it as cancelled. I don't want to be petty, or bother you in any way.)

O Mitya, why aren't you franker about things? You know you are always found out. I had no idea you were contemplating getting it together, that *he* knew all about it, that it was to be a 'surprise' for you, etc., etc.

It was rather a shock to me, I must confess, as I know you wouldn't dream of being so foolish as to spend £300 on a statue – knowing how hard up we both are – that you were never going to set eyes on.

---

[1] former.　　[2] Colonel Reginald A. Cooper, close friend of Harold Nicolson. He had served with Harold at the embassy in Turkey.

So it must mean that you have every intention of returning to your statue at the end of 6 weeks?

O darling, if you would *only* be frank. You would never find me unsympathetic. It doesn't make me angry, it only makes me sad, when you withold not all – but half your intentions.

As to chepescar,[1] you *know* that what I told your mother is true, namely that I would never force you to do anything against your will. You are perfectly free to do as you like, and as seems to you most advisable. Tout comprendre, c'est tout pardonner.[2]

As to my other reason for disliking your friend, it was a purely personal one. I can't bear his finicky appearance, and finicky, mincing way of talking. I did NOT enjoy my tea. I must keep out of that quarter as they make me see RED!

I longed for a real person to come into the room, a real man, or a real woman, absolutely without pose or pretension of any kind, say, '*Lingard*'.[3] He would have made them look silly. Someone BIG! You're big – you would have done. I don't mean physically. But someone built on broad and ventilated lines – pas même[4] – anything REAL. Anything that didn't calculate, and analyse, and explain. Anything that was a stupid, primitive impulse. A cowboy, a skipper, an engine driver – Anything drunk, or cursing, or loving, or hating, or quarrelling – O my God, Mitya, you don't know how *small* they are, those people, you can't or *won't* see through them.

With all their civilization and intellect, they are not worth one of the *farmers* on your father's estate – and you know I'm not wrapped up in farmers. Mais au moins j'y vois clair.[5] . . . I am always – being a liar – seeking passionately for truth, TRUTH in people, *real* people, not shams, and sycophants, and humbugs. I think truth, and breadth and fearlessness are the greatest things in life. I'm neither truthful, nor broad, nor fearless – only one thing can be said in my favour: au fond, I am always thrilled by the *right* things. I don't do them, alas! but I admire them. . . .

O Mitya, I sat yesterday and listened to those people, talking . . . talking . . . talking well, talking competently, even originally. . . . And I saw the room in exquisite taste (I thought the house lovely), its glittering tea things, harmonious proportions . . . and through it all, and far beyond it saw . . . sand . . . hundreds of miles of sand . . . sand, and a crude blue sky . . . and a tiny, solitary figure on a camel.

[1] escaping together.   [2] To understand all is to forgive all.   [3] See note 1, p. 237.   [4] not even.   [5] But at least I see this clearly. . . .

... I got nearer ... the figure dropped and sagged ... the face was haggard and ghastly, the hair white ... with sand ... only the eyes burnt, searched, hoped ... sublime, and parched and fearless, riding either to Immortality or your death, or both; you would have understood. ...

16 November 1920

... Why am I always told that things are much more difficult for you than for me? If you really mean to chepescar, what conceivable difference can it make if you go away for a weekend now or not? When (?) you chepescar it won't be remembered whether you went away for the weekend or not. I'm sorry to sound so brutal. ...

And you needn't put on a shocked face and say 'that's all you care about', because you know it isn't the case. But I *do* care about that. Je ne te le cache pas: je trouve que m'en suis assez privée: ce régime ne me convient pas à bon entendeur salut.[1]

Have you any idea how perfectly vile Brighton would be? It makes my blood boil to think that when you have been there with _____ there have been no recommendations – and that you belonged to *that* for five years – with *no interference*! O God what a nightmare!

When are you going to see about your PASSPORT???

16 November 1920

Yesterday I wrote you a frantic letter ... because I was exasperated by your lack of enthusiasm over my suggestion.

What I say still holds good. In the long run who will remember if you spent the weekend with me or not? More especially, as he has only just had three weeks' holiday. However if you won't, you won't and the real reason is this: you loathe and dread a scene with him, and nothing in your mind is worth that. I will cease to bother you about it, poor Mitya.

With you, it's just *talk* – but with me it is urgent, compelling, almost terrifying in its insistence. But we'll leave it at that. ...

[1] I don't hide it from you: I think I have been deprived enough of it: this diet isn't good for me, if the shoe fits, wear it.

Look here, we'd better have this out. I have got to this stage: a day here and a day there is of no real use to me. Mais ça me fait patienter.[1] I must have months.

O give me what I want. You say nothing about chepescar. You take no steps. . . .

O darling, what I could give you if you would let me! Je me ferai toute neuve pour toi. . . .[2]

16 November 1920

My love, my darling, I am writing to you with tears pouring down my face – Oh Mitya, my heart is simply breaking. . . . We hardly ever see each other now – we are parted and kept apart as we never were before I went to Holland. . . .

If you love me at all, you must see the truth of this, see the necessity to chepescar. . . . Faresti ciò che tì ho promesso quella benedetta notte che abbiamo soldato [?] insieme – un mesa fa – più due mesa fa.[3]

If things were different, et tu l'avais voulu, j'aurais humilié ma chair pour toi. J'aurais subi ce qui me semble l'horreur suprême – J'aurais eu un enfant pour te faire plaisir si tu l'avais exigé.[4] O God, don't think I would say such a thing lightly; if you had put it to me hypothetically a year ago I should have said NO without hesitation – but now je t'aime infiniment plus.[5] . . . I wouldn't say such terrible things if I didn't mean them; I am too superstitious, too reverent. I lay my whole heart and soul at your feet –

[1] But it keeps me waiting patiently.   [2] I will make myself over for you.
. . .   [3] I will do what I promised you that blessed night when we pledged our troth together – a month ago – more than two months ago.   [4] and if you desired it, I would have humiliated my flesh for you. I'd have submitted to what seems to me the supreme horror – I'd have had a child to give you pleasure, if you wished it.   [5] I love you infinitely more. . . .

6 o'clock in the morning

O my darling, I awoke trembling from a dreadful dream of you and your mother. I think you both laughed and mocked me, and since you had no further use for me – O God, it's too awful....

How I wish I was Harold Nicolson! He can be with you as much as he pleases. His words come back to me: 'I have always had everything I wanted' – and I am as the beggar at your gate....

21 November 1920

I am writing to you in the train, half choked by smoke and fog – one man is smoking a pipe and the other a cigar. I don't know which makes me sickest. ... Darling, the Pigeon[1] has made a discovery! It adores Dotty Wellesley's[2] poems. It went and bought them all by itself. [A pencil drawing of a pigeon turning the pages of a book]. I think they're so good! They are so *naughty*. That's what I like about them – so un-smug. I loved the one about Atlantis and I liked the war ones. If I knew nothing about her, I should say they were the poems of an unhappy, captivating woman....

My sweet, I continue my letter. Poor E.[3] has just returned from hunting, in an awful state. It appears that Denys lamed his first horse, and killed the second, I think by making them jump impossible obstacles, though they didn't actually say so. He himself was not hurt.

It makes me sick to think of animals, especially horses, suffering. I know I shall have a row with him when he comes in.

I can't begin to tell you how I have missed you all day....

24 November 1920

... Men tiliche, I have had an amusing day. I was made love to in Spanish after lunch, in Italian after tea, and shall be made love to in American after dinner.

---

[1] Violet herself.   [2] Lady Dorothy Wellesley, wife of Lord Gerald Wellesley, an intimate friend of Vita. (Violet and Lord Gerald had been engaged in 1913.)   [3] Not identified.

I had tea at the Carlton and pretended to myself it was the Hotel de Paris. I can never hope to describe to you the magic that hotels and cafés have for me! I think to sit in a very crowded, smoky café on a boulevard, with a tzigane[1] orchestra playing, say, 'Le plus joli rêve'.[2] ... in its most debauché manner, to speculate as to what love affairs with almost everyone in the café would be like, is the most delectable occupation in the world.... That is one of my conceptions of Bliss. Another is to ride with a gale of wind blowing through one's hair – I love that.

A third is to go to a play with Julian, and wander home through deserted streets, knowing that....

[Telegram]
27 November 1920

HAVE FINISHED MY BOOK

29 November 1920

'Heritage' was like a flute, 'Challenge' was like a lyre, the 'Dragon in Shallow Waters' is like an organ, and 'Battledore and Shuttlecock'[3] is like – a concertina! Worse – it has a concertina-ish atmosphere – it suggests slums and banana skins and guttersnipes. This is just to prepare you for what it's like. (I have got a nice lot of 'nature notes' for you to do.)

O Mitya, won't it be awful if you turn it down – I shall never hold up my head again. Please be kind to it, and descend from Olympus where I have no place.

My wretched book! It has got to be re-inforced and re-inforced – at present it trembles on long, weak, lanky legs, like a foal – and it's just as wistful! We must really work at it this week – how divine it will be.

HAI SCRITTO?[4] Si crede qui ch'io vada a casa tua, ma è miglio cosi.[5]

---

[1] gypsy.   [2] 'The most lovely dream'.   [3] The title of Violet's novel.
[4] HAVE YOU WRITTEN?   [5] It's believed that I'm going to your house, but it's better that way.

Sunday 2.30 I have just rung you up, but they say they can get no answer – where have you gone?

You've got to give my book – Bovril,[1] you know. It wants bovrilling. We've got to pull it through. . . .

I am going to Clemence Dane's at 4. She's asked me to bring the book, but I flatly refused. . . .

Have just rung up Kemptown. My precious, I've only just heard about your mother.[2] I am so sorry, but hope it is not serious.

29 November 1920

My own darling sweet, I am so dreadfully distressed about your mother. I know how you will worry about her, and how nervous you are. I do hope she will be better tomorrow. I have said a little prayer that she may be. I hate to think of her being in pain. I fervently hope, darling, that she will be better enough for you to go away on Wednesday, but I shall quite understand that you can't leave her if she isn't. . . .

In the train
4 December 1920

. . . I am sorry I was silly about my book; it's only because I have no confidence and feel so forlorn about it. It is so bad compared to yours – and I have tried so hard that it shouldn't be.

Please, *please,* do the bits I asked you to do, about the bonfire and the 'gratitude' – the latter is so very important. I will try to get more of it into shape by Monday to show you. I am so shy about its inferiority: please understand, darling; and what makes me even shyer is that yours are so good.

O Mitya, please go on loving me in spite of my faults. . . . All my beastliness – or nearly all of it – is superficial and the outcome of one thing: au fond, I am full of humility and distress. There is nothing but love in my heart for you.

. . . Above all, I must have patience and confidence – confidence in you and your resolution, for which I bless you every hour of

---

[1] beef tea.   [2] Lady Sackville was ill.

the day. I humbly ask your forgiveness for all jealousy, temper, impatience, intolerance, narrow-mindedness, and lack of charity I have shown. I only blame you for one thing: that is for neither beating me nor hurling a jug of cold water at my head.

[December 1920]

You were so radiantly, so primitively beautiful, so free, so omnipotent, Dionysius, any woman would have willingly offered her life and her soul to satisfy the most fugitive of your caprices! . . .

I had a conversation of some hours with M.de M.[1] who is a great friend of the Grand Duke Dmitri![2] – another piece of fate that fits accurately into the puzzle! Mitya, I know where I would live – sartute, minus Bolsheviki, minus wars, minus revolutions, *plus* your liberty and mine – Russia, indubitably! Mitya, he says that Russians are the only people who know how to live, who understand love in its manifold manifestations – who sacrifice *everything,* wives, husbands, homes, and children, unswervingly, relentlessly to the caprice of the moment! Divorce, he says, is made excessively easy, – is consequently excessively frequent –

The Past Master in the art of living is the Grand Duke Dmitri! I feel there's nothing I don't know about him. L. said he was the most magnificent young man he knows – of marvellous physical beauty, and unparalleled audacity! – He is 26 and again I quote M. de L. 'No woman has ever been able to resist him' – He has liaisons in every part of Russia, but such is his charm that his liaisons forgive him when he deserts each in turn for someone new! He never flirts; each time he is madly in love, they all end fatally on the poor victim in an incredibly short space of time. She is just 'taken off' somewhere – and I suppose Dmitri does the village idiot stunt at the booking office! He is a marvellous horseman, boxer, fencer. His palace is beautiful, but almost too flamboyant and barbaric – He loves jewels, and is recklessly extravagant. He has, it appears, wonderful taste and each of his 'chères amies' would easily eclipse Mrs Astor as far as jewels and clothes are concerned –

[1] Not identified.   [2] Grand Duke Dmitri Pavlovich (1891–1942), son of the younger brother of Tsar Alexander II. He had been obliged to leave Russia after his participation in the assassination of Rasputin and was a friend of Denys Trefusis, who was a passionate Russophile and had lived in Russia before the Revolution.

What a picture! I might ask M. de L. if his intimes call him Mitya! – Dmitri, Dionysius! But Dionysius wins –

Who cares for the snug, the domestic, the complacent of this world? You know as well as I do that they *don't count*! . . .

Mitya, it *can't* be done – one day, and one day soon, you will have to choose . . . the mistake you make is thinking you can *have your cake and eat it*.

Dionysius and 'Mar'[1] – how pitiful, how absurd – what a target for Dionysius! . . .

[December 1920]

O Mitya, what is the use of disguising it? What is the use of feigning indifference? What is the use and the sense of this criminal separation? It is such wanton waste, such a deliberate, monstrous suicide. What is the good of my writing to you? . . .

I know it is useless to remonstrate with you, only everything is so dreadful, and there is so very little time left – O mercy, what a fool you are – but perhaps you don't care. . . .

Anyhow, I asked Loge the other day if he would be surprised if I ever committed suicide and he said: 'No, not in the least. I think it's a very natural thing to do if one is very unhappy. As you know I set no value on human life. If one is very wretched, and making everyone else wretched, it is the most decent thing one can do.'

. . . O Mitya, what are you making of four lives? Is it very satisfactory? 'And have you found the best for you, the rest for you?' . . . Are you happy? Is Harold happy? Am I happy? Is Loge happy? Instead of four utterly miserable people, you could have two flawlessly happy ones; the other two would be wretched for the time being, but, believe me, they would eventually get over it, and find two worthier objects of their affection.

21 December 1920

. . . You must never never have cause again to say what you said to me yesterday. I would sooner become a maternity nurse than lose one particle of your love. I will become whatever you want me to

[1] Harold's nickname for Vita which Violet is mocking.

become, only you must never say that again. I have been so straight and true to you, and it *doesn't* come naturally to me.

I may be a beast to other people – but O! I *do* love you – I will devote my life to proving it to you. You shall see. I will become considerate, conscientious, hardworking, thrifty, a good needle-woman and washerwoman and cook, and knife and boot cleaner. ... I am determined that you shall admire and love my character as well – You have no idea how it terrifies me when I think you *only want* me in one way – because I know it is the most precarious of all foundations. When you said that thing to me last night, I felt as though a piece of ice were being slipped into me.

O Mitya, how terribly vulnerable one is when one loves....

Are you going to talk to your mother? ... I cling ferociously to my conception of what a Julian should be: whole-hearted, reckless, *faithful,* fierce, *truthful,* responsive, jealous, generous. Do I fall very short?

I am so pathetically full of misgivings. I don't satisfy you as a companion. I am not clever enough. ... I am not intellectually stimulating. My limitations are coming so forcibly before me – acariâtre,[1] spiteful, narrow-minded, fanatical, crazy, stupid (no small talk in current events, etc.). O Mitya, I can't go on – the fact remains, je t'adore, tu es toute ma vie.[2]

I wish you were going to be with me for Xmas much as I hate it. Xmas is all part of the other life, part of the life that keeps you from me. You should be spending Xmas eating a stolen chicken on a treacherous fire of sticks, your eyes and hair full of the acrid smoke, and the flames glinting on the gold of your earrings....

North Mymms Park,
Hatfield
26 December 1920

Mitya, I can never thank you enough for the lovely fur. As you know, I have never had one and have really longed for one for ages. Your fur was my only parcel, as I predicted. It was infinitely sweet of you to give me such a lovely present....

It is so dreadful, Pat having gone. I really feel absolutely alone,

[1] quarrelsome.   [2] I adore you, you are my whole life.

severed from everyone I care for. Yesterday I cried so, I could hardly see. . . .

North Mymms Park,
Hatfield
27 December 1920

I got two short letters from you yesterday, for which I was extremely grateful. I have never been so bereft, so utterly forlorn and friend-less – I am so unhappy, darling. Won't you help me? I have literally no one left but you.

Men chinday is gone, Pat is gone, there is no one left who cares whether I am unhappy or not. . . .

31 December 1920

. . . You do not know what the human heart can suffer. You were so stiff on the telephone. Think how much happier your life is than mine. Do try to love me. This time last year it wasn't necessary for me to say this. It breaks my heart to have to say it now.

3 January 1921

. . . I hated so leaving you last night. It seemed so ironical and disgusting that you should be coming back to the station to fetch him [Harold]. I had a haut-le-coeur[1] when I thought of it – surtout dopo quello ch'era successo.[2]

Remember, je compte sur toi[3] to fix things up before I see you. . . .

---

[1] sick feeling. [2] especially after what had transpired. [3] I count on you.

8 January 1921

Tu m'as fait infiniment de la peine hier. Toi qui détestes faire de la peine aux gens. Tu m'an as fait à moi.[1] And I didn't deserve it. O Mitya, I wish you hadn't. I love you just as foolishly and insanely as ever – only a little differently with the ideal, exalted, spiritual side sadly attenuated. I *did* trust you so. That's what hurts. It will prey on my mind terribly, feeling I *can't* trust you. ... Mitya, we were everything to one another. I can't bear that we should be less – it is so dreadful, unfaithfulness. If we are unfaithful, it is the first step towards dissolution, and it leads to *rottenness*.

It would begin in small ways, then spread and spread till it corrupted everything; then indeed love would be but lust, lust undiscriminating, as ready to take you for a few hours' pleasure as anyone else – love degraded, obscene where it had once been whole-hearted and beautiful.

I would sooner leave you a million times than that it should come to this. ...

[January 1921]

Now listen: Either I go to *Paris* Saturday, Sunday, or Monday – not later because I shan't be well, or else I stay on for another week until I am well again, and go then. If you will find it equally easy to go a week from Wednesday next, 21st, say so, darling, and couldn't you join me in Paris, and we would proceed to Carcassone to-gether, which would be so much nicer?

Denys doesn't care a damn whether we start to-gether or not, as gossip leaves him cold. ... Of course we would have to go south by day, and by a _____. So we should be quite certain of meeting no one if that is what tiri chinday minds about. ...

[1] You hurt me badly yesterday. You who detest hurting others. You have hurt me.

268

March to November 1921

Back in England in March 1921, Violet's situation was now desperate. Denys refused to have anything to do with her and Alice Keppel was unrelenting in her abuse. In the spring Violet accompanied her mother to Florence and Rome, and was forbidden to correspond with Vita. Her letters to Pat Dansey, to be passed on to Vita, are as pathetic as Pat Dansey's betrayal was cruel. Violet's desolation increased when she realized that Vita had stopped writing to her. In July she went back to Holland and pleaded with Pat to join her, but was refused. By November 1921, the letters ceased altogether.

9 March 1921

Men colochin, I am sitting here waiting for my uncle. I simply cannot tell you how wretched I am and how utterly forlorn. I know he will be beastly to me. M'lle says I can hope for no mercy. She has got to act as a sort of gaoler to me to prevent my seeing *anyone*.

They do not wish me to see a soul and have told her she has got to live in the house. I now feel I would sooner be by myself as she nags and shrieks at me without ceasing. I think what she secretly means to do is to come and live with me for good. I would sooner have died than have her.

Another letter from men chinday that simply breaks my heart. There isn't much doubt as to what would become of me if you let me down. How lucky you are to be with somebody who cares for you and is anxious to spare you and shelter you as much as possible.

M'lle says, which I'm *sure is untrue*, that Harold told everyone that Denys has deserted me. Anyhow I am past caring. I am utterly broken and defenceless, but I *do* trust and believe in your resolution – if I didn't – O God. . . .

They are (my family) evidently determined that I shall pay to the uttermost farthing. They have taken an inventory of all my things, preparatory to letting the house, with them. Needless to say, I shan't be consulted.

Why did I ever come back. It's going to kill me. Melle said: 'The Cubitts[1] are furious!' As though they had to bear the brunt.

You are the only thing that stands between me and dissolution.

[1921]

... My silly, inconsequent, banal little room looks sillier and emptier than ever! This room has only one merit: It has perhaps one or two clues to the character of its occupants, but nothing vital: *List of things to be taken away*
> The porphyry man
> My Tanagra Head of a Greek Matron
> The little alabaster bust of the Vestal Virgin
> The Persian bowl
> The Egyptian beads
> The Persian Fish
> The Canton Enamel cups
> The Persian Picture
> Two Pictures of Mitya
> AND THAT'S ALL

It will be as though I had never lived here, so little has my personality impressed itself upon this house....

12 March 1921

Darling, I am writing to you in the train on my way back from Devonshire. I might have spared myself the trouble, for when I got within 1 1/2 miles of his house,[2] his mother, with a red lantern, suddenly sprang up from nowhere, barring the road. She said she had been *warned of my arrival*, and that she knew the exact hour etc.

A horrible suspicion shot through my mind, namely, that you had wired anonymously, which would have been terribly underhand. And she told the chauffeur to drive me straight back to where we came from, adding that he [Denys] was 'adamantine'. It was

[1] The family of Sonia Keppel's husband.   [2] The Trefusis's, where Denys was staying.

most unpleasant. We had motored 12 miles and it was past 9, and a terrible road across Dartmoor. I can't believe, darling, that you would have let me go all that way in order to play such a low trick on me, and only want your reassurance.... It was too horribly humiliating a scene in front of a tittering chauffeur. I shall never forget it.

... You mayn't believe it, but I have a certain degree of pride and last night's scene has wounded it horribly.

O God, and this time last week we were at Carcassonne....

Darling, please destroy all my letters, in case they were 'got hold of'. I have promised that all letters should be destroyed, and you must please do the same.

Yesterday I hit M'lle because she goaded me too far. She never ceases, even in the train. I know I shall kill her.

14 March 1921

The servants told me last night that this house was watched and that I was probably being shadowed.... I am watched not only from without but from within. They are sending me stark staring mad.... Melle never leaves me for one instant. She knows exactly when I go out, when I come in; in fact she nearly always goes out and comes in with me – when I write a letter, when I go upstairs. I might be a criminal; it's too awful when one is dreadfully unhappy to be perpetually in the society of a spiteful, ignorant, stupid woman who shrieks abuse at one from morning till night.

If my uncle can't come here, she will stay as long as I do. I can't have five unspied on minutes even in my own house. They have reverted to treating me as if I were a child.... Your letter of yesterday made me feel that even *you* might turn against me....

17 March 1921

I was so upset by what the lawyer told me that I nearly fainted in the taxi coming home; I had to put my head between my knees. It was such an awful shock, can you wonder I spoke to you as I did? ... *Je t'aimerai quoi-que tu fasses, toujours, toujours, toujours. Seulement, ça me dégoûte, tu comprends,*[1] when you (apparently) say that you

[1] *I will love you whatever you do, always, always, always.* However, this disgusts me, you understand.

will give me up when I'm down, knowing that it is indirectly owing to you that I am brought so low.... I *have* been true to you in all essentials, though panic and misery may have made me tell lies at the moment. I simply don't know how to envisage life without you.... Je n'ai rien qui m'y rattache; quoique tu penses de moi je t'aime et t'ai aimée de tout mon coeur, de tout mon âme, et tu *sais* que c'est vrai. Si nous nous séparons, ce sera la fin de toutes choses, le néant absolu....[1]

18 March 1921

I can no longer put my despair and unhappiness into words ... My heart broke when I realized there was nothing left to hope for. It is so awful that my mind is quite glazed and petrified.

I wander about as though I were in a trance ... I wonder, quite dispassionately, what I shall do when I realize quite, quite irrevocably – because I'm only beginning to realize – that it is finished, short of your doing something you're not prepared to do, something I should never dream of asking you. I don't answer for what I shall do then.

Yesterday they told me you were so 'sensible' and that you had said I was always ringing up and sending notes when all you asked was to be left alone; also that even if there was no 'procès'[2] you thought it would be much better to give me up....

Don't worry about my doing imprudent things. I'll be as quiet as a mouse with a hole in its heart through which its life ebbs quite quietly. (I wonder how long I shall stand it?) I'm afraid that Denys is determined on a 'procès' –

A quite disinterested third person who knows us both fairly well, saw him [Denys] yesterday, by appointment, and far from what Harold alleges that he told him – he told this woman that it was exclusively on your account that he left me....

He also said that he disliked me and that nothing would induce him ever to set eyes on me again. He added that he had us all absolutely in his power and that, if he wanted to, he could ruin all our lives for ever and ever –

He tells all these details to anyone who chooses to listen to them

[1] I have nothing that attaches me to life; whatever you may think of me, I love you and have loved you with all my heart, with all my soul, and you *know* this is true. If we separate, that will be the end of everything, the absolute ... emptyness.
[2] trial.

apparently. Whatever people don't know, he tells them ... which will of course finish me. I don't care a damn what he does to me, but I do care quite dreadfully what he does to her [Alice Keppel] and I feel he won't spare her. It is useless my writing to ask him to, because he said yesterday to this woman that he would not read any further communication from me!

My poor mother is coming straight through from the Riviera. I don't know that she has even got a sleeper. She is going to stay here. I would far rather she hadn't come, as at least she would have been spared a little by being abroad.

It will break her heart. How I wish I had been frank with her from the first. I expect she will want to sell the house and all my things. Of course I shall let her, if she wants to sell them....

18 March 1921

Please destroy
These intolerable days of solitude and misery!

The awful monotony of meal after meal alone with M'lle! The horror of never having anyone intelligent or sympathetic to talk to. How lucky you are! How I envy you!

This morning I said: 'Why don't you go away too?' and you answered blandly, 'Why should I?'

Why should you indeed: you have all you want – a lovely place to live in, love, affection, understanding. How can I help feeling bitter?

Suppose there were no procès: then you would be intrinsically intact: Long Barn, Harold, the children, your books, your animals, all your possessions.

And what should I have?
NOTHING.

No one who loves me and lives with me, no possessions, no reputation, no hope, nothing.

I ache with the sense of the appalling unfairness. What a triumph and what a proof, that in spite of it all, I still manage to love you above everything!

[March 1921]

What a pity you are such a fool, Mitya. I was overjoyed at hearing your voice, and all I get from you is flippancy and indifference. I *hated* you for it. *Beware*, Mitya, beware of laughing at my love. By Heaven, you will regret it if you do. Who are you that you should presume to do such a thing? If I can love, I can also hate, and I could hate you more than anyone in the world. You have had what dozens of people (and I am not exaggerating when I say dozens) have grovelled and gone down on their knees for. I have loved you. I have given you everything. I have withheld nothing and you seem to think I am here at your beck and call, to come if you raise a finger, or to stay away as long as it is your pleasure.

Damn you, I say. Curse your insolence. I am not your slave. How dare you trifle with my most sacred sentiments!

26 March 1921

... I am dazed with grief. ... I don't know what is to happen to me. I can never speak to anyone. Men chinday said yesterday she did not want me to see Pat, as I might talk to her about you.

I am so tortured that my own pain is almost indecent to me; it is like having a dreadful, gaping wound unbandaged. She will not consent to my writing to you. I said I could not promise that. She said, if I wrote, would I show her the letter. I said yes, but I cannot show this one. You've no idea what I suffer. ...

I pray frenziedly to God to help me – as I feel the waters mounting higher and higher. ...

Men chinday told me yesterday that Harold had said he would leave you if you ever saw me again.

You have chosen, my darling; you had to choose between me and your family, and you have chosen them. Of course you are quite right. I do not blame you. If, one day soon, I seek for what escape I can find, you must not blame me. ...

29 March 1921

Once upon a time, there were two thieves. One day one was caught and put in prison; the other escaped and prospered.

The one who was in prison cried through the bars to the one who was free: 'The injustice of this is eating into my soul – for pity's sake commit some theft and then perchance you will be caught and allowed to share my cell, for you are as guilty as I am.' 'Not so,' said his former accomplice, 'I was not more prudent than you. It so happened that they caught you and that I escaped. Be patient and long-suffering, and at the end of several years they will set you free.' 'But how do I know that at the end of that time, I may still reckon on your friendship?' wailed the other thief. But the free one waved to his friend vaguely, and replied: 'Who knows?'

The one in chains protested: 'But it is monstrous! We have both committed the same offence; *you* return to a loving and respectable family who welcome you as the Prodigal Son, you live amongst tolerant friends who do not disown you, you are free to exercise all your faculties, free to divert yourself, free to wander, free to love, free to exercise your youth, your temperament – whereas I languish here in prison, despised and rejected of men, deprived of liberty, deprived of love, obliged to stifle my youth and my temperament, knowing that the slightest lapse, the most trivial rebellion will bring the universe about my ears. Watched, hunted, spied upon – it is too much. I would sooner strangle myself!'

The other held up his shocked hands: 'How can you say such things! You have a nice, kind jailor, a clergyman who visits you once a week and tries to reform your deplorable character, and from your little window you can watch other people being happy – What more can you want? You are ungrateful!'

And he went away pained, and a trifle disgusted.

S'il n'y avait que cela![1] But that, bad as it is, is not the worst; the worst is that I love you wholly, insanely, hopelessly. And it's that that is killing me.... If only you would map out some sort of existence for me, with some sort of reward at the end – something to pin my hope to. *One cannot live without hope.*

You said: 'None for the present' – but is there any in the future? That's what I want to know.... I would far far sooner you told me the truth outright, than that you subjected me to this lingering torture. It is crueller far, than any truth could be. Are you prepared

[1] If it had only been that!

to give me up altogether? That is what I must, what I have every right to know, what I *insist* on knowing.
Please burn this letter.

My dear Vita,

I have thought a great deal since seeing you. My dear, don't think I mean to be unkind or that I don't sympathize – but, I am *sure* the best way of helping Violet is to make a *complete* break – no writing, no communication with her. I am sure that as long as you both keep in touch, Violet will always have some hopes that one day in the near future you will go off with her. The thing *must* end for both your families' sake and surely it would be far wiser and better for you both not to prolong the misery? I think Violet stands a far better chance of forgetting if you make a firm stand for a *complete* break. Vita, give Violet no promises and exact none from her. It may seem cruel for the moment but it will be true kindness eventually.

I won't try to bias Violet either way – but, Vita dear, do think it over – do be warned by someone who is fond of you both and has no ideas beyond helping you both.

I have got second-sight, Vita, if I choose to use it and I could astonish you if I told you all I know. I am so fearful for the future if you are not wise.

Bless you,
Yours Pat

My precious Misskins, This is a pestilential place, smug little hills dotted over with villas, and museums and churches that have been so much photographed and written about that one is fed up to the eyes with them long before one sets foot inside. It amuses me to think I have been brought here to be 'reformed' – The Italian Society here is the most corrupt I have ever run across, except perhaps Rome. They are mercenary, vicious, lewd, stupid. If one lived here long enough, I tremble to think what one would become. So much for the *Italian* set. The *foreign* set – Russian, Greek, French, American, English – is worse. The only Englishmen who reside here are men of a certain description, nearly all clever. The cosmopolitan set is clever, there's no doubt about it, diabolically, nauseatingly clever. O Pat, it's so awful for me to have lost *everything*, never to be with a decent person. Men chinday doesn't realize this because she doesn't speak Italian. But her temper is such at present, that I would rather be with those sort of people than with her. Then, not hearing a word from ____ [Vita]. Am I already forgotten? I would be content with *messages*. But *nothing*! ... It's a fortnight tomorrow since I heard. If I am forgotten, I had better try and become like the people I have all around me. In my present appalling loneliness and unhappiness the only thing that keeps me straight is hoping that I am cared for. Do please show this letter. O Misskins, I care so dreadfully, it gets worse and worse. You see, I've got nothing to fill my life, even in a small degree. Writing simply does not count. All I wish for is a message. However paradoxical this may sound in a way, it is true: love is *clean*, wherever you find it, and I may have love no longer. O Misskins, I think you are the only person who loves me in the world. God bless you for it. But I am not with you. It seems so odd to have lost V. and D., my freedom, my home, my money, all at one fell swoop. I begin to think the sort of reckless, exorbitant love I gave is the one unjustifiable crime in this world. One should love prudently, reasonably, comfortably; not dash one's glove in the face of the world. O Misskins, what should I do without your letters? I *am* so grateful for them.

Mama made me cry and cry last night. She said if she had been me she would have killed herself long ago! Will you tell [Vita] he can telegraph anything he likes in Italian, if he signs himself Scovello.

[A fragment of Violet's novel sent presumably to Pat Dansey to be passed on to Vita]
2 May 1921

Con wrote her long letters from all over the world that he never posted. He wrote them because he *had* to, as spasmodic, desperate outlets for his misery.

He was never separated from her; she accompanied him everywhere: she was in the contour of clouds, the sough of bells, the rush of rivers; most of all was she near him in the train. He would almost catch himself saying: 'Look, darling, look, doesn't that remind you of –' and for this reason, he would have liked to be always in the train, never stopping more than a night in any place. Sometimes he would lean back and close his eyes, always imagining that she was bending over him. He was so unhappy that he made a compact with unhappiness: 'Very well, I will allow you to have dominion over me for a fixed length of time; I will submit to your despotism, *but* at the end of that time I will gather together all my strength that will have lain fallow for months, and I will wrench myself free at any cost. Provided she loves me still I will wait and suffer in crouching patience, but at the end of that time I mean to fight for my life, for the right to happiness that is every human being's inheritance. We all entitled to some measure of happiness on earth, and I mean to make a bid for it or die in the effort.' At which the misery that ruled him, taunted and furious, would drive its nails into his flesh and goad him with fresh insults and fresh tortures – not knowing that *so long as she loved him* it could not kill him, could not subdue the fierce faith that lit him and secretly mocked his tormentors. So long as she loved him intrinsically he was invulnerable.

He prayed to be reassured from time to time; he prayed for his life really, for that meant his life. With indifferent eyes he wandered from place to place, impervious to beauty, to ugliness, to cold, to warmth, to all the things that usually meant so much to him.

He was detached, isolated, grimly, rawly aloof.

The slave who, beneath blows and ill-treatment, secretly fashions the key to his escape.

[Pat Dansey to Vita]
53, Cumberland Mansions, Bryanston Square, W.1.
12 May 1921

My dear Vita,

I received the enclosed [Violet's letter to Pat] this morning. It has been following me round the country. That is the reason it is so late in arriving. Did I send you a letter in which there was some mention of a coloured photograph? It – the photograph – has just turned up.

I wrote on Tuesday when I got back here and sent the message you gave me. It is always difficult to write because I should imagine all letters are subject to being opened.

Yours ever,

Pat

Just having finished this note to you, a second note has arrived which I send. If you happen to be in London and have a spare second, do come and see me. She [Violet] goes to Rome from 17th to 20th. She noted that on the back of the envelope.

[Violet's letter to Pat Dansey]
My own darling Misskins, I do hope you are back from Scotland by now.... I wonder if you have got the elaborate photograph and photograph apparatus I sent you by Rebecca West,[1] because it really is as though you were face to face with the person. She will know what to do with it. I wish so that Rebecca W. hadn't gone; she was the only person worth speaking to in Florence, and one of the most human, genuine people I have ever come across – brilliantly clever, with the only true conception of cleverness – namely, that it is of such secondary importance, and that one's emotions matter so

---

[1] Rebecca West (1893–1983); prolific author and a leading personality of the British literary scene; she had become prominent in the 1910s through her writings for radical feminist and socialist periodicals. Her friendship with Violet from the early 1920s lasted until Violet's death. In her review of *Portrait of a Marriage* (*Sunday Telegraph* 28 October 1973), she wrote that Violet 'was enormously gifted; she was a superb linguist, she had real literary talent, far more than Vita, and artistic talent also.... She was written down by many as amoral, but she achieved one real moral triumph. She had been reared in a society whose money, privilege and power had gone to its head, and she had been trained to be a snob. Yet she realized that anybody who painted a good picture or wrote a good book or put in a good day's work at the Pasteur Institute was superior to herself. Apparently arrogant, and apt to find out at any moment that she was descended from Louis XI by yet another line, she was in reality humble ...'

infinitely more. She was very kind to me, because she knew I was desperately unhappy, though of course, I couldn't tell her why. Since I've been away – 3 weeks tomorrow – I have only had one rather smug message from Julian with whom I have managed to correspond fairly frequently. There is no earthly reason now why he shouldn't write Post Restante *here* and at Rome. Please tell him so; also he might send me parts of his book. There are heaps of ways in which he might keep in touch with me. I am simply starving for a letter from him. He has never sent me his book of the newspaper cuttings or anything. He knows perfectly well why I have been exiled to this pestilential place, and that I endure everything patiently provided I feel he cares for me. The message he sent me might have been from anyone. What is he made of? Doesn't he realize how unhappy I am, how I miss him, how wretched I am in this beastly place? If he wrote occasionally P.R. and sent me parts of his book as he did before, I should not feel so utterly deserted, and cut off from him. O Misskins, do show or send him this letter. Men chinday is as difficult as ever. I can do nothing with her.

Last week I was in bed two days with fever. I am getting terribly thin – don't go by the photograph; it was done two days after I got here! And I can hardly drag myself about. I do hope I'm not going to be really ill here. Surely Julian can't have forgotten me so soon. I worry myself sick about him. It is awful. Please, please see him. I am on the verge of bankruptcy, but that's a detail. It has now transpired that I have been horribly swindled by the cook and Osborne[1] – So I haven't a penny in the world! O Misskins I feel really like Job – one thing after another – but I could put up with everything bravely, if *only* I could hear –

[Pan Dansey to Vita]
53, Cumberland Mansions, Bryanston Square, W.1.
12 May 1921

My dear Vita,

Miss Rebecca West pranced into the flat this afternoon with the photograph (which is excellent). I don't know how quite to pack it for safety, as I am so afraid of the thing smashing which would be tragic. If you are not likely to be up I must see how I can manage to pack it.

[1] Not identified.

I have never seen any-one *so* ugly as Miss Rebecca West! She took my breath away! My manners fled and I quite forgot to ask her anything about Violet. I am sure she meant to talk, but really she *is* ugly – without warning!

Yours ever,

Pat

[Violet to Pat Dansey]
Rome
27 May 1921

My own darling Misskins, I am so worried because I haven't had a line from you for ages. I do hope you aren't ill?

As for me, I'm half dead. The heat of Rome is past description; last night I lay stark naked on my bed and gasped! It was far too hot to sleep. The heat is making me terribly thin, also the unnecessarily strenuous life I lead – Dances and luncheons and dinners all day and every day and malaria hanging over the whole place like a great dark bird waiting to swoop.

This palace is situated in the heart of the ghetto where all the crimes are committed, but it is on a little sort of hillock and has a beautiful garden with fountains that play day and night beneath my window. . . .

We return to Florence on Wednesday. Men chinday now completely ignores me. It's as though I didn't exist. She says that her affection for me is dead, and that after Sonia's baby is born, I may do what I like.

. . . O my darling Misskins, do write to me – My thoughts never leave England for a minute. I have only one preoccupation: chepescar.[1]

[Violet to Pat Dansey, who in turn sent it to Vita]
[May 1921]

My own darling Misskins, you never fail me! I will go to Cook's about the money this morning. I am very grateful indeed, as I hadn't a penny. I hope my cheque may arrive either tomorrow or the next

[1] to escape.

day. Do you know you have never let me down over anything? Bless you for it. I heard from [Julian: scored over] two days ago; he says he also wrote to Rome but the letter can only have arrived after I left, as it certainly wasn't there before.

... It was a good thing the letter arrived when it did, for I had decided to go to Greece that day to join a man at Brindisi (who bores me infinitely) and who wanted me to run away with him for some little time. From Brindisi we were to go to Greece. Honestly, Pat, I was so desperate, so convinced that Julian didn't care a hang what became of me, that I meant to do this. It would have been insane, as I didn't even like the man, but it would have got me away....

[A postscript added by Pat Dansey addressed to Vita]
I received this letter this afternoon. It seems to have been some time in coming. I wonder if Mrs Keppel will come over for her sister's funeral?

Love from
Pat

[Pat Dansey to Vita]
53, Cumberland Mansions, Bryanston Square, W.1.
7 June 1921

... I sent your telegram [to Violet] quite early Saturday morning. I almost daily receive a telegram – all of which I answer in some form which I hope may give her momentary peace. I would give so much if she could re-gain her happiness, but sometimes I wonder if she could ever be happy in *being* happy. Do you know what I mean?

Yours ever,
Pat

[Telegram from Violet to Pat Dansey]
7 June 1921

PLEASE MAKE JULIAN WRITE

[Violet to Pat Dansey]
9 June 1921

My precious Misskins, Please forgive the curtness of my telegram
re the cigarettes, but I only had enough money with me for two
words!! and now I have hardly any money at all!! I hate always
bothering you about something – but the cigarettes here are so vile,
one really can't smoke them.

The heat has been terrible; everyone is going away. You *will*
come to Holland, won't you? ... Julian sent me a telegram for my
birthday, but hasn't written.

Darling, one humorous thing has happened: I have got mixed up
in a Sicilian vendetta!! It is too absurd: An elderly Englishman fell
in love with me here ages ago, when I first arrived. It appears that
he once had a liaison with a Sicilian called Chichina d'Orsay – the
name is so marvellously appropriate.

Well, she arrived here about a week ago, saw me constantly with
this man (to whom I have assigned a perfectly avuncular role in my
life) and jumped to the conclusion that I was having a affair with
him. Ever since then, she has *shadowed* him herself day and night;
she has got hold of me several times, and told me the most ignoble
things about him. She goes about telling everyone I am this poor
respectable old father-of-a-family's mistress; she had a scene with
him in the middle of the street in the course of which she told him
he was wasting his affections on me; as I was secretly living with
somebody else, ending up by telling him that if he didn't cease
seeing me, she wasn't answerable for what might happen to him!!
He has since been told that she belongs to a secret society – the
Maffia I think it's called – which do away with people. ... My poor
old friend is in a blue funk, but sees me tremulously all the same!
Strange as it may seem – for he is neither young nor attractive –
this woman is crazily jealous of him, and as no one understands
jealousy better than I do, I have tried to make him go back to her,
which he absolutely refuses to consider! The whole episode is
worthy of being 'filmed'.

She 'lies in wait' for him everywhere – on his doorstep, in the street, outside his club, and worst of all, outside this house!

It is rather tiresome, for if I am going to be stilettoed, I certainly don't want to be stilettoed by her, on account of a man almost old enough to be my father!

If I didn't care so idiotically for Julian I should not lead the life of chastity I am leading at present, and which I shall continue to lead so long as I think he cares for me. To be accurate, there are at present seven men who want me in a certain capacity; I don't care a hang about any of them.... Do not misunderstand me: none of these people *dream* of matrimony! Julian and Denys between them have completely ruined my chances of respectability for ever. Whatever I become, it would be their fault.

... Julian doesn't write, and I can't – except through you – write to him. It is awful to be completely cut off.

My life is empty and futile and wasted.

[Violet to Pat Dansey]
17 June 1921

My darling Misskins, I am dismayed and appalled by your letter. It will be too dreadful if you don't come to Holland. I implore you on bended knees to come. I have been so looking forward to seeing you again – it is the one thing that has kept me going. Also I am most frightfully run-down; if you don't come I shall get no change of air to speak of as Clingendaal is so relaxing. The doctor says it is imperative that I should have one – and I can get my mother's consent for us to go away somewhere in Holland. She absolutely forbids me to set foot in England till September. If you don't come, I am done, morally and physically.... I think of him from morning till night – it is an obsession and as time goes on it gets worse instead of better....

I have now got rid of all the men who cared for me in a filthy way; I told them I could never think of them, as I cared for somebody else. So now, I am as lonely and bereft as when I first came.

[Pat Dansey to Vita]
53, Cumberland Mansions, Bryanston Square, W.1.
21 June 1921

My dear Vita,

I have sent your enclosures this morning. I do hope it will be all right about the press notices. I told her to be sure and send them back. But she is so forgetful.

Her letter came last night. Also, the telegram. I have written to her once or twice P.R. So it may be meant for me! I think my letters are probably inspected! So when I write I never say any-thing which might lead to trouble for her.

When I have written to her P.R. it has been to calm her down — or try to. Goodness only knows *what* she means to do in September. I am nervous at moments as to what madness she may commit. I don't see my way to going to Holland. I am sure there is some mad idea at the back of her mind. I am afraid in September there will be trouble if she comes back to England.

[Pat Dansey to Vita]
53, Cumberland Mansions, Bryanston Square, W.1.
22 June 1921

My dear Vita,

I had another letter from Violet this evening! She wants to know if you won't write to her P.R. The Hague so as she may find a letter when she arrives there. My dear, she is hopeless with letters! She wrote to me on the back of my own letter in which I had abused old Daisy[1] rather freely! She had probably left that about for Mr R.[2] to read! It really isn't to be wondered at if we don't write, or if we only write to say 'today it is cold — yesterday it was hot'. She also wants to know if you have any plans for her future. God! what a life, poor darling. She is very unhappy and missing you beyond all endurance. I am afraid I cannot bear her to be so unhappy, but what can we do. I am *so* sorry for her.

Vita, what is to be done? Do you think she will be happier when she is in Holland? I honestly don't want to go. I have a lot of visits to pay in July, and I hate old Daisy as much as she hates me! Surely, if she is coming back in September, she can bear 2 more months?

[1] Baroness de Brienen, the owner of Clingendaal.   [2] Not identified.

Violet wants to know if I don't see you. I have told her you are *rarely* in London, and when you are you do manage to see me. . . . I feel grey hairs springing out all over my head whenever I see her handwriting.

I am going down to Sussex from Friday till Monday, and you will have a little peace. . . .

[Violet to Pat Dansey]
Clingendaal, The Hague,
8 July 1921

My own darling Misskins, Daisy says you can come here any time between now and the 24th and between the 1st and the end of August. I shall be *miserable* and *frantic* if you don't come. She and Mama both expect you to propose yourself. There is going to be no one here at all except from the 24th to the 1st, Daisy's friends. There isn't going to be a single soul I can talk to the whole time I'm here. So I implore you on *bended knees to come.* . . .

Mama leaves here on the 20th for London, so I shall be here all alone till the beginning of September – not later than the 1st I hope. Tell Frank, if he is still in London, I couldn't get into the Hague to send him a telegram, and I hate sending them from here, as they say I'm so extravagant. . . .

They have sold my house for £200!! I spent nearly £3000 on it – and even the 200 Mama is taking 'to pay for the carpet'. It really is rather a shame as I am so terribly hard up, and shall have very little money in future. Heaven knows what is going to become of me! The one thing that keeps me going is that I feel I am still cared for.

[Violet to Pat Dansey]
Clingendaal, The Hague
9 July 1921

My blessed Misskins, You have GOT to come here. There won't be a soul to disturb us – only Daisy at meals – who has said heaps of charming things about you and would really love you to come. I went into the Hague to see the doctor and various other things. He says my heart is still strained and that I ought not to tire myself.

I shall tire myself if I have to keep begging you to come! You can't refuse, knowing how much pleasure it would give me. . . .

Mama goes back to England on the 21st to look after Sonia, who expects her infant at the beginning of August. Poor little thing. I *do* feel sorry for her: it is terrible to think of what she will have to go through.

It is rather sad to think of my poor house going for absolutely nothing – and the infortunate things I collected being jolted off to another warehouse – homeless as their mistress. I have literally nothing in the world. I feel as though I had been attacked by highwaymen and left bruised, naked and bleeding by the roadside – And Fate gleefully shouts: 'There! *Now* let's see what you can do! You had all sorts of other defences, other protections, now you've only got yourself.'

'You've got your brain, as a last resource, you've got your body . . . but *you've got nothing else*.' You don't know how exposed I feel. But the only thing I hope and trust I've got: the love of the highwayman! . . .

[Violet to Pat Dansey, and forwarded to Vita]
Clingendaal, The Hague
19 July 1921

My own darling Misskins, This morning I was so upset, because Mama said if she ever gave a party again she couldn't ask me. It is a small thing, but it hurt my feelings, though by now I'm sure I oughtn't to have any left. I live in a sort of stagnant hopelessness. . . .

I have nearly finished 'Women in Love'. Of course, it is quite neurasthenic, hysterical, but there are some beautiful things like jewels in a manure heap. The sex obsession is too disgusting, don't you think? The part where Hermione drops the lapis lazuli bell on 'Birkin's' head isn't meant to be funny, but I'm afraid I giggled over it. Also it is quite obvious from the relationship of 'Birkin' and 'Gerald' what sort of man Mr Lawrence is: He gives himself away at every turn. . . .

My novel progresses very slowly, alas! To think I have been writing it for over two years and it isn't finished yet because I keep rewriting. I think it's because I couldn't bear to part with it. It is everything to me, inevitably: Lover, Husband, Child, Friend. . . .

[Violet to Pat Dansey, and forwarded to Vita]
Clingendaal, The Hague
23 July 1921

... I am so conscious of being no longer young. I never forget
it for a moment. Also, I suppose one shouldn't mind one's looks
beginning to go, but somehow one can't help it. I look ten years
older than when you saw me last year. Each day I mercilessly look
at myself in the looking glass – and see my chin beginning to sag
and my throat getting all wrinkled. Soon I shall be quite plain and
there seems to be nothing to look forward to. You are the only
person who cares what becomes of me, outside my family.... It is
so humiliating.

... It's awful to feel that one had left all one's life behind one,
that all that's left is to get older and plainer every day. I'm such a
coward. I'm frightened of death too. I shouldn't be if I had been
good, but alas! I have not been good....

I have no spirit, no fighting capacity left – but, O Pat! I *do* believe
in another better world.

[Violet to Pat Dansey]
Clingendaal, The Hague
11 August 1921

My darling Misskins, Will you forgive me if I write you another
dejected letter? I do feel so *out* of everything; I am never asked to
take part in the numerous expeditions, dinners, dances, etc. that the
others get up. I am always left out. I am always alone.... O Pat, I
am one vast ache.

Julian has apparently forgotten me, and so has everyone else –
except you. Nobody ever writes to me; even Hugh Walpole won't
make an effort to come here, and doesn't answer my letters. It is a
hopeless position. My whole life seems ruined. I see only too clearly
that it would be impossible for me to live in England. I cannot bear
being snubbed and mortified. I am too proud. I prefer to live among
people of a different class altogether, who would not look on me as
a pariah and a déclassé....

People are *merciless*. Denys's sister, who is staying here, never lets
me forget for one moment. O God, how unfair it all is! I do really,
really want you to evolve some plan, some theory by which to
regulate my existence....

53, Cumberland Mansions, Bryanston Square, W.1.
15 August 1921

My dear Vita,

A letter like the enclosed reduces me to abject pity and unhappiness for the wretched child. I would gladly do any-thing to help her. But, what *can* I do? I have written her a most urgent appeal to give you up in *all ways* – for as long as there is any connection between you two the world will never allow the scandal to be forgotten. *Curse* the malicious tattlers who did all the harm, *curse* them. I have done my best to impress Violet that there can be no future for her as long as people are not made to understand that the mad friendship between you two is over and not to be revived.

Poor child, I am afraid she has not much future ahead. O Vita, Vita, why didn't you leave her for the first 6 months after she was married? Now the harm is irretrievably done. Doubtless you can be strong, but it is too late. I am sorry. I did not mean to upbraid! The tragedy was that in those days you looked upon me as an enemy. I wasn't and never have been. *You* were the enemy, but, the point is, how can Violet be helped?

I think it is cruel the way she is being treated, and that sort of treatment is not going to make people forget the scandal – is it? I simply don't know what to do. Shall I go and see her mother and try to make her see that treating V. as a pariah does more harm than good? But to make this effective I want a guarantee that all the malicious tongues shall be silenced – how can I do that? I do think people are beastly. They might give that poor little thing a chance. She has been terribly punished.

Vita, will you put all feelings aside from your personal point of view, and tell me quite candidly and truthfully what you consider would really be the best for V. in the future? I swear on my honour – unless you tell me to – I should never repeat your views to any-one. You must remember I have no friend of Violet's to whom I can talk and I do get fearfully worried and unhappy when she writes such sad and pathetic letters....

[Pat Dansey to Vita]
53, Cumberland Mansions, Bryanston Square, W.1.
1 September 1921

My dear Vita,

Don't come up specially. I can easily be in London on the 13th. If you aren't too busy, will you lunch with me here? But, you may find you have a lot to do, in which case, you arrange a time which is most convenient to you.

You mustn't be under the impression any-one is forcing Violet go to back to Denys. It was *entirely her own suggestion, and her mother refuses* to advise her one way or the other. Personally, well, the less I say on the subject the better! But — I'm damned if she ever dupes me again! I shall start a business as a clairvoyant! I had a feeling V. was doing exactly what she has done.

Don't worry, and try not to be unhappy. I *know* it is not going to be worth it. If Violet did not claim my friendship, I think I might save you a lot of unnecessary pain. But, that is where my part is so difficult. I only send you the message about coming to see me Tuesday to force her to tell you her plans. Bless you,

[Violet to Pat Dansey, forwarded to Vita]
This is the first time I have ever used a type writer: please
    forgive mistakes. Please make a point of coming to see our friend on the thirteenth.will you send me Dannunzios poems.
            Iwant them to look up some thin g Laudi will do
                you might enclose something of yours dont forget
        the photograph.my typeing is ludicrous and Ido feel so mis-
erable
            Bless you always
                            darling sweet

[Pat Dansey to Vita]
53, Cumberland Mansions, Bryanston Square, W.1.
10 November 1921

My dear Vita,

Violet asked me to send you the enclosed [novel fragment].

I think you *will* be taken in by V. and I think she will get round you — that is your business. I shall never be able to save you. V writes me letters at every second of the day, asking if you care fo her. I have told her that *my own opinion* was that you would *never* lead the mad life of the past 3 years again. Beyond that I have said nothing. Personally, I would not bet 6d that in less than 3 months' time you are not again on the old footing with V.!!

Oh Vita, she *is* hopeless. I hate the way she tricks and deceives people who have done everything for her. She has promised over and over again not to lie to me, but still she does it.

When I next see you I am going to ask you to do something for me – nothing very serious! I wouldn't ask you – but I cannot ask V. as I don't trust her not to lie to me. . . .

[Fragment from Violet's novel]
Chapter 7

Full of hope and confidence, he opened the letter. Though he had felt it previously to see if it was thick and had realized with a sickening sense of disappointment that it only contained one sheet, he was nevertheless unprepared for the few sparse sentences that met him. He had looked for definite, conclusive relief of his fears and misgivings. He found . . . nothing of the kind! A few scattered endearments to cover the paucity of information. A nervous, furtive letter; brief, because unwilling to commit itself, nervous, because it realized that in no way would it come up to the recipient's expectations. Even as he read it, it shied away from him.

He was a divining rod for truth, for sincerity. Apprehensive, the antennae of his extreme sensibility detected the note of falseness in that letter – worse, the note of cowardice, of guilt . . . the cowardice of the last sentence: 'Am I never to see you again in this life?' Thrusting the responsibility on *him*, knowing all the while that it depended on *her*, on her decision, on her courage, whether she saw him again or not. The recurrent question: Are you faithful? Without any allusion to her own faithfulness, which he hideously began to doubt for the first time. . . .

But no, surely, it was not possible. After she had deprived him of all that made life worth living, while she herself was spared, it was inconceivable that she would be guilty of this supreme horror – knowing him stripped, destitute, cheated, starved, but in spite of everything, loyal and loving. . . .

No, no, no! Tormented, he fled from this monstrosity.

Suddenly a redeeming hypothesis presented itself: Supposing she hadn't had his letter after all, supposing she had really not had his question?

But why? She had known there would be such a letter. He had taken the precaution of letting her know, days beforehand. Or did she merely pretend, so as to have an excuse for not answering this question? The uncertainty lacerated him. He felt sick, exterminated. He was too weak, too poor to wrestle with the problems of trickery and deception. Surely people wouldn't give a beggar a false coin?

The words of the Italian rang in his ears: 'She is beautiful, she is charming, but she is not frank, not straight. I could never trust her. She was full of withdrawals, evasions; she would never give a straight answer to a straight question. Il y a quelque chose qui sonne faux chez elle'[1] and Con remembered his shudder, and the words that mutilated still more horribly: 'I don't know if she is in love with her husband, but she certainly loves him. Perhaps he is the only person she ever cared for really?'

And this was Con's Diana, to whom he had sacrificed everything!

[Pat Dansey to Vita]

53, Cumberland Mansions, Bryanston Square, W.1.
12 November 1921

'That brilliant creature Vita Sackville-West' is a darling, I think, to have sent me her book of poems. I am dreadfully proud to have been given them. Vita, thank you a thousand times.... I spent the whole of last night dreaming about you. I expect it was because I had taken your poems to read in bed. Queer dream it was too....

I had another letter from Violet last night. For the moment she is occupied on a quest after her own heart! – So perhaps peace for a bit. Oh Vita, there is something in connection with a theory that V. got into her head and which she wrote me 7 pages about. It tickled me to death. I long to tell you, but, I suppose I never can. And I know it would amuse you as much as it did me.

Love from Pat

---

[1] There is something in her that strikes a false note.

Evening

Vita dear, I do hope you won't think my first letter to you was meant to be disagreeable? Indeed, it wasn't, but the same post that brought me Violet's letter brought another from someone telling me what V. was up to, and I felt livid with her.

My God! I simply fail to see why people don't see through her.

Love from Pat

Postscript

After their move to Paris, Violet and Denys gradually established an affectionate, if distant, companionship until his death, from tuberculosis, in 1929. That year the first of her novels was published. In 1952 her autobiographical work, *Don't Look Round*, followed. She did not remarry and apart from seeking refuge in England during the war – when she made contact again with Vita – Violet lived as an expatriate in France and Italy, moving in international society and art circles, until her death in 1972. Vita and Harold remained together and in 1930 purchased the ruin of Sissinghurst Castle in Kent and began to create its now famous gardens.

But during the half century that remained to Violet the embers of the 'great love' continued to burn and threatened to rekindle with passion during the Second World War, as the moving letters written by Vita to Violet at that time fully testify.

One of Violet's favourite books, *The Unquiet Grave* by 'Palinarus' – her friend Cyril Connolly – is inscribed to her: *'quand bleuira sur l'horizon la Desirade?'*[1] And in the book Violet marked vehemently with a red crayon the following passage:

> We love only once, for once only are we perfectly equipped for loving: we may appear to ourselves to be as much in love at other times – so does a day in early September, though it is six hours shorter, seem as hot as one in June. And on how that first great love-affair shapes itself depends the pattern of our lives.

Not long before Violet's death, a faithful friend, François

---

[1] *when the Desirade will become blue on the horizon'*, from Apollinaire's poem 'Descendant des hauteurs òu pense la lumière', from *Alcools*. As Connolly's lines were written during World War II, it is probably an allusion to Violet's desire to return to France, since 'bleuira' means that the coastline is at last being seen from the sea.

Mitterrand, paid her a last visit in Florence. He left the villa greatly moved and made the following note in his journal:

> ... in the great house the memory persisted of singular passions of which I had registered the last cries. I had not asked Violet any questions. She had not made any confidences to me. There appeared occasionally at L'Ombrellino the signs of ancient storms and torments that half a century had not entirely dispelled ... I knew that an epoch was drawing to an end, or rather, were fading away the traces of a time elsewhere already vanished, although until now preserved here by the firm hand of Violet.

Index

Dower House *see* Sonning-on-Thames

The Dragon in Shallow Waters (Vita Sackville-West), 34, 238–9, 247 & n, 249 & n, 262

'Duckrus' *see* Winnington-Ingram, Mrs

Duntreath Castle, Stirlingshire, 9, 61: Violet's visits to, 41, 55, 57–60, 209, 232–8

Duveen, Sir Joseph, 11

Ebury Street (Nicolsons' home), 19, 22, 73, 74, 97

Edel, Leon, 1

Eddy (Violet's cousin), 237, 238

Edmonstone, Sir Archibald (Uncle Archie), 58n, 233

Edmonstone, Admiral Sir William, 2

Edmonstone, Willie, 58

Edward VII (Prince of Wales until 1901), 2; Alice Keppel's relationship with, 2–4, 6–7, 11, 46–7; death of (1910), 3, 12, 55; Violet's relations with, 6–7

The Edwardians (Vita Sackville-West), 5

Fairbairn, Nancy *see* Cunard

Fairbairn, Sydney, 100n

Falmouth, 39

Fitzhardinge of Berkeley Castle, Lord, 19, 73, 219n

Florence, 11, 15, 60, 192, 200, 232, 233, 269, 276–7, 279, 281, 294; Vita's and Harold's honeymoon in (1913), 18

Foster, Muriel, 97

Fromm, Erich, 46

Fuenterrabia, 147

Gaigneron, Comte Jean de, 228 & n

George V, King, 12

Gien, Hotel du Rivage, 37, 175–6

Glendinning, Victoria, *Vita*, xi, 16

Glinka, Mikhail, *A Life for the Tsar*, 125 & n

The Good Humoured Ladies ballet, 124 & n

Goudeket, Maurice, 255n

Granby, Marquess of, 14

Grenfell, Julian, 18, 56, 214 & n, 238

Grieg, Edvard, 83

Grimthorpe, Lord, 56

Grosvenor, Rosamund, Vita's friendship with, 11, 12, 13, 15, 16, 17, 55, 56, 73, 163

Grosvenor Street (Keppel house at no. 16), 12, 14–15, 21, 55, 60–5, 110, 192, 199, 200, 202, 203; Violet's coming-out ball at (1912), 15

Hardinge of Penshurst, Lord, 3

'Hadji' *see* Nicolson, Harold

Hardy, Thomas, 91; *Jude the Obscure*, 98

Hay, Ivan, 14, 15

Heidelberg, 72

Hendaye, Grand Hotel Eskualduna, 147–8, 150

Heneage, Dorothy, 18, 19, 74–5 & n

Heritage (Vita Sackville-West), 27, 110, 127, 173, 174, 262

Hill Hall, Theydon Mount, Epping, 97, 170

Horner, Edward, 14

Hugo, Victor, *Lucrèce Borgia*, 157n, 158

Hunter, Mrs Charles, 16, 97

'Hwth', 152–3